OUTCOMES-BASED GOVERNANCE

A MODERN APPROACH TO CORPORATE GOVERNANCE

OUTCOMES-BASED GOVERNANCE

A MODERN APPROACH TO CORPORATE GOVERNANCE

MERVYN KING, SC
FABIAN AJOGWU, SAN

Outcomes-Based Governance

A Modern approach to Corporate Governance

First published 2020

© Juta and Company (Pty) Ltd
1st Floor, Sunclare Building, 21 Dreyer Street,
Claremont 7708

www.jutalaw.co.za

ISBN: 978 1 48513 568 5

Cover Design: Drag & Drop
Typesetter: CBT Typesetting & Design

Acknowledgement

The world of corporate governance is indeed intriguing and ever relevant to the business world. It is our passion for good corporate governance and its ability to transform businesses and in turn economies that has enthused the writing of this book. Our preoccupation with corporate governance over the years has produced codes in South Africa and Nigeria respectively, and we thank all who supported these efforts. More specifically, the *King IV Code* and the *National Code of Corporate Governance* 2018 have provided a strong platform for the discussions in this book.

A number of institutions deserve special mention for their commitment to the development of Corporate Governance – the Institute of Directors South Africa, Society for Corporate Governance Nigeria, the Johannesburg Stock Exchange, Nigerian Stock Exchange, the Financial Reporting Council of Nigeria, Nigerian Communications Commission, Central Bank of Nigeria, Securities and Exchange Commission, etcetera.

We thank Okechukwu Ekweanya, Ruth Barnett, Oludolapo Makinde and Chinonye Nnaji for their immense contributions. Much appreciation goes to Kenna Partners for being of significant support in the course of writing this book and to our families for their support and encouragement during the literary preoccupation.

We also would like to express our appreciation to our learned colleague and banker, Mr. Sim Tshabalala, for writing the foreword to the book.

Professor Mervyn King, SC
Johannesburg

20 February 2020

Professor Fabian Ajogwu, SAN
Lagos

20 February 2020

Prologue

Organisations in the twenty-first century have witnessed significant changes and challenges relating to sustainable development. These challenges have been triggered by a number of factors, such as the reality that organisations and individuals are using up natural resources at a faster rate than nature is able to replenish same, the world has witnessed a number of financial crises that crumbled not only organisations but also whole economies. These crises revealed weaknesses within organisational leadership and structure and have created a world characterised by vocal calls for real transparency.

These requests have been amplified by the rise of social media, an awakening on the part of stakeholders, (investors in particular) to the need to protect their investments and the society at large is beginning to demand certain non-traditional obligations from organisations as corporate citizens. Technological disruptions and developments have also been relentless in changing the traditional roles and functions of organisations and business models and industries as we knew them.

It is in light of these developments that the essence of corporate governance as a tool for engendering sustainable development and increased stakeholder confidence has become more relevant than ever as most corporate failures have been attributed to the failure of corporate governance. It is against this backdrop that corporate governance principles, codes and regulations have developed over the past few years to ensure that the challenging realities of a changing world are adequately catered for.

The *King IV Code* of South Africa has been revolutionary in this regard as it provides a framework for considering the governance of corporate entities from an outcomes-centric approach. The Nigerian National Code of Corporate Governance 2018 takes a cue from King IV, albeit from a principles-driven angle. Although the concept of governance outcomes is not revolutionary, it is hardly mainstream; it is innovative, and in most jurisdictions, untested. Outcomes-based governance entails considering the positive effects and benefits that an organisation can reap if the underlying principles of good governance are properly applied and fully achieved. It promotes the idea that there is a need to consider the potential benefits of effectively implementing governance inputs as opposed to isolated actions, details, or procedures. The principles of an outcomes-focused approach have become crucial in equipping the board in whom the primary duty of corporate governance lies, with the tools required to achieve sustainable development and stakeholder confidence.

Various trends and components of contemporary corporate governance have also emerged in recent years to assist the corporation in developing management quality and responsiveness towards the interest of all its financial stakeholders and society at large. Some of these emerging trends are inclusive capitalism, long-term sustainability, rights relations, integrated reporting, and technology governance. All the trends are interrelated and result in one goal; the long-term existence and profitability of corporations. As new corporate governance trends have emerged, so has the role of the board of directors and other persons key to the development of an organisation such as the company secretary, auditor, institutional investors and even the government and regulators evolved. Importantly, in recent years, a new role of a Corporate Stakeholder Relationship Officer has been developed to handle the task of communicating with stakeholders and informing management of their legitimate and reasonable needs, interests, and expectations (NIEs).

The major aim of this book is to demystify outcomes-based governance and emerging corporate governance trends and aid their adaptability in emerging economies. The idea is that good corporate governance is not only for large organisations but also useful for small and medium-sized enterprises (SMEs) which make up most businesses in emerging economies and the world generally, hence organisations and economies however small should ensure to adopt best practices from inception.

The authors of this book bring in their substantial experience and knowledge from two countries (Nigeria and South Africa) and it is our hope that enterprises and individuals who are keen on expanding their corporate governance practices find this book helpful.

Professor Mervyn King, SC   **Professor Fabian Ajogwu, SAN**
Johannesburg   Lagos

20 February 2020   20 February 2020

Professor Mervyn King, SC

Mervyn King is a Senior Counsel, a former Judge of the Supreme Court of South Africa and former Judge at the International Chamber of Commerce's International Court of Arbitration in Paris. He was the first president of the Commonwealth Association of Corporate Governance and a former Governor of the International Corporate Governance Network. He is Chairman Emeritus of the Global Reporting Initiative, Chairman Emeritus of the International Integrated Reporting Council and Chairman Emeritus of the King Committee on Corporate Governance that birthed the revolutionary *King IV Code* which introduced an outcomes-based approach to corporate governance in South Africa.

He is currently a member of the Private Sector Advisory Group to the World Bank on Corporate Governance and was a member of the international advisory boards of Stern Stewart (UD), Tomorrow's Company and the Central European Corporate Governance Association. Professor King, SC chairs the Asian Centre of Corporate Governance and was the chair of the United Nations (UN) Committee on Governance and Oversight.

He is an honorary fellow of several businesses and accounting organisations and holds honorary doctorates from universities in South Africa, the United Kingdom (UK) and Australia. He has acted as an Inspector of Companies and a Commissioner of Inquiries into the affairs of companies. He has chaired many meetings for the compromise of creditors of companies and the rearrangement of shareholders' interests. He has spoken at conferences and lectured on corporate issues in 60 countries. Professor King, SC is a regular speaker on radio and television talk shows and ran his own television series, 'King on Governance'. He now sits as an arbitrator and mediator and is a founding member of the Arbitration Foundation of Southern Africa.

Professor Fabian Ajogwu, SAN

Fabian Ajogwu is a Senior Advocate of Nigeria with Kenna Partners; and Lagos Business School Professor of Corporate Governance. He is an alumnus of the Saïd Business School, Oxford University, and an alumnus of the Lagos Business School. Professor Ajogwu holds a doctorate degree in law from the University of Aberdeen, Scotland; an MBA from the IESE Business School, University of Navarra, Barcelona; and law degrees from the University of Nigeria, and University of Lagos.

He serves on the boards of Novare Group in Nigeria, ARM Harith Infrastructure Ltd, NES Global Ltd, Stanbic IBTC Holdings Plc, and Guinness Nigeria Plc. He has served as Honorary Counsel to the State of Israel, and the Republic of South Africa. Professor Ajogwu assisted the Securities and Exchange Commission in drafting Nigeria's pioneer Code of Corporate Governance. He chaired the Nigerian Communications Commission Committee on Corporate Governance, and served on the Financial Reporting Council of Nigeria's Committee on the 2018 National Code of Corporate Governance.

Professor Ajogwu is a Fellow of the Society for Corporate Governance Nigeria, Nigerian Institute of Chartered Arbitrators, African Leadership Initiative West Africa, Henry Crown Global Leadership of the Aspen Institute and AIFA Reading Society. He served on the board of the Lagos Court of Arbitration, the Governing Council of the Nigerian Institute of Chartered Arbitrators. He served on the Governing Council of Pan-Atlantic University (Lagos Business School), the General Council of the Bar, and the Council of Legal Education (Nigerian Law School) as the statutorily referred Distinguished Legal Author, and serves as the Chairman of the Body of Senior Advocates of Nigeria Subcommittee on Continuing Legal Education. He is a member of the London Court of International Arbitration, and the International Council for Commercial Arbitration and was a member of the Lagos Court of Arbitration. He is Chairman of the Nigerian Climate Innovation Centre.

Professor Ajogwu, SAN is the author of a number of authoritative texts, including – *Corporate Governance & Group Dynamics; Corporate Governance in Nigeria: Law and Practice; Mergers & Acquisition in Nigeria: Law and Practice; Commercial Arbitration in Nigeria: Law and Practice,* to name but a few.

Foreword

It is great honour to provide a foreword to *"Outcomes Based Governance: A Modern Approach to Corporate Governance"*.

It is undeniable that sound corporate governance is crucial to the profitability and sustainability of businesses, and to their capacity to fulfill their social purpose.

Corporate Governance has come into sharper public focus in recent years, first due to a number of major scandals (for instance, at Enron and WorldCom) and then owing to the global financial crisis of 2007–2008, which led to an unprecedented loss of trust in the global financial system in general, and in the governance of several major financial firms in particular.

Greater attention to good Corporate Governance is unarguably essential to preventing market abuse, enhancing a company's value, and enabling sustainable growth, profitability and equity valuation. Further, good Corporate Governance contributes substantially to capital market deepening and, ultimately, to the liquidity and soundness of investment portfolios.

This may sound dry and abstract, but what it means in practice is that good Corporate Governance powerfully promotes inclusive and sustainable economic growth and human development.

There is an argument that Corporate Governance has been over-sold and that its promises are hollow. The authors' view – which I share – is that the opposite is true. It has never been more necessary than it is now for corporate governance principles to be adopted proactively and ingrained in the culture of every organisation. There is, therefore, still a great deal of work to do to explain and embed good Corporate Governance in Africa – and it is this task to which this book makes a very distinguished contribution.

Outcomes Based Governance: A Modern Approach to Corporate Governance makes a very strong case for a holistic approach to Corporate Governance, in terms which firms and their directors are enjoined to focus on intended outcomes as opposed to isolated actions. The authors do not mince their words. This is a bold proposal. The adoption of an outcomes-based approach to corporate governance requires that companies move beyond traditional governance and organisational principles and move towards embracing purpose-led inclusive capitalism, integrated reporting, active corporate citizenship, and careful technology governance.

Talking of technology, the book argues that technology can revolutionise corporate governance by improving and automating the compliance process. I have seen this firsthand in governance and practice in the banking sector and so it is refreshing and timely to see this development extensively covered here.. The book goes on to explain how block chain technology in particular can enhance corporate governance by eliminating a complex web of intermediaries and enabling transactions to be verified in a timely and cost effective manner.

This book will be very useful in classrooms where Corporate Governance theory is taught, and equally valuable in the board rooms where Corporate Governance is practiced.

I commend the Learned Authors, Professor Mervyn King, SC and Professor Fabian Ajogwu, SAN for their extraordinary and lifelong dedication to defining, promoting and practicing good Corporate Governance in Africa. Their knowledge and practical experience of Corporate Governance are unmatched and their insights are of immense value both to students and to practitioners.

Sim Tshabalala
Group Chief Executive
Standard Bank Group Limited
Johannesburg,

20 February 2020

Table of Contents

Chapter 1

INTRODUCTION

1.1 DEFINITION OF CORPORATE GOVERNANCE

The term 'corporate governance' can be analysed from different perspectives, and as such, there is a plethora of literature debating the 'correct' definition of corporate governance. We shall consider, in this chapter, a few definitions put forward by different authors. It is, however, important to note that regardless of the definitions that these authors attribute to the term, the core notion of corporate governance relates to the means by which a corporation assures investors that it has established a well-performing management who are able to ensure that corporate assets provided by investors are being put to appropriate and profitable use.[1]

Mike Wright defines corporate governance as the rights and responsibilities of different stakeholders and its consequences for the process in terms of which companies are controlled and operated.[2] The Cadbury Report on the Financial Aspects of Corporate Governance defines it as a system by which companies are directed and controlled.[3] Matthiessen, however, provided a broader and all-encompassing definition, describing corporate governance as:

> A field of economics that investigates how to secure or motivate efficient management of corporations by the use of incentive mechanisms, such as contracts, organisational designs, and legislation. It is often limited to the question of improving financial performance, for example, how the corporate owners can secure or motivate the corporate managers in order to deliver a competitive rate of return.[4]

Corporate governance entails:

> ... holding the balance between economic and social goals and between individual and communal goals. The governance framework is there to encourage the efficient use of

---

[1] Chairperson: Ira M Millstein, (1998), Corporate Governance, Competitiveness and Access to Capital in Global Markets (a report to the OECD).

[2] M Wrights, D Siegel, K Kasey & I Filatatchey (eds) *Oxford Handbook of Corporate Governance* (2013) University of Cambridge Faculty of Law Research Paper No 54/2011 ECCGI – Law Working Paper No 184/2012.

[3] R Smerdon *Cadbury Report on The Financial Aspects of Corporate Governance, A Practical Guide to Corporate Governance*.

[4] H Mathiesian *Managerial Ownership and Financial Performance* (unpublished PhD thesis, Department of International Economics and Management, Copenhagen Business School, 2002).

resources and equally account for the stewardship of those resources. The aim is to align as nearly as possible the interests of individuals, corporations, and society.[5]

Corporate governance has been defined by focusing on its purpose; thus:

> Corporate governance is intended to regulate the conduct of directors, accountability to shareholders, recognition of the interest of their stakeholders and the need to encourage investment to flow where it could be most productive by raising in this case the Nigerian corporate governance standards to be international practices in comparable jurisdictions. This would appear to be the reason and purpose of corporate governance.[6]

It is also helpful to examine the definitions of various codes of corporate governance attributed to the term corporate governance. For example, the 2014 Central Bank of Nigeria Code of Corporate Governance for Banks and Discount Houses in Nigeria states that:

> The term corporate governance refers to the rules, processes, or laws by which institutions are operated, regulated and governed, it is developed with the primary purpose of promoting a transparent and efficient banking system that will engender the rule of law and encourage the division of responsibilities in a professional and objective manner. Effective corporate governance practices provide a structure that works for the benefit of stakeholders by ensuring that the enterprise adhered to accepted ethical standards and best practices as well as formal laws.

The most cited definition of corporate governance in recent times comes from the Organisation for Economic Co-operation and Development (OECD). The OECD defines corporate governance as:

> A set of relationships between a company's management, its board, its shareholders and other stakeholders. Corporate governance also provides the structure through which the objectives of the company are set, and the means of attaining those objectives and monitoring performance are determined.[7]

For purposes of this book, we adopt the definition of corporate governance espoused in the *King IV Report on Corporate Governance for South Africa* (*King IV Report*).* It defines corporate governance as 'the exercise of ethical and effective leadership by the governing body towards the achievement of the following governance outcomes: ethical culture, good performance, effective control, and legitimacy'. This definition embraces a broader meaning by putting the company into a wider context of societal obligation. The reason for adopting this definition is that it not only defines corporate governance but also examines the aims and purpose behind effective corporate governance. It is also the view of the authors that corporate governance remains a critical driver of corporate accountability, commer-

---

[5] Foreword by Sir Adrian Cadbury to MR Iskander & N Chamlou *Corporate Governance: A Framework for Implementation* (2000).

[6] FI Ajogwu *Corporate Governance in Nigeria: Law and Practice* (2007).

[7] OECD *Principles of Corporate Governance* (1999).

* Refer to our King IV IP Policy on our website: (https://www.iodsa.co.za/page/KingIVIPpolicy).

cial prosperity, and business sustainability in that it connects the mission of the company with the objectives of its stakeholders.

It is not only necessary to define corporate governance, but its workings and determinants must also be mentioned. O'Donovan takes the view that sound corporate governance relies on external marketplace commitment and legislation, plus a healthy board culture which safeguards policies and processes.[8] The codification of corporate governance principles and best practices are designed to reinforce specific provisions of the law. It further aims to introduce best practices and regulations that are critical to the discharge of the duty of accountability of the board and management to the organisation. In some cases, existing law may either have lacunae or be insufficient to address corporate governance issues; therefore, the codes of corporate governance come in handy to fill the gap created by law.[9]

1.2 THE ESSENCE OF CORPORATE GOVERNANCE

Corporations have evolved and have now become powerful and dominant in terms of their capabilities and influence; however, with such power invariably comes abuse. Shareholders are losing trust in the management of corporations, which in turn affects the market value of the corporation.[10] Corporate governance is an important tool with which to manage organisations in the current complex, global environment. This book proposes that for corporate governance to be effective, it must be carried out mindfully with the end goal and purpose for which it is in place remaining the primary focus; hence the title *Outcomes-Based Governance*.

Corporate governance experts have long attempted to prove the link between good corporate governance practices and the success of firms.[11] Although it is not easy to fully and unequivocally quantify the relationship between good corporate governance and a firm's specific performance results, good corporate governance practices enhance a company's value and consequently attract investment. It contributes to the sustainable growth and profitability of a company as well as its growth and profits. For companies listed on a stock exchange, the most commonly discussed benefit of good governance is its effect on share value, liquidity, and investor portfolio composition.[12] O'Donovan goes on to note that the 'perceived quality of a company's corporate governance can influence its share prices

---

[8] G O'Donovan 'Change management: A board culture of corporate governance' (2003) 6 *Corporate Governance International Journal* 28.

[9] FI Ajogwu *Corporate Governance & Group Dynamics* (2013).

[10] A Crane & D Matten *Business Ethics: Managing Corporate Citizenship and Sustainability in the Age of Globalization* (2007).

[11] OECD 'The Tangible Benefits of Good Governance' available at https://www.oecd.org/daf/ca/corporategovernanceprinciples/43654500.pdf (accessed on 18 August 2019).

[12] O'Donovan (n 8 above).

as well as the cost of raising capital'.[13] On a national scale, countries that adopt good corporate governance models attract more foreign direct investments.

The root of most corporate failures stems from an entity's corporate governance practices failing.[14] For instance, the research leading up to the 2014 Nigeria Code of Corporate Governance for Public Companies indicated that weak corporate governance has been responsible for most of the recent corporate failures in Nigeria.[15] This nexus can also be seen in the Nigerian banking industry; the consistent corporate failures of many banks in Nigeria have resulted in financial crises over the last two decades that called for increased regulation by the relevant regulatory agencies of the industry.[16]

1.3 THEORIES OF CORPORATE GOVERNANCE

Corporate governance is often analysed around major theoretical frameworks. Corporate governance theories and models have furthermore evolved and will continue to evolve. The evolution of corporate governance is unending. The foundational theories of corporate governance commenced with the Agency-Shareholder Theory, expanded into Stewardship Theory and Stakeholder Theory and, in recent times, are evolving into various other theories such as feminist ethics theory, resource-dependence theories, discourse theory, business ethics theory, etcetera.[17]

An analysis of the theories of corporate governance is important as the theory adopted determines the effectiveness of the governance of a corporation. Research has shown that companies that adopt the best forms of corporate governance enjoy higher returns.[18] For the purpose of this book, the most common of the theories will be examined, namely the Agency Theory, Stewardship Theory, Shareholder Theory, and Stakeholder Theory.

1.3.1 Agency Theory

As far back as the discussions of Adolf Berle and Gardiner Means in 1932, corporate governance has focused mainly on the separation of ownership which in turn resulted in principal-agent problems arising from the disper-

---

[13] OECD (n 11 above).

[14] K Aina 'Board of directors and corporate governance Niger' (2013) 1 *IJBFME* 21–34.

[15] Securities and Exchange Commission *Code of Corporate Governance for Public Companies* (2014).

[16] ID Nworji, O Adebayo & A Olanrewaju 'Corporate governance and bank failure in Nigeria: Issues, challenges and opportunities' (2011) 2 *Research Journal of Finance and Accounting*.

[17] H Abdullah & B Valentine 'Fundamental and ethics theories of corporate governance' 2009 *Middle Eastern Finance and Economics Issue* 4.

[18] NM Saad 'Corporate governance compliance and the effects to capital structure in Malaysia' (2010) 2 *International Journal of Economics and Finance*.

sed ownership in the modern corporation. This theory regards corporate governance as a mechanism where the board of directors is a crucial monitoring device to minimise the problems brought about by the principal-agent relationship. In this context, agents are the executives hired to manage the organisation, while principals are the owners (or shareholders) and the boards of directors act as the monitoring mechanism.[19]

Eugene Fama and Micheal Jensen established the Agency Theory by asserting that a corporation is, in fact, a series of contracts. They posit that the separation of ownership and control can be explained as a result of an 'efficient form of economic organisation'.[20] Jensen and Meckling further defined the agency relationship and identify agency costs. They define the agency relationship as 'a contract under which one or more persons (principal) engage another person (agent) to perform some service on their behalf which involves delegating some decision-making authority to the agent'.[21]

The assumption under this theory is that principals of an organisation do not directly manage the company, as such they suffer an agency loss (a lesser return on investment). The theory argues that agents/managers tend to act in their interest rather than in the interests of the company for the benefit of its shareholders and stakeholders; therefore they need to be monitored and controlled in order to ensure that they do their primary job.[22] Eisenhardt notes that there is a tendency of the agent to act in their own interest as opposed to in the interests of shareholders, hence the need for corporate governance is to curtail the agents by having a board of directors who will control the actions of the management by providing a framework and policy for business, and also ensure that the management complies with such policies as well as the applicable laws and regulations.[23] It is for this reason that a board developed from the perspective of the Agency Theory tends to exercise strict control and supervision of the performance of the agent to protect the interests of the principal.[24] Hence, the board of directors is actively involved in most of the managerial decision-making processes.

---

[19] WFW Yusoff & IA Alhaji 'Insight of corporate governance theories' (2012) 1 *Journal of Business & Management* 52–63.

[20] EF Fama & Michael Jensen 'The separation of ownership and control' (1983) 26 *Journal of Law and Economics* 301.

[21] MC Jensen 'Agency costs of free cash flow, corporate finance and takeovers' (1986) 76 *American Economic Review* (Papers & Proceedings) 323.

[22] Ajogwu (n 9 above).

[23] KM Eisenhardt in her two classics 'Agency theory: An assessment and review' (1989) *Academy of Management Review* 57–74 and 'Agency– and institutional – theory explanations: The case of retail sales compensation' (1988) 31 *The Academy of Management Journal* 488–511.

[24] Amy J Hillman & Thomas Dalziel 'Boards of Directors and Firm Performance: Integrating Agency and Resource Dependence Perspectives' (2003) 28(3) *The Academy of Management Review* 383–396.

Under this theory, maximising the shareholders' wealth is paramount, and that is the sole focus of the directors.[25]

1.3.2 Stewardship Theory

The major difference between the Agency Theory and Stewardship Theory is that the latter argues that shareholder interests are maximised by shared incumbency of these roles while the Agency Theory argues that shareholder interest requires protection by separation of the incumbency roles of the board and executives of the company.[26] The basis of the Stewardship Theory is that managers/executives of a company are the stewards of the owners; as a result, they both share common goals.[27] The theory proposes that the board should not be too controlling, as agency theories advocate; rather, the board must play a supportive role. The theory further advocates for constant training and mentoring of executives to ensure higher performance and also proposes shared decision-making between the groups.[28] Macgregor takes the view that people can be trusted to act in public good in general and in the interest of shareholders in particular. The original corporate concept takes the view that man is essentially trustworthy, able to act in good faith in the interest of others with integrity and honesty. This is implicit in the fiduciary relationship required of directors.[29]

The problem with the stewardship theory is that it proceeds from the notion or ideology that people can be trusted to act in the public good in general and in the interest of shareholders, examples abound of outright breach of fiduciary duties.[30]

1.3.3 Shareholder Theory

The Agency and Stewardship theories of corporate governance both lead to one conclusion regardless of their differences; which is that profit maximisation for the owners (shareholders) should be the paramount focus of corporate governance. Noble Laureate Milton Friedman strongly argues in favour of this theory. His capitalist perspective clearly considers that a firm is owned by and operated for the benefit of the shareholders, and he notes

---

[25] A Ghula, K Binish, R Zeeshan & A Alia 'Theoretical perspectives of corporate governance' (2014) 3 *Bulletin of Business and Economics* 166–75.

[26] L Donaldson, JH Davis 'Stewardship Theory or Agency Theory: CEO governance and shareholder returns' (1991) 16 *Australian Journal of Management*.

[27] JH Davis, FD Schooman & L Donaldson 'Toward a stewardship theory of management' (1997) 22 *The Academy of Management Review* 20–47.

[28] Chamu Sundaramurthy & Marianne Lewis, 'Control and Collaboration: Paradoxes of Governance' (2003) 28(3) *The Academy of Management Review* 397–415.

[29] F Herzberg, B Mausner & B Snydeman *The Motivation to Work* (1959).

[30] For example, the financial statements of Cadbury Nigeria Plc show a financial loss to the tune of NGN13 billion as a result of a breach of fiduciary duties by the board; and a breach of trust by the managers of Oceanic Bank of Nigeria leading to losses in excess of NGN150 billion.

that there is only one social responsibility of a business which is to apply its resources towards increasing its profits; however same should be done within confines of law and principles of business, that is, there must be open competition without deception or fraud. The shareholder approach is so socially ingrained into the financial community and is proliferated in and enforced in practice.[31]

The most popular proponent canvasser of this theory was Professor Adolf Berle. In the celebrated Berle/Dodd debate, he argued that 'all powers granted to the management of a corporation are exercisable only for the benefit of all the shareholders. Berle argues that corporations are simply vehicles for advancing and protecting shareholders' interest; hence, corporate law and governance should be interpreted to reflect this.

The major effect of adopting the Shareholder Theory of governance on the company is that it attracts short-term and passive investors whose sole aim is to derive quick turnover on their investments and cash out. The Shareholder Theory may not be considered as an obsolete theory of doing business as companies have realised that there are disadvantages to concentrating solely on the interests of shareholders, as it is geared towards short-term profit maximisation at the expense of the long-term sustainability of a business entity.[32]

1.3.4 Stakeholder Theory

The Stakeholder Theory is another theory of corporate governance, which looks further than the traditional members of the corporation recognised by the Agency Theory (managers, directors, and shareholders). It focuses on the effect of corporations on all identifiable stakeholders of the corporation and posits that corporate governance should take into consideration the interests of each stakeholder in its governance process. Under this theory, stakeholders are divided into internal and external stakeholders. Internal stakeholders consisted of the directors and employees as they are involved in the corporate governance process while the external stakeholders include creditors, customers, suppliers, auditors, government agencies, and importantly the community at large.[33] Unlike the Agency Theory in which the managers are working and serving for the stakeholders, stakeholder theo-

---

[31] DK Saint & AN Tripathi 'The shareholder and stakeholder Theories of Corporate Purpose' available at http://knowledgeworkz.com/samatvam/newsletter/The%20Shareholder%20and%20Stakeholder%20Theories%20of%20Corporate%20Purpose.pdf. (accessed on 18 August 2019).

[32] Corplaw 'Shareholder and Stakeholder Theories of Corporate Governance available at http://www.corplaw.ie/blog/bid/317212/Shareholder–Stakeholder–Theories–Of–Corporate–Governance (accessed on 18 August 2019).

[33] The Business Professor 'Stakeholder Theory of Corporate Governance' available at https://thebusinessprofessor.com/knowledge–base/stakeholder–theory–of–corporate–governance/ (accessed on 18 August 2019).

rists suggest that managers in organisations have a network of relationships to serve and this network is more important than the owner-manager-employee relationship as in Agency Theory.[34] Donaldson and Preston argued that this theory focuses on managerial decision-making and interests of all stakeholders have an intrinsic value, and no sets of interests are assumed to dominate the others.[35]

The Stakeholder Theory is often misunderstood to mean that a company's focus is not profitability, even though the theory's ultimate objective is the concern's continued existence, it must be achieved by balancing the interests of all shareholders, including the shareholders, whose interests are usually addressed through profits.[36]

The problem with the Stakeholder Theory is that executives can conceal their true intent by publicly asserting a colourable justification to support an initiative on behalf of another stakeholder and most importantly, the fact that balancing the interests of all stakeholders may be extremely difficult and often in fact, impossible.[37]

1.3.5 Resource-Dependence Theory

The Resource-Dependence Theory argues that a company's success can only be achieved by the maximisation of its powers of the resources necessary for its operations. It essentially concentrates on the role of the boards in being the key sources of securing and acquiring the crucial resources of the organisation by their external linkage to the environment.[38] Through these linkages, it brings in different resources, such as information, skills, raw materials, etcetera. Organisational performance is reliant on the power of a company to avail the required and scarce resources.

On the one hand, the Agency Theory suggests the importance of boards in monitoring the managerial activities, on the other; resource-dependence theory highlighted another role of board director as the resource providers. Also, Ruigork, Peck and Tacheva considered the boards as the boundary

---

[34] H Abdullah & B Valentine 'Fundamental and Ethics Theories of Corporate Governance' (2009) 4 *Middle Eastern Finance and Economics* 88–96.

[35] T Donaldson & L Preston 'The stakeholder theory of the corporation: Concepts, evidence, and implications' (1995) 20 *Academy of Management Review* 65–91.

[36] HJ Smith 'The Shareholders vs Stakeholders Debate' available at https://sloanreview.mit.edu/article/the-shareholders-vs-stakeholders-debate/https://sloanreview.mit.edu/article/the-shareholders-vs-stakeholders-debate/ (accessed on 18 August 2019).

[37] L Hsieh 'Long-term value and shareholder theory of corporate governance, available at http://www.eiuperspectives.economist.com/strategy-leadership/long-term-value-and-shareholder-theory-corporate-governance (accessed on 18 August 2019).

[38] T Afza & MS Nazir 'Theoretical perspective of corporate governance: A review' (2014) 119 *European Journal of Scientific Research* 255–64.

guards that shelter the necessary firm's resources like capital, knowledge, skills, and projects partnership agreements.[39]

Furthermore, Aguilera, Filatotchev, Gospel and Jackson argued that the stewardship and stakeholder theories cover the restraining assumptions of the agency perspective, but still these theories do not provide the broader view of the corporate governance that makes it connected with the diverse organisational environments. Hence, the Resource-Dependence Theory has covered this space.[40]

1.4 ORIGIN AND HISTORY OF CORPORATE GOVERNANCE

Charting a definitive historical beginning of corporate governance poses a great difficulty, as corporate governance has been in existence since the use of corporate forms of business ownership and consequently, the possibility of conflict between investors and managers. However, the term 'corporate governance' became popular in the United States (US or USA) in the 1970s. It has since become the subject of global debate and has been well-entrenched in regulatory shorthand worldwide.[41]

Following the aftermath of the Wall Street Crash of 1929, legal scholars such as Adolf Berle, Edwin Dodd, and Gardiner Means pondered on the changing role of the modern corporation in society. The classical mono-graph of Berle and Means, 'The Modern Corporation and Private Property' in 1967, continues to have a profound influence on the concept of corporate governance in scholarly debates.[42] The concept 'corporate governance' started to appear in American law in journals in the 1970s and was exported from America to other countries.[43] However, some have linked the history of corporate governance down to the Netherlands. The Netherlands has the oldest stock exchange market in the world, and its entrepreneurs largely invented the joint-stock corporation. They also established the world's first great limited liability company, The Dutch East India Company in 1602. The world's first great corporate governance dispute followed in 1922, with shareholder complaints about inadequate disclosure and dividend pay-outs.

---

[39] W Ruigrok, S Peck, S Tacheva, P Greve & Y Hu 'The determinants and effects of board nomination committees' (2006) 10 *Journal of Management & Governance* 119–48.

[40] RV Aguilera, I Filatotchev, H Gospel, & G Jackson 'An organizational approach to comparative corporate governance: Costs, contingencies, and complementarities' (2008) 19 *Organization Science* 475–92.

[41] PA Gourevitch & J Shinn *Political Power and Corporate Control: The New Global Politics of Corporate Governance* (2005).

[42] FI Ajogwu *Corporate Governance in Nigeria: Law and Practice* (2007) 4.

[43] The concept first appeared in the Federal Register in America; the official journal of the Federal Government as the Federal Securities Exchange Commission started to treat managerial account-ability issues as being part of its regulatory permit.

The concerns of investors had to be resolved, and this is said to have led to the first talks of the governance of companies.[44]

Although the history and origin of corporate governance pose great difficulty to narrate, what is clear is that corporate governance has existed for as long as companies have been in existence, however, as a field of study, it is less than 70 years old. What is also clear is that corporate governance came about to deal with corporate wrongs such as loss of ethics, short-term goals, and considerations, collusion between directors and auditors, loss of investments, etc. This can be seen through various scandals worldwide that led to strong corporate governance reforms worldwide, such as the Bank of Credit and Commerce International (BCCI) scandal in the United Kingdom (UK), the Imclone Systems scandal in the USA and many more.[45]

There is little literature on the history of corporate governance in African countries. For the purpose of this book, an insight will be given into the development of corporate governance in South Africa and Nigeria.

1.5 HISTORY OF CORPORATE GOVERNANCE IN SOUTH AFRICA

The development of corporate governance in South Africa is not linked to any significant crises of corporate failure as is the story for many other countries, it was rather, as a result of concerns of unhealthy competition that began after South Africa's transition to democracy and re-entry into the global economic space.[46]

Corporate governance in South Africa began to develop with the establishment of the King Committee on Corporate Governance ('King Committee') by the Institute of Directors in South Africa (IoDSA) in 1992. The King Committee released the first King Report in November 1994.[47] The first King Report offered to companies and state-owned enterprises, a coherent and disciplined governance framework relevant to local circumstances. Importantly it was practical in its guidance. The King Committee

---

[44] RK Morck *The Global History of Corporate Governance around the world: Family Business Groups to Professional Managers* (2007)

[45] N Devi A Brief History of Corporate Governance, Agra University available at https://www.docsity.com/en/a-brief-history-of-corporate-governance-corporate-governence-lecture-slides/81334/ (accessed on 18 August 2019).

[46] P Armstrong *Status Report on Corporate Governance Reform in Africa. Prepared on behalf of the Pan–African Consultative Forum on Corporate Governance* (2003).

[47] CA Mallin 'Handbook on International Corporate Governance' available at https://epdf.pub/handbook-on-international-corporate-governanceec28966954d9be3c45a88aada145f00279128.html (accessed on 18 August 2019).

has no official mandate, unlike nearly all other similar initiatives globally, and thus its recommendations are self-regulatory.[48]

The second King Report (King II) came about in 2002 following an assessment of the developments that had taken place in the South African economy and in the global markets since 1994. Just like the first King Report, it was not driven by any major crisis in the corporate sector. However, coincidental with this review, several crises came to light, in both private and public-sector companies, that provided stimulus to this second review.[49] A particular emphasis in the second King Report was on the qualitative aspects of good corporate governance. The second King Report was not designed as a regulatory instrument but was really developed to identify core areas of good practice for boards, directors, and companies, which extended beyond the existing legal and regulatory framework to embrace several aspirational issues. Given the difficulties of applying the guidelines across the entire South African economy, the guidelines contained in the second King Report focused primarily on companies quoted on the Johannesburg Stock Exchange (JSE), financial institutions, and public-sector enterprises and agencies at the national and provincial levels, as they fell within a structured and more readily regulated environment, against which the standards of corporate governance can be more easily identified and measured.[50]

There has also followed the *King III Report** of 2009 which integrated strategy and sustainability to all other aspects of governance and applied to all entities, public, private, and non-profit. Compliance with the *King III Report* was a listing requirement of the Johannesburg Stock Exchange. As Professor Melvyn King noted in his interview to CSJ in July 2017, what was happening was companies wishing to do a rights issue, or companies applying for a listing were being asked to complete an application register which listed the 75 principles of *King III* and required the company to disclose whether it followed each principle and if not explain why. However, this a mindless checklist approach to governance.

The latest iteration of the report is the *King IV Report* of 2016, which was brought about as a result of significant corporate governance and regulatory developments, locally and internationally since the *King III Report*. The *King IV Report* contains 16 basic principles and comes up with practices which if adopted, would lead to the achievement of the principles.[51] The *King IV Report* adopts an outcomes-based approach to corporate

---

[48] Mallin (n 47 above).

[49] P Armstrong *The Evolution of Corporate Governance in South Africa*. Speech delivered at the 4th Annual AIG Corporate Governance Seminar on 4 August 2004.

[50] Armstrong (n 49 above).

* Refer to our King IV IP Policy on our website. (https://www.iodsa.co.za/page/KingIIIPpolicy).

[51] Institute of Directors in New Zealand 'The Future of Governance' available at https://www.iod.org.nz/Portals/0/Branches%20and%20events/Auckland%20branch%20docs/2017%20do-

governance; its structure and principles are designed to evade the risk of tick-box compliance.

While the regulators urge companies to follow the Code, the recommendations of the *King IV Report* are very flexible, and they have not imposed any mandatory obligations for companies to abide by, neither do they have proper legal backing.[52]

1.6 HISTORY AND ORIGIN OF CORPORATE GOVERNANCE IN NIGERIA

The emergence of corporate governance principles in Nigeria can be traced, essentially to the Companies and Allied Matters Act of 1990, which replaced the Companies Act of 1968.[53] The corporate governance principles of Nigeria have closely mirrored those of the UK.[54] For example, the Nigerian Companies Act of 1968 was modelled after the UK Companies Act of 1948. The Companies of Act of 1948 contained detailed provisions regarding the running of the affairs of companies and the roles of the boards of directors and that of members in general meetings. The 1968 Act, however, failed to adequately appreciate the economic realities of Nigeria and the Companies and Allied Matters Act of 1990 (CAMA) ultimately replaced it. Although when CAMA was promulgated, the term corporate governance was yet to emerge as a distinct concept in Nigeria,[55] it contains provisions which are fundamental to corporate governance practice in Nigeria such as required accounting and auditing standards, oversight management, etc. The Act also codifies the fiduciary nature directors' duties and responsibilities (see sections 279, 280, 282 and 283 of the Act).

Shortly after the enactment of CAMA, global corporate challenges fostered conversations on corporate governance; as a result, a number countries reviewed their corporate governance practices in Nigeria, the concept of corporate

---

cuments/Rpt%20-%20The%20Future%20of%20Governance%20by%20Prof%20King-csj_2017_july_mervyn.pdf (accessed on 18 August 2019).

[52] Prof Mervyn King is not the co-author of the King IV Report. The King IV Report was jointly created by many members of the King Committee Task Team as well as input from members of the King Committee—primary contributor was the Project Lead and all individuals assign ownership to the IoDSA as members of the King Committee. Kindly correct same. Furthermore Prof Mervyn King is no longer the Chariman of the King Committee and is now just a member of the King Committee. It is important to note that the co–author, Professor Mervyn King, is the chairperson of both the King Committee on Corporate Governance in South Africa, and the International Integrated Reporting Council. Since the 1990s, South Africa's Kings Reports on Corporate Governance have consistently been at the leading edge of governance best practice and Professor Mervyn King has been at the forefront of the development of Corporate Governance in South Africa.

[53] JB Marshal 'Corporate governance practices: An overview of the evolution of corporate governance codes in Nigeria' (2015) 3 *International Journal of Business & Law Research* 49–65.

[54] BJ Inyang 'Nurturing corporate governance system: The emerging trends in Nigeria' (2009) 4 *Journal of Business Systems, Governance and Ethics* 1–13

[55] Marshal (n 53 above).

governance codes first came from the banking and finance industry through the Code of Corporate Governance for Banks and Other Financial Institutions in Nigeria (the Code) issued by the Bankers' Committee in August 2003. This was in response to the financial crisis in Nigeria before the 2000s and the fact that CAMA did not address the challenges posed by the corporate world. Virtually all crisis in the financial sector had been linked to failed corporate governance practices. The Code addressed issues of corporate governance practices, such as the responsibility of the board, risk management, board relation with shareholders, etcetera

The Atedo Peterside Committee set up by the Securities and Exchange Commission (SEC) in 2003, developed a Code of Corporate Governance for Public Companies.[56] Although a welcomed development, the rapid changes in the corporate world coupled with many corporate scandals across the globe made the provisions of the Code inadequate to cope with the corporate challenges and new developments in the sector.[57] SEC, unfortunately, failed to react and bring the provisions of the Code in line with corporate realities. However, the emergence of sector-specific codes were able to achieve this, such as the Central Bank of Nigeria Code of Corporate Governance for Banks Post Consolidation 2006, Code of Corporate Governance for Licensed Pension Operators 2008, Code of Corporate Governance for the Insurance Industry 2009, Code of Corporate Governance for the Telecommunication Industry 2014 and the Code of Corporate Governance for Banks and Discount Houses in Nigeria and Guidelines for Whistle Blowing in the Nigerian Banking Industry 2014. These Codes regulate the guideline for corporate governance in their respective sectors/industries.

Due to the numerous shortcomings of the 2003 SEC code, SEC constituted a National Committee, headed by Mahmoud, SAN to review of the 2003 SEC Code and to address its weaknesses by improving the mechanism for its enforceability and to also identify weakness and constraints to good corporate governance and proffer solutions.[58] The 2003 Code was replaced with the Code of Corporate Governance for Public Companies 2011. The Code is regarded as the minimum standard for public companies in Nigeria. The purport of the Code is to ensure the highest standards of transparency, accountability, and good corporate governance, without unduly inhibiting enterprise and innovation. In that same year, the Financial Reporting

---

[56] The co–author Professor Fabian Ajogwu worked on the drafting of this pioneer code, under the chairmanship of Atedo Peterside. The Financial Reporting Council of Nigeria has inaugurated a Technical Committee to review the suspended National Code of Corporate Governance (NCCG) and develop/recommend a revised Code. Professor Fabian Ajogwu is a member of this committee.

[57] The Corporate Prof 'Historical development of Corporate Governance in Nigeria' available at http://thecorporateprof.com/historical-development-of-corporate-governance-in-nigeria/ (accessed on 18 August 2019).

[58] Corporate Prof (n 57 above).

Council of Nigeria Act 2011 was enacted and contained details and impactful provisions on the operation of Nigerian corporations.

In line with the dynamic nature of the capital market and challenges in the corporate world, the SEC further amended the 2011 Code in 2014 to reflect evolving international best practices. Majorly, the Code was upgraded from a moral-suasion based voluntary code to a mandatory code and provided minimum corporate governance standards to be met. [59]

The Financial Reporting Council of Nigeria (FRCN), issued a three-in-one National Code of Corporate Governance in October 2016. Specifically, the three codes issued were, the National Code of Corporate Governance for the Private Sector in Nigeria, public-sector Governance Code in Nigeria, and the Not-For-Profit Organisations Governance Code. The Code of Corporate Governance for the Private Sector was to harmonise the various sector codes previously in existence. The Federal Government, through the Minister for Industry, Trade, and Investment, suspended the Codes and following this, the FRCN inaugurated a technical committee to review these suspended codes.

The said technical committee produced the Nigerian Code of Corporate Governance, 2018. The Code consolidates the Codes for private and public companies; however, the Code for Not-for-Profit entities remains suspended. Before the suspended Codes and the 2018 Code, a shortcoming of the development of Corporate Governance in Nigeria was that most private companies were not mandated to comply with the principles. This was likely premised on the notion that it is public companies that control the economy; however, this notion is misplaced as companies can shape the economy regardless of if they are private or not. For example, MTN Nigeria only recently went public. It had derived a total revenue of about N870 billion in 2017, while still a private company.[60] Although private at the time, its system of corporate governance ought to have been monitored as a result of the wider implications the failure or negative activities of such a company could have on the Nigeria Economy. The 2018 Code applies to all companies as it makes no distinction between Private and Public Companies or Public Interest Entities. The Code adopts the 'apply and explain' approach, which requires companies to adopt the practices in the Code and explain the reasons for adopting them in line with their activities.[61] It requires companies to demonstrate how the specific activities they have undertaken best achieve the outcomes intended by the corporate governance

---

[59] Marshal (n 53 above).

[60] O Obi-Chukwu 'MTN reports N870 billion revenue from Nigeria alone in 2017 HY' available at https://nairametrics.com/mtn–reports–n870–billion–revenue–from–nigeria–alone–in–2017–hy/ (accessed on 18 August 2019).

[61] *The National Code of Corporate Governance* (2018).

principles specified in the Code;[62] this is in a bid to prevent a box-ticking exercise. Importantly, the Code is scalable to suit the type, size, and growth phase of each company while still achieving the outcomes envisaged by the principles.[63]

The 2018 Code is divided into six key governance pillars and 28 principles:

- ☑ Board of Directors and Officers of the Board (Principles 1–16)
- ☑ Assurance (Principles 17–20)
- ☑ Relationship with Shareholders (Principles 21–23)
- ☑ Business Conduct and Ethics (Principles 24 and 25)
- ☑ Sustainability (Principle 26)
- ☑ Transparency (Principles 27 and 28)

Under each principle, the Code provides recommended practices for its implementation.

KEY DEVELOPMENTS IN THE NIGERIAN CODE OF CORPORATE GOVERNANCE 2018

1. **Whistle Blowing (Section 19):** The Code mandates Boards to design a whistleblowing framework allowing for confidential disclosures by employees.

   Information Technology (Section 11.5.6.6): The Code requires the board to constitute a committee responsible for providing oversight for risk management related matters within the organisation. In particular, the Code notes that the committee is responsible for reviewing the company's Information Technology (IT) Data Framework on an annual basis. The framework is to include the development of IT Strategy, management of risks relating to third-party and outsources IT service providers' assessment of value delivered to the Company through investments in IT and periodic independent assurance on the effectiveness of the Company's IT arrangements.

2. **Tenure (Section 12.10)** The Code provides that Independent Non-Executive Directors have a **maximum** tenure of three terms of three years each.

3. **Corporate Governance Evaluation (Section 15):** The Code introduced a corporate **governance** evaluation to be performed annually which will focus on the implementation of the Code, and the summary of the report included in the company's annual report and investors' portal.

---

[62] Code (n 61 above).
[63] Code (n 61 above).

4. **Remuneration Governance (Section 16)**: The Code provides that remuneration policies are also to be disclosed in the annual reports alongside remuneration for all directors. The Code further **excludes** executive directors from earning sitting allowance at board and committee meetings and non-executive directors from earning performance-based pay. Interestingly, the Code provides that companies implement a clawback policy to recover excess or underserved reward, such as bonuses, incentives, a share of profits, stock options, or any performance-based rewards, from directors and senior employees.

5. **Risk Assessment (Section 1.9 and 17.5)**: The Code mandates companies with complex **operations** to undertake at least annual a risk assessment covering all aspect of the company's business and to approve the establishment of a framework that defines the company's risk policy, risk appetite and risk limits.

6. **Auditors (Section 20)** The Code extends the role of auditors and mandates them to report any **observed** instance where the company or anyone associated with the company commit an indictable office under any law.

7. **Environment, Social and Governance (ESG) Activities (Section 28.2.l)**: The Code requires that a company's corporate governance report includes ESG activities, sustainability policies **and** programmes covering social issues such as corruption and community service.

8. **Company Secretary (Section 8)**: The Code mandates the Board to empower the company secretary properly as well as provide for the company secretary's performance, evaluation, appointment, and removal.

1.7 THE CHANGING ROLE OF THE GOVERNING BODY IN THE GOVERNANCE OF CORPORATE ENTITIES

The board of directors is the primary governing body of an entity; they link the key players in an entity together. The board of directors is central to corporate governance as it provides a link to other participants, such as shareholders and management.[64] Their role has been at the centre of the policy debate concerning governance reform and the focus of considerable academic research.[65]

The board is usually made up of executive and non-executive directors. Executive directors are full-time employees of the company and therefore have a dual relationship with the company as they also work in a senior capacity, usually concerned with policy matters or functional business areas

---

[64] S Jan & M Sangmi 'The Role of the Board of Directors in Corporate Governance' 2016 2(5) *Imperial Journal of Interdisciplinary Research (IJIR)* 707–715 at 707 available at https://pdfs.semanticscholar.org/ab6c/60705060fa198a543890d4968925943cc71c.pdf (accessed 18 August 2019).

[65] R Adams, BE Hermalin & MS Weisbach 'The Role of Boards of Directors in Corporate Governance: A Conceptual Framework and Survey' 2008 *National Bureau of Economic Research.*

of major strategic importance.[66] While non-executive directors are not employees of the company and are not involved in its day to day running, they provide a balancing influence and help to minimise conflicts of interest. They also scrutinise the performance of the executive directors and provide an external perspective on risk management.[67]

There are majorly two models of boards; unitary and two-tier. The unitary model is adopted by countries like the UK, USA, and South Africa, under this model, the board of directors is comprised of both executive and non-executive directors. However, in many countries, companies adopt a two-tier structure where there is a separation of those responsible for supervision from those responsible for operations. The supervisory board generally oversees the operating board.[68] A criticism of the one-tier structure is the high concentration of power which resides in the hands of the Chief Executive Officer (CEO); however, the presence of the non-executive directors should curtail this.

The board is the link between the company and its stakeholders. As a result, it is entrusted with great power and responsibility to ensure efficient governance of a company. Determining the role of the board often proves very difficult as companies are different all over the world and the perceived role of the board is ever-changing in accordance with the theories of corporate governance or the laws/code in place at a particular period.

Possible answers as to the role of the board range from being simply legal necessities to the overall management and control of the entity.[69]

Undeniably, one of the main if not the main role of the board is to establish the culture, value, and ethics of the company. The King Report identifies with this noting the following to be the roles of the board:

- To define the purpose of the company
- To identify the value drivers by which the company will perform its daily duties
- To identify the stakeholders pertinent to the business of the company
- To develop a business model which creates value in a sustainable manner
- To ensure implementation of strategy by way of informed oversight
- To ensure adequate and effective controls
- To ensure that the company is seen to be a responsible corporate citizen

---

[66] ACCA Global 'Corporate Governance' available at http://www.accaglobal.com/content/dam/acca/global/PDF-students/2012s/sa_oct12-f1fab_governance.pdf (accessed on 18 August 2019).

[67] D Higgs *Review of the Role and Effectiveness of Non-Executive Directors* (2003).

[68] ACCA Global (n 66 above).

[69] Ibid (22).

☑   To ensure conscious corporate leadership.

Boulton also noted that the generally accepted roles of the boards are:

☑   establishing objective, corporate strategies and broad policies of the company;
☑   asking discerning questions;
☑   providing advice and counsel;
☑   serving as a sort of discipline; and
☑   acting in crises situations.

However, the role of the board can be said to be above and beyond the roles set out above.

Simply put, the board is the custodian of the company, and in recent times, boards have expanded their roles beyond conventional governance to include strategy development and stakeholder relations. Leading boards recognise that they bear responsibility for allocating resources and to do so, must be increasingly aware of the strategic options available to the company. Directors have dug deeper to concern themselves with market conditions, customers, and competitors.[70] This is as a result of the external pressure on the company; stakeholders, particularly civil society, which demand more attention and and pressing boards to remain alert and vigilant and also to anticipate important issues and opportunities before they materialise.[71] There is also pressure from regulators for boards to not only ensure the long-term sustainability of the business of the company but to ensure that companies are run according to best governance principles.

Boards today play an active role in mindfully applying good governance principles. Boards constantly question how their decisions impact on the four outcomes of good governance. Evolving duties of the board include informed oversight, conscious that it is the conscience of the company which as an incapacitated artificial person has no conscience.

1.8 CONCLUSION

This chapter has provided the definitions of corporate governance and the theories and the historical development of corporate governance. As can be inferred from the above discussions, corporate governance is a complex term that has stirred much academic and regulatory debate. As a result of the academic nature of the term, transferring its principles into a codified regulatory framework and enforcing same provides much difficulty. It is also difficult to attribute effective corporate governance to positive business

---

[70] C Skroupa 'How Boards of Directors Shaping to Meet New Challenges' *Skytop Strategies* (2017) available at https://skytopstrategies.com/how-boards-of-directors-are-shaping-to-meet-new-challenges/ (accessed on 18 August 2019).
[71] Skroupa (n 70 above).

achievements. Hence to reduce the unwillingness of companies to apply the ethics and principles of corporate governance, an approach must be taken to tie corporate governance to its outcomes. This is the exact aim of this book. The following chapters will delve deeper into understanding the term corporate governance in a bid to propose and structure an outcomes-based system of corporate governance that will provide companies with an incentive to mindfully apply the necessary principles of good corporate governance.

Chapter 2

CORPORATE GOVERNANCE MODELS: A COMPARISON

There are various corporate governance models operating in different parts of the world, and there is an ongoing debate over which one is the best or most effective model. This is so given the fact that each model has its own advantages and disadvantages. The most popularly identified models are the Anglo-US model, the Japanese model, and the German model.

2.1 THE ANGLO-US MODEL

This is also known as the unitary board model (or the 'Anglo-Saxon' approach) in which all directors participate in a single board comprising both executive and non-executive directors in varying proportions.[1] This model applies mostly to corporations in the developed nations of the UK, the US, Australia, Canada, New Zealand, India, and other commonwealth countries.[2]

The Anglo-US model was adapted from and influenced by the systems of governance followed in the USA and the UK and is essentially shareholder-oriented. It is characterised by share ownership of individual and institutional shareholders not affiliated with the corporation. It is a well-developed legal framework defining the rights and responsibilities of three key players – management, directors, and shareholders (which form what is commonly referred to as the 'corporate governance triangle'), and a set of procedures for interaction between shareholder and corporation as well as among shareholders.[3]

One important characteristic of the Anglo-US model is that it prescribes the separation of share ownership and control in most publicly-held corporations. The value herein is that investors avoid legal liability for the acts of the corporation and simply contribute capital and maintain

---

[1] AC Fernando *Business Ethics and Corporate Governance* 2 ed (2012).
[2] Fernando (n 1 above).
[3] Emerging Markets ESG 'Three Models of Corporate Governance' available at http://www.emergingmarketsesg.net/esg/wp–content/uploads/2011/01/Three-Models-of-Corporate-Governance-January-2009.pdf (accessed on 2 March 2018).

ownership of their shares.[4] Investors can avoid liability by ceding the management and control of the corporation to management that, in turn, oversees the affairs of the corporation. This gives rise to what is referred to as 'agency costs'. The separation of shareholder and management has, however, resulted in a situation wherein the interests of the shareholders and management may not always coincide. Countries using the Anglo-US model have attempted to reconcile this conflict in several ways. One such way is prescribing that the board of directors be elected by shareholders and to require that boards act as fiduciaries for shareholders' interests by overseeing management in the best interests of the company.

It is also pertinent to point out that players in the Anglo-US model included shareholders (most often shareholders who are institutional investors), directors, management, government agencies, stock exchanges and consulting firms that advise entities on corporate governance.[5] Supervision is exercised mostly by investors who express their favour or disapproval for the actions of management by buying or selling shares of the company and voting during the general meetings of shareholders.[6] It is for this reason that stock exchanges, by establishing listing, disclosing, and meeting other requirements, play a crucial role in this model.

A further prominent feature of the Anglo-US model is the fact that the board of directors includes 'insiders' and 'outsiders'. An 'insider' is a person employed by the corporation (an executive, manager, or employee) or a person who has a significant personal or business relationship with the corporation's management.[7] An 'outsider' is a person or institution who has no direct relationship with the corporation or its management.[8] Insiders are often referred to as executive directors while outsiders are considered non-executive directors or independent directors.

In the Anglo-US model, shareholders may exercise their voting rights without being present at the annual general meeting (AGM) in person; shareholders may vote by proxy, and so forth. It is also common practice to have a corporation's performance and corporate governance monitored by institutional investors and financial specialists such as rating agencies, auditors, a variety of specialised investment funds, venture capital funds, or funds that invest in start-up corporations.[9] This model also allows shareholders to submit proposals known as shareholder proposals which may

---

[4] B O'Connell 'Models of Corporate Governance' available at https://bizfluent.com/list–6710522–models–corporate–governance.html (accessed on 23 February 2018).

[5] Emerging Markets ESG (n 3 above).

[6] CEOpedia 'Anglo–Saxon Model of Corporate Governance' https://ceopedia.org/index.php/Anglo–Saxon_model_of_corporate_governance (accessed on 2 March 2018).

[7] *The National Code of Corporate Governance* (2018).

[8] Code (n 7 above).

[9] Code (n 7 above).

then be added to the agenda for the company's AGM. The proposal must, however, relate to the company's business activities. Shareholders with at least 10 per cent total share capital are also allowed to convene an extraordinary general meeting of shareholders.[10]

Overall, the protection of shareholder interests is the chief characteristic of the Anglo-US Model and the fundamental principle behind its existence and global acceptance as the most favourable model of corporate governance.[11] The Anglo-US model, however, has a shortcoming, which is that the same person often serves as the chairman of the board and as the CEO of the enterprise. This has the potential to result in several abuses and a concentration of power in the hand of one person.

2.2 THE JAPANESE MODEL

This is the business network model, which reflects the cultural relationships seen in the Japanese *keiretsu* network, in which boards tend to be large, predominantly executive, and often ritualistic.[12]

The Japanese model comprises of a broad level of ownership by banks and their affiliated companies, '*keiretsu*,' industrial groups linked by trading relationships and cross-shareholdings of debt and equity.[13] The key players under this model are the banks, the *keiretsu*,[14] management, and the government.[15] The board of directors of corporations that adopt the Japanese model comprises almost solely of insiders. There is usually a low or non-existent level of input by external shareholders.[16] Although equity financing is important for Japanese corporations, insiders and their affiliates are the major shareholders in most Japanese corporations. Consequently, they play a significant role in individual corporations and in the system as a whole.[17]

The Japanese system of corporate governance is multifaceted, centring around a main bank and a financial or industrial network or *keiretsu*.[18] In

---

[10] C Thomas (ed) *Theories of Corporate Governance: The Philosophical Foundations of Corporate Governance* (2004).

[11] Implicity 'The Anglo– American Model of Corporate Governance– Basic Overview' available at https://implicity.wordpress.com/2009/09/15/the–anglo–american–model–of–corporate–governance–basic–overview/ (accessed on 9 March 2018).

[12] JB Marshal 'Corporate governance practices: An overview of the evolution of corporate governance codes in Nigeria' (2015) 3 *International Journal of Business & Law Research* 49–65.

[13] Code (n 7 above).

[14] *Keiretsu* means group or system. The Keiretsu network is a set of companies with interlocking business relationships and shareholdings.

[15] Ibid

[16] F Allen & M Zhao *The Corporate Governance Model of Japan: Shareholders Are Not Rulers* (2007).

[17] Allen & Zhao (n 17 above).

[18] In the Japanese model, the four key players are: The main bank (a major inside shareholder), affiliated company or *keiretsu* (a major inside shareholder), management and the government.

this model, the financial institution plays a crucial role in governance. One of the distinctive features of this model is that the main bank and the shareholders jointly appoint board members and a president, who consults both the supervisory board and the executive management.[19] The board of Japanese corporations tends to be comprised mostly of executive managers who head major departments and a central administrative body.[20] Another important power that the main bank and *keiretsu* exercise under this model are the removal and replacement of directors in the event of the company's profits reducing over an extended period.[21]

Under the Japanese model, the composition of the board is dependent on the company's financial performance. Another common practice in Japan is the appointment of retiring government bureaucrats to corporate boards.[22] Government policy also plays a crucial role under the Japanese model and, as such, government ministries have been extremely influential in developing industrial policy.[23]

Several corporate actions require shareholder approval under this model, such as payment of dividends, allocation of reserves, capital authorisations, amendments to articles of association, the election of directors, the appointment of auditors, and payment of certain bonuses to directors and auditors such as retirement bonuses. Further, non-routine corporate actions such as mergers, takeovers, and restructurings also require shareholders' approval.[24]

The Japanese Model also contains certain disclosure requirements. For example, companies are mandated to disclose the following information in their annual report and/or agenda for an AGM:

- ☑ the company's financial data on a semi-annual basis;
- ☑ the company's capital structure;
- ☑ particulars of persons proposed as auditors;
- ☑ particulars of each nominee to the board such as the director's occupation, relationship with the corporation, and ownership of shares in the company;
- ☑ the maximum amount of compensation payable to the board members and other executive officers
- ☑ information on corporate restructurings; and

---

[19] JB Marshal (n 12 above).

[20] S Claassen, S Djankov & LHP Lang 'The separation of ownership and control in East Asian corporations' 2000 *Journal of Financial Economics.*

[21] Claassen et al (n 20 above).

[22] Emerging Markets ESG (n 3 above).

[23] A major shareholder in the corporation in the Japanese https://www.coursehero.com/file/p69mte3c/A-major-shareholder-in-the-corporation-in-the-Japanese-model-In-the-Japanese/

[24] Code (n 7 above).

☑   information on amendments to articles of association.[25]

The annual reports and materials for the AGM are required to be made available to all shareholders and shareholders are entitled to vote by proxy or vote by mail.[26]

The main strength of the Japanese corporate governance model lies in its ability to ensure that outside stakeholders like shareholders and creditor are given an internal function.[27]

2.3 THE GERMAN MODEL

The German model is also referred to as the two-tier board model of corporate governance or the Continental European approach. It is also the model adopted in Holland and to a certain extent, France. Under this model, corporate governance is the function of two boards, namely, the upper board (*Aufsichtsrat*) that plays a supervisory role over the executive board (*Vorstand*) on behalf of stakeholders. The objectives of this model are societal-oriented.[28] The distinguishing characteristics of the model are the board structure and rights afforded to shareholders.

The supervisory board is responsible for appointing and dismissing the management board as well as advising the management board and approving their major decisions. A corporation's Articles of Association usually sets the financial threshold of corporate acts requiring supervisory board approval.[29] The management board is composed entirely of insiders, that is, executives of the corporation whereas the supervisory board is composed of labour/employee representatives and shareholder representatives. The management board is solely responsible for the management of the company and its business activities.[30]

In respect of shareholders' rights, Germany legally prescribes voting-right restrictions which prohibit shareholders from voting only a prescribed

---

[25] Prior to 1981, Japanese law did not permit shareholders to put resolutions on the agenda for the annual meeting. A 1981 amendment to the Commercial Code states that a registered shareholder holding at least 10% of a company's shares may propose an issue to be included on the agenda for the AGM.

[26] Ibid.

[27] H Sakai & H Asaoka 'The Japanese Corporate Governance System and Firm Performance: toward sustainable growth' 2003 *Research Center for Policy and Economy*. Mitsubishi Research Institute, Inc. available at http://www.esri.go.jp/jp/prj/int_prj/prj–rc/macro/macro14/05mri1_t.pdf (accessed 8 March 2018).

[28] JB Marshal (n 7 above).

[29] P Nunnenkamp 'The German model of corporate governance: Basic features, critical issues, and applicability to transition economies' Kiel Working Paper, No 713 (1995) *Institut für Weltwirtschaft* (IfW).

[30] Sections 76(1) and 78(1) of the Aktiengesetz (AktG), translated as the German Stock Corporation Act.

percentage of the corporation's total share capital, regardless of the amount of shares the shareholder holds in the company.[31]

German corporations traditionally prefer bank financing over equity financing. As a result, the German stock market capitalisation is small in relation to the size of the German economy.[32] Also, individual stock ownership in Germany is relatively low. As such, the German corporate governance model aims to preserve relationships between banks and corporate shareholders.[33] In Germany, corporations are also shareholders and may invest long term in other companies even when it has no industrial or commercial affiliation to the company.[34]

The German model has policies in place to foster harmony between the corporation and its stakeholders.[35] Employees are able to elect a third of the members of the supervisory board (usually trade union representatives) depending on the corporation's size (except for corporations in the coal, iron, and steel industries because different regulations apply to them). This right is known as codetermination (*Mitbestimmung*), and it is regulated principally by the *Mitbestimmungsgesetz* of 1976 (Codetermination Act of 1976). It is applicable to public and private companies with over 2 000 employees. Where the company has between 500 to 2 000 employees, one-third of the supervisory board must be selected. The ideology behind codetermination is to promote trust, transparency, and harmony.[36]

The German model, like the Japanese mode, requires certain information to be disclosed in the company's annual report and/or agenda for an AGM.[37] Certain corporate actions such as payment of dividends, allocation of reserves, elections to the supervisory board, the appointment of auditors and the ratification of management acts require shareholder approval.[38]

---

[31] 'Corporate Governance in Germany: A model out of time?' *The Economist* available at http://www.economist.com/node/3600260 (accessed on 26 February 2018).

[32] Ibit.

[33] LA Bebchuck 'The case for increasing shareholder power' (2004) 118 *Harvard Law Review*.

[34] In 1990, corporations held 41% of the German equity market, and institutional owners (primarily banks) held 27%. Neither institutional agents, such as pension funds (3%) or individual owners (4%) are significant in Germany. Foreign investors held 19% in 1990,

[35] B Tricker & The Economist Newspaper Ltd *Essentials for Board Directors: An A–Z Guide* 2 ed (2003, 2009).

[36] See, JP Charkham *Keeping Good Company* (1995) 13 and 14 for a historical background of employees on the board.

[37] This includes: corporate financial data (required on a semi–annual basis); data on the capital structure; limited information on each supervisory board nominee (including name, hometown and occupation/affiliation); aggregate data for compensation of the management board and supervisory board; any substantial shareholder holding more than 5% of the corporation's total share capital; information on proposed mergers and restructurings; proposed amendments to the articles of association; and names of individuals and/or companies proposed as auditors.

[38] A Cadbury *Report of the Committee on the Financial service Aspects of Corporate Governance* (1992).

2.4 ANALYSIS OF THE THREE MODELS

The criteria for comparison of these models are based on several factors, some of which are:

☑ the key players in the corporate environment;
☑ the share-ownership pattern;
☑ the composition of the board or boards of directors;
☑ the regulatory framework;
☑ the mission of the board;
☑ delineation of the duties and responsibilities of the board of directors;
☑ disclosure requirement for publicly-listed stock corporations;
☑ corporate actions requiring shareholder approval;
☑ rights of shareholders;
☑ rights of stakeholders; and
☑ interaction among key players.

Overall, many countries across the world consider the Anglo-US model more favourable and it is therefore widely adopted. In contrast to the Anglo-US model, unaffiliated shareholders have little or no voice in Japanese governance.[39] As such, the Japanese model does not make sufficient provision for truly independent directors (directors representing outside shareholders). In contrast to the Anglo-US model, representatives of unaffiliated shareholders seldom sit on Japanese boards.[40]

In both the Japanese and the German model, banks are key shareholders and have overlapping roles since they also provide services to corporations. This is unlike the Anglo-US model, where antitrust laws prohibit such relationship. Under the Anglo-US model financing is obtained from a various sources, including the securities market.[41]

Although under both the German and Japanese models, bank representatives are elected to the board, under the Japanese model, this is usually only done where there is a corporate failure or financial decline.[42]

The Anglo-US model has the strictest disclosure requirements, unlike the Japanese model. Under the Anglo-US model, for instance, there is a requirement for quarterly disclosure of financial data, whereas, under the

---

[39] CJ Crawford *The Reform of Corporate Governance: Major Trends in the U.S. Corporate Boardroom, 1977–1997* (unpublished doctoral dissertation, Capella University, 2007).
[40] M Ungureanu & AI Cuza *Models and Practices of Corporate Governance Worldwide* (CES Working Papers) (2013).
[41] A Cadbury *Report of the Committee on the Financial Aspects of Corporate Governance* (1992).
[42] Cadbury (n 14 above).

Japanese model, the requirement is on a semi-annual basis.[43] There is also a significant difference in acceptable accounting standards in both models.[44]

Another angle of comparison lies in the fact that whereas American corporations are managed under the supervision of a single board, German corporations are organised under the Stock Corporation Act of 1965 and have a two-tier system. The essence of the two-tiered structure is the explicit representation of other stakeholder interests besides shareholders and also because no major strategic decisions can be made without the cooperation of employees and their representatives.[45] Both the role of the supervisory board as well as the role of the unitary board arises out of a need to control management.

Looking closely at the role of the board in the Anglo-US model and German model, it is clear that whereas the role of the unitary board is to monitor management primarily in the interest of shareholders, the supervisory board's task is supervision in the interest of a wider range of stakeholders of the company.[46] The supervisory board theoretically plays a monitoring role somewhat similar to that played by independent directors on a unitary board.[47]

In conclusion, the effect of corporate governance is far-reaching in economies as it links to good governance systems. Thus, there is the need for a state – especially emerging economies – to identify the appropriate model that could harness the potentials of all key players in the corporate governance circle and promote corporate restructuring and technological modernisation.

2.5 PROBLEMS OF CORPORATE GOVERNANCE MODELS IN EMERGING MARKETS

Emerging markets play a key role in the global economy because of their rapidly growing and improving legal infrastructures. For investors, this not

---

[43] L Bebchuk & J Fried *Pay Without Performance – the Unfulfilled Promise of Executive Compensation* (2004).

[44] S Ross 'What are different Corporate Governance Systems around the world?' available at https://www.investopedia.com/ask/answers/051115/what–are–some–examples–different–corporate–governance–systems–across–world.asp (accessed 23 February 2018).

[45] G Tuengler 'The Anglo–American board of directors and the German supervisory board – Marionnettes in a puppet theatre of corporate governance or efficient controlling devices?' (2000) 12 *Bond Law Review* 230.

[46] M Bradley 'The purposes and accountability of the corporation in contemporary society: Corporate governance at a crossroads' (1999) 62 *Law and Contemporary Problems* 9 at 53.

[47] CJ Meier-Schatz 'Corporate governance and legal rules: A transnational look at concepts and problems of internal corporate management control' (1988) 13 *The Journal of Corporation Law* 431 at 443 fn 67.

only offers an attractive opportunity but also presents multifaceted risks.[48] For this reason, it is necessary to structure an appropriate framework for a model of corporate governance in emerging markets such as South Africa and Nigeria. Corporate governance in countries like South Africa and Nigeria have taken their roots from the above-discussed models, most especially the Anglo-US model. However, these models have been adopted without adaptations to fit the peculiarities of the economies of these emerging markets. The adoption of these models in emerging markets wrongly assumes that the market conditions present in developed economies are equally present in emerging economies.

It is important to identify the distinctive challenges of corporate governance in corporations in emerging markets. Some of the issues include the existence of a principal-principal conflict (as opposed to the principal-agency conflict particular to developed corporations) between controlling shareholders with concentrated ownership and minority shareholders coupled with the weak legal protection of minority shareholder. There is also extensive family ownership and control even over business group structures.[49] It has further been identified that there is lack of information contained in stock or share prices. Furthermore, the legal framework in emerging markets has been criticised. This is not to say that emerging economies have no legal framework for corporate governance, in fact as already noted, emerging economies have traditionally adopted the legal frameworks of developed economies, particularly the Anglo-US system in response to international demands or corporate failures.[50]

There is, however, a lack of regulations concerning key components of corporate governance such as accounting requirements, information disclosure, securities trading, and even when present, there is a lack of enforcement or inadequate enforcement.[51] What is predominant in emerging markets is the presence of informal institutions playing a greater role in shaping corporate governance, this results in novel problems.[52] It is, however, important to note that in recent times economies such as those of South Africa and Nigeria are moving towards creating a model of corporate governance that can be termed as 'outcomes-based', this proposed model of corporate governance will be discussed in detail in the following chapters.

---

[48] G Dallas 'Corporate Governance in Emerging Markets' (Harvard Law School Forum, August, 2011) available at https://corpgov.law.harvard.edu/2011/08/24/corporate–governance–in–emerging–markets/ (accessed 16 April 2018).

[49] MN Young, MW Peng, D Ahlstrom, GD Bruton & Y Jiang corporate governance in emerging economic: A review of the principal–principal perspective (2008) 45 *Journal of Management Studies*.

[50] Young et al (n 49 above).

[51] Young et al (n 49 above).

[52] Young et al (n 49 above).

Chapter 3

EMERGING TRENDS IN CORPORATE GOVERNANCE

As has been highlighted in Chapters 1 and 2, corporate governance is an ever-changing concept, influenced by cultural, political, educational, and societal occurrences. Since the emergence of the term 'corporate governance', there has been a constant evolution of its composition. In the past decade there has been a shift in corporate governance from mere compliance and check-box ticking to an actual consideration of the effects of governance on a corporation. Importantly, there has been a marked shift to ethical and strategic governance. In terms of strategy, over the past ten years, boards have been restructured and managed to become tools of strategy based on information and data shared by directors and managements alike. Corporations have become increasingly receptive to the notion that a more engaged board is today's business reality as such engagement translated into benefits for the corporation.[1]

Various trends and components of contemporary corporate governance have emerged in recent years to assist the corporation in developing management quality and responsiveness towards the interest of all its financial stakeholders and society at large.[2] A very important development worthy of mention is the fact that the pendulum is also swinging back from boards being concerned solely with shareholders to a recognition of the importance of a broader set of stakeholders the interests of which the board must also consider. Boards and governance scholars are now more readily perceptive and understanding of the fact that a board's role does not stop at merely protecting the interests of its shareholders but can also draw links to shareholder interests from the interests of other constituents, such as employees down to even the environment.[3] These emerging trends are as a result of the business realities of the twenty-first century and include:

- ☑ inclusive capitalism;
- ☑ long-term sustainability;

---

[1] A Skeet 'Corporate Governance Continues to Evolve' (2018) Markulla Center for Applied Ethics available at https://www.scu.edu/ethics/focus–areas/business–ethics/resources/trends–in–corporate–governance/ (accessed 30 April 2018).

[2] V Rajendran 'Corporate governance practices – Emerging trends' (2012) 1 *TRANS Asian Journal of Marketing & Management Research*.

[3] Skeet (n 1 above).

☑   corporate citizenship;
☑   right relations;
☑   ethics of matching supply and demand;
☑   multiple stakeholder considerations;
☑   integrated reporting;
☑   technology governance;
☑   corporate security;
☑   internal audit; and
☑   outcomes-based governance.

These emerging trends listed above are related and eventually result in one goal, which is the long-term existence and profitability of corporations. The three emerging trends highlighted in the *King IV Report* (inclusive capitalism, a shift to long-term sustainability and integrated reporting as opposed to siloed reporting) will be considered in this chapter. The key trends of technology governance, corporate security, internal audit and assurance and corporate citizenship will also be discussed due to their key significance. Finally, the all-encompassing trend of 'outcomes-based corporate governance' under which all other emerging trends have emanated will be considered.

3.1 INCLUSIVE CAPITALISM

Capitalism is one of the world's major economic systems which has been given several definitions. Black's Law Dictionary[4] defines capitalism as 'an economic system that depends on private ownership of the means of production and on competitive forces to determine what is produced'. On its own part, the New Webster's Dictionary of the English Language (International Edition), defines capitalism as 'an economic system in which the means of production, distribution and exchange are privately owned and operated for private profit'.

A third and similar definition of capitalism can be found in the Merriam-Webster Online Dictionary and reads as follows:

> an economic system characterized by private or corporate ownership of capital goods, by investments that are determined by private decisions, and by prices, production, and the distribution of goods that are determined mainly by competition in a free market.

Lynn Forester de Rothschild and Dominic Barton declare,

> '[C]apitalism is the greatest engine for prosperity the world has ever seen, and part of its success lies in its capacity to adapt'.[5]

---

[4] BA Garner *Black's Law Dictionary* 7 ed (1999).
[5] LF de Rothschild & D Barton 'A Case for Inclusive Capitalism' *The Guardian* available at https://www.theguardian.com/commentisfree/2012/may/15/case–for–inclusive–capitalism (accessed 18 May 2018).

The use of the term 'inclusive' as an adjective to complement the noun 'capitalism' implies that there is something inherently exclusive about a capitalist system. Inclusive capitalism originates from philosophical questions that predate modern-day capitalism. These questions regard people's motivations, such as are people motivated by self-interest? The society's interest? Or somewhere in between? In simple terms, inclusive capitalism is a global effort to engage leaders across businesses in the movement to make capitalism more equitable and sustainable.[6]

The term inclusive capitalism was made popular by Prahalad in the 'bottom of the pyramid' discourse. This idea was lent support by the likes of the South African President Thabo Mbeki in 2002 when Hewlett-Packard launched a three-year public-private partnership at the 2002 United Nations (UN) World Summit on Sustainable Development in Johannesburg aimed at creating breakthrough models of sustainable development and not altruism.[7] In 2014, a non-profit organisation known as the 'Coalition for Inclusive Capitalism' was founded by Lady Lynn de Rothschild as an initiative to convene Fortune 100 CEOs, asset managers, and political leaders in order to help restore capitalism as an engine of broadly-shared prosperity.

The objective of the organisation is to encourage businesses to make changes and expand their investment and management practices to regain public trust and influence the future of capitalism.[8] The organisation has set the tone of the inclusive capitalism trend in corporate governance and has a number of supporters such as former US President Bill Clinton, Carlos Slim and even Pope Francis. The organisation has also succeeded in receiving the commitment of top organisations such as Vanguard, Unilever, and PepsiCo to its goals.[9] The coalition discusses inclusive capitalism in the following words:

> Inclusive capitalism provides that firms should account for themselves, not just on the bottom line, but on environmental, social and governance (ESG) metrics. Every firm has a license to operate from the society in which it trades. This is both a legally and socially defined license. Firms must contribute proportionately to the societies in which they operate. Without fairly contributing, firms free-ride on services that other people have paid for. Firms that practice unsustainable activities, disrespect their stakeholders and the communities in which they operate will find their licenses threatened, first by the

---

[6] De Rothschild & Barton (n 5 above).

[7] R McaFalls 'Testing the limits of 'inclusive capitalism': A case study of the South Africa HP i–Community (No 28, is Corporate Citizenship Making a Difference?) 2001 *The Journal of Corporate Citizenship* 85–98.

[8] Inclusive Capitalism 'About Us" available at https://www.inc–cap.com/about–us/ (accessed on 18 May 2018).

[9] Businesswire 'Global Private Sector Leaders Make Commitments to Investment and Business Practices That Stimulate Long-Term Value Creation at the 2016 Conference on Inclusive Capitalism in New York City' available at https://www.businesswire.com/news/home/20161010005815/en/ Global–Private–Sector–Leaders–Commitments–Investment–Business (accessed on 20 May 2018).

engaged consumer, then by government. Conversely, Firms actively practicing proper Inclusive Capitalism will see their license strengthened.[10]

Inclusive capitalism has been described as an action that can move a population out of poverty while driving economic growth that is more inclusive, sustainable, and fair. The emergence of inclusive capitalism in corporate governance is in line with Professor Merrick Dodd's side of the Berle/Dodd debate which argued for a view of the business corporation as an economic institution which has a social service as well as a profit-making function.[11] Inclusive capitalism adopts the idea that a corporation ought to do more than just make a profit but should also aim to have a positive impact on the society at large by means of corporate social responsibility (CSR) instruments and fostering community engagement.[12] Inclusive capitalism is related to CSR, however, it goes beyond CSR because it focuses on the ways in which corporations can jointly foster responsible behaviour, fairness and integrity.[13]

Inclusive capitalism in the corporate governance framework is centred on long-term value creation, always building on principles such as ethics and transparency. It is a more responsible form of capitalism which puts people at the heart of decision-making, with the aim of creating jobs, promoting investment, contributing to public finances, fostering innovation, protecting the natural environment, and ensuring the wellbeing of citizens. It has become the essential responsibility of corporations to materialise these concepts. To take full advantage of this, companies practising inclusive capitalism require stable and predictable regulatory frameworks which allow them to design and implement responsible and sustainable business models.[14]

The ideal of inclusive capitalism is that companies must ensure that all stakeholders, not just shareholders, derive benefits from a business. The Henry Jackson Initiative for Inclusive Capitalism suggests that there are three ways for a corporation to achieve inclusive capitalism. They are:

☑   education for employment;
☑   support for SMEs; and
☑   improvement in corporate management and governance for the long term.

---

[10] 2016 Conference on Inclusive Capitalism held in New York City.

[11] LA Stout 'Bad and Not–so–Bad Arguments for Shareholder Primacy' (2002) *Cornell Law Faculty Publications* 448, available at https://scholarship.law.cornell.edu/facpub/448/ (accessed on 28 September 2019).

[12] M Boleat 'Inclusive Capitalism: Searching for a purpose beyond profit' 2014 *Ethical Business Finance* https://www.theguardian.com/sustainable–business/inclusive–capitalism–purpose–beyond–profit (accessed on 30 May 2018).

[13] Boleat (n 12 above).

[14] IS Galan 'The Meaning of Inclusive Capitalism' *Huffington Post* available at https://www.huffingtonpost.com/inclusive–capitalism/the–meaning–of–inclusive_b_8922230.html (accessed 30 May 2018).

The most important of the three is generally agreed to be the long-term improvement in corporate management and governance. A destabilizing aspect of contemporary capitalism is that the pressures of today's short term-focused market lead to management focusing more sharply on short-term regulations that provide short-term profits than on the long-term requirements of the business. This ought to be replaced by long-term thinking on the part of corporations.

The important question to be asked is what corporations seek to gain in the pursuit of inclusive capitalism and the simple answer to this is that it is the capitalist economy that enables corporations to thrive and thus, capitalism cannot be allowed to fail. The argument is that if the capitalist system becomes more inclusive it becomes more sustainable. Sustainability of the capitalist system leads to the long-term existence and profitability of a business corporation.[15] The potential benefits associated with the long-term nature of inclusive capitalism are:

- ☑ harvesting an illiquidity risk premium;
- ☑ providing ballast to the capital market;
- ☑ investing in innovations that sustain the enterprises and society over time; and[16]
- ☑ creation short, medium, and long-term value.

It is noteworthy that twenty-first-century corporations have started adopting inclusive capitalism measures on an ever-growing scale. This trend was highlighted at the 2016 Conference on inclusive capitalism held in London. To emphasise the newly acknowledged importance of inclusive capitalism measures in corporate governance, below are some quotes from the speeches of renowned CEOs of thriving corporations:

> Richard Edelman, the president and CEO of Edelman:
>
> The best CEOs are taking a different view, a commitment to solving societal problems while achieving top results for their corporations.[17]

Harry Samneu, CEO of RBC Investor & Treasury Services:

> Corporations have a vested interest in developing their employees, which increases economic value for their organisation and the economy as a whole. The next step is for the private sector to recognize that it is essential to invest in social infrastructure to underpin a dynamic and robust economy and ensure its longevity. These investments include but are not limited to, education, healthcare, housing, and public transportation. They must be designed to promote and protect equal access and opportunity.

---

[15] The Henry Jackson Initiative *Towards A More Inclusive Capitalism* (2012).

[16] DF Carney (ed) *Inclusive capitalism The Pathway to Action*, 'Thoughts form the 2015 Conference on Inclusive Capitalism (26 June 2015) available at <http://www.inc–cap.com/wp–content/uploads/2015/07/Book–2.pdf> (accessed 30 May 2018).

[17] Carney (n 16 above).

Lynn Forester de Rothschild of EL Rothschild and Dominic Barton of McKinsey & Company, note that:

> The idea that underlies our notion of inclusive capitalism is the need to manage companies for the long term. Companies that manage for the long-term worry about the skills and development of their recruits, build sustainable and loyal supplier bases, find ways to counter the short-term pressures of the market and consistently foster lasting relationships with all their stakeholders.[18]

It is therefore imperative for a twenty-first-century corporation to consider seriously the ideals of inclusive capitalism. For inclusive capitalism to be achieved, the approach of boards must be changed, board members need to consider that increasing shareholder value is just one amongst several objectives and desired outcomes. The job of the board is to balance multi-stakeholder interests; hence boards should set long-term goals for people, the planet and profits; oversee the production of integrated annual reports that monitor progress in all aspects of a corporation's business and ensure that the remuneration of top executives is aligned to achieving these goals.

The enabler for the change towards inclusive capitalism is a drive by investors to reward good business. It is neither achieved by a box-ticking focus on governance nor by obsessing about quarterly financial results, but by a shift towards measuring longer-term business performance and wider social impact.

In the context of emerging markets such as most markets in Africa. Tony O Elumelu, the chairman of Heirs Holding explains that in the context of Africa, inclusive capitalism and 'Africapitalism' must emphasise the obligation of the private sector towards the socio-economic development of Africa and advocate greater coordination and collaboration by diverse economic actions. Inclusive capitalism must be part of the solution to Africa's long history of economic and social inequality. He further notes that there is a compelling need to generate social capital in a sustainable and self-reinforcing manner if market-based systems are to continue to flourish. Corporations in emerging markets must recognise that their long-term sustainability is dependent on their obligation to contribute to the wellbeing of the wider society and this in turn would benefit the corporation.[19]

3.2 SHIFT IN FOCUS TO LONG-TERM SUSTAINABILITY

Sustainability has many definitions but from a corporate perspective, sustainability means that companies should consider the future in their decision-making actions with the aim of using their resources for creating

---

[18] De Rothschild & Barton (n 5 above).
[19] Carney (n 16 above).

value in the long run.[20] Corporate sustainability is the process by which corporations through corporate governance ensure positive impact on environmental, social, economic and sustainable development. A new prerequisite for a fully functioning corporate governance reflects sustainability through the entire process of business management.[21] The concept encompasses a long-term vision that characterises socially responsible companies. This approach requires the balance of interests of all those who contribute to the company's current and future success by means of sustainable value creation that satisfies both shareholders and other stakeholders in the long term.

Sustainable development is not limited to matters such as economic viability of a corporation or CSR.[22] Sustainable development rather meets the needs of the present without compromising the ability of future generations to meet their needs. It is against the backdrop that corporations are corporate citizens and an integral part of society hence, they must consider the needs, interests and expectations of society and its other stakeholders.[23] Sustainability is also related to capitalism as sustainable capitalism refers to an economic system in which value is created in a sustainable manner for the long term. The period indicated by the long term is dependent on the corporation's objective alongside the risks/opportunities presented by the external environment and stakeholders.[24]

This relatively new trend also focuses on ways to encourage investors and finance providers to extend their investment horizons. It fosters the idea that the performance in terms of an all-inclusive value should be assessed over the longer term and the capital market system must reward long-term decision-making.[25] It is important to note that corporate sustainability does not mean that value creation of shareholders and their adequate remuneration is less important. Rather it means that meeting the needs of stakeholders other than share holders also creates shareholder value and ownership satisfaction, guaranteeing the firm's competitive advantage in the long term.[26]

In the past, institutional investors often had a myopic obsession with short-term performance. Historically investors pressed boards and managers

---

[20] DM Salioni, F Gennari & L Bosetti *Sustainability and Convergence: The Future of Corporate Governance System*: Department of Economics and Management, University of Brescia, Contrada Santa Chiara (2016).

[21] M Krechovska & PT Prochazkova 'Sustainability and its integration into corporate governance focusing on corporate performance management and reporting' (Elsevier University of Wet Bohemia, Faculty of Economics Husova 11, Plzeh 306 14, Czech Republic.

[22] IODSA *King IV Report on Corporate Governance* (2016).

[23] Salioni et al (n 20 above).

[24] *King IV Report* (n 22 above).

[25] Salioni et al (n 20 above).

[26] FE Harrison, J Wicks, A Parmer & B de Colle *Stakeholder Theory. The State of the Art* (2010).

to deliver high returns promptly and often pushed for corporate managers to be highly responsive to the immediate pressures and incentives of the capital markets.[27] This has now changed; investors are aware of the perceived benefits of long-term investments which include long-term value as it focuses on future challenges. Increasingly, investors are diversifying their portfolios and investing in corporations with a commitment to corporate sustainability.[28]

According to the UN Global Compact:

> Corporate sustainability is imperative for businesses today, essential to long-term corporate success and for ensuring that markets deliver value across society and to push sustainability deep into the corporate DNA, companies must commit at the highest level.[29]

Marjella Alma, the CEO and co-founder of the business intelligence technology company, 'eRavalue' mentions that heightened expectations of leadership to adopt a holistic, long-term approach to managing ESG impact is the 'new normal'[30]

RobecoSAM, an investment specialist agency focused exclusively on sustainability investing, notes what they look out for before investing in a company:

> We're interested in who within a company is responsible for sustainability issues on both a strategic and an operational level,' said Matthias Müller, a senior analyst. We look for a specific board committee formally responsible for sustainability and/or if executive managers sit on a sustainability committee that sets the company's corporate responsibility agenda.[31]

RobecoSAM also assesses 'whether companies apply environmental and/or social success metrics for senior management compensation or other financial indicators. Implementing sustainability performance into the management incentive system should assure that sustainability initiatives are managed properly,' Müller said.[32]

The evolution of corporate governance to consider long-term strategy and risk/opportunities while not easy is vital to achieving sustained value. In the process of solving the complex and multifaceted challenges of today's

---

[27] LE Strone Jr. 'One fundamental corporate governance question we face: Can corporations be managed for the long term unless their powerful electorates also act and think long term?' (2010) 66 *The Business Lawyer.*

[28] I Knoepfel 'Dow Jones Sustainability Group Index: A global benchmark for corporate sustainability, corporate environmental strategy' (2001) 8 *Corporate Environmental Strategy* 6–15.

[29] *UN Global Compact. Guide to Corporate Sustainability* (2015).

[30] M Flynn & M Wallace 'Corporate governance and sustainability: Who's connecting the dots?' available at https://www.greenbiz.com/article/corporate-governance-and-sustainability-whos-connecting-dots (accessed 30 May 2018).

[31] Carney (n 16 above).

[32] Carney (n 16 above).

world, businesses must understand the effects of economic, social, and environmental systems and how they interrelate and affect one another. By adopting an approach of long-term sustainability, the business gains the support and value of shareholders and stakeholders to sustain the future.[33]

A sustainable approach to business can result in a competitive advantage and a long-term success factor. Sustainable governance requires that the boards of directors consider economic, social, and environmental expectations in an integrated way no matter what ownership structure and formal rules of corporate governance apply to the company, just like inclusive capitalism. This mitigates the traditional difference between insider and outsider systems of corporate governance.[34]

The first responsibility for sustainable corporate strategies lies with the board of directors – their cooperation is necessary for the transfer of principles of sustainability into the goals and behaviours of the whole organisation. International guidelines emphasise the role of the board in the realisation of sustainable goals. Boards of directors have the ability to combine leadership with control and effectiveness with accountability that will primarily determine how well companies meet society's expectations of them.[35] Several studies have investigated the links between corporate governance structures and corporate sustainability, showing the importance of the board's approach to these matters. A board's commitment and sustainable corporate engagement reflected in goals, strategies, operational activities, and accountability can be a major factor in overcoming the traditional differences in corporate governance structures, stimulating a gradual sustainable convergence between outsider and insider systems. The board's commitment to sustainability can be carried out by establishing devoted committees and other organisational positions. A sustainability-oriented board can be a force to be reckoned with especially if the board maintains a constant dialogue with all the stakeholders and ensure that sustainability is dynamically integrated into corporate objectives and business operations to create a shared sustainability culture.

3.3 CORPORATE CITIZENSHIP

Businesses today face a complex and often contradictory set of stakeholder expectations. They are called on to engage with activists as well as analysts, to manage market risks as well as social and environmental risks and to be held accountable for their financial and non-financial performance. Businesses are also expected to compete often with non-traditional partners and unfamiliar issues. There is pressure from governments, consumers, trade

---

[33] Carney (n 16 above).
[34] Salioni et al (n 20 above).
[35] A Cadbury 'Thoughts on corporate governance' 1993 *Corp Gov* 1 at 5–10.

unions, etcetera for organisations to demonstrative performance in terms of their corporate and citizenship and not note in market growth.[36]

The concept of corporate citizenship is closely linked to the ideals of inclusive capitalism and sustainability. Corporate citizenship deals with companies taking into account not just their impact on the economy but also on society and in so doing assume responsibilities that go well beyond the scope of simple commercial relationships.[37] It expresses the conviction that companies must not just engage with their stakeholders but are themselves stakeholders alongside the governments and civil society. Therefore, organisations must commit to sustainable development and address paramount global issues. Because these issues increasingly impact business, it is in the corporation's enlightened self-interest and goal of sustainability to address issues that are both good for the corporation and society. This has become extremely important in a time of increasing globalisation and diminishing state influence.[38]

Organisations must aim to do minimal harm in terms of negative economic impact, bad labour practices, corruption, etcetera. This calls for management strategies such as compliance with internationally accepted and best norms, guidelines, and standards. Secondly, organisations must aim to do good in terms of creating new value for both the business and its stakeholders in the community or communities in which it operates.[39]

In leading companies, corporate citizenship is moving beyond the boundaries of legal compliance and traditional philanthropy to become a more central factor in determining corporate success and legitimacy, with implications for corporate strategy, governance, and risk management.[40] Good corporate citizenship can provide the following business benefits:

1. *Reputation management:* Reputations are built over time by the ability of an organisation to balance the expectations of multiple stakeholders. A study of 'America's Most Admired Companies' as listed in Fortune magazine, found that a good corporate reputation increases the length of time a firm spends earning above-average financial returns and decreases the length of time that firm spends earning below-average financial returns.[41] A company's reputation can also affect its

---

[36] J Nelson, 'Corporate Citizenship in A Global Context' (2005) Corporate Social Responsibility Working Paper No 13 available at https://sites.hks.harvard.edu/m–rcbg/CSRI/publications/Workingpaper_13_nelson.pdf (accessed on 10 September 2018).

[37] AD Little 'The Business Case for Corporate Citizenship' available at http://www.csrwire.com/pdf/Business–Case–for–Corporate–Citzenship.pdf (accessed 10 September 2018).

[38] S Klaus 'Global Corporate Citizenship: Working with Governments and Civil Society' (2008) 87 *Foreign Affairs* 107–18.

[39] Klaus (n 38 above).

[40] Little (n 37)

[41] G Dowling *Creating Corporate Reputations: Identity, Image and Performance* (2001).

attractiveness as a prospective employer, hence influences recruitment, motivation, and retention.

2. *Risk profile and risk management:* Companies are constantly facing a widening range of risks. One way to substantially reduce an organisation's perceived risk is by directly being involved in systematically managing social issues under their control and influence.

3. *Investor relations and access to capital:* Investors are becoming more aware of the non-financial aspects of business management. There is a range of indices that rate corporate performance on environmental and social performance. Funds are increasingly being managed in line with socially responsible investment (SRI) principles, hence portfolio managers screening out of businesses that do not meet high SRI principles or use their influence to improve the ethical performance of these corporations.

4. *Competitiveness and market positioning:* With the level of public interest on environmental and societal issues, corporate citizenship offers organisations a platform to appeal to the public by adopting these high environmental and social standards in their business activities.

5. *Operational efficiency:* Corporate citizenship can result in bottom-line improvements. For example, reducing material use and waste can save money while simultaneously reducing environmental impact.

6. *Licence to operate:* As was discussed under inclusive capitalism, every company has a license to operate and the perceptions that stakeholders have of a company's corporate citizenship performance can significantly affect the business's licence to operate.

3.4 INTEGRATED REPORTING AND THINKING AS OPPOSED TO SILOED REPORTING

Social and environmental (sustainability) reporting has been evolving since the 1970s, with accelerated growth in reporting since the turn of the century. This evolution can be seen in the vast volume of literature documenting sustainable reporting's development. Social and environmental reporting can be considered a way of legitimising a company to its stakeholders, as companies seek to persuade society that they have stakeholders' interests at heart and that they share common objectives.

3.4.1 Siloed Reporting and Its Dangers

Siloed reporting is the traditional means of reporting and reflects the data silo culture in organisations. A data silo is a repository of fixed data that remains under the control of one department and is isolated from the rest of the organisation, much like grain in a farm silo is closed off from outside elements.[42] Data silos are increasingly present in large organisations because each organisational unit is often dispersed with varying goals, priorities and responsibilities. Also, in large organisations departments tend to compete, resulting in data silos.[43]

Data silos have faced increased criticism because they impede productivity and negatively impact data integrity.[44] Siloed technology and request management results in disconnected reporting channels. It is crucial to note that management base their decisions on the information they receive and when the information is not effective or accurate, the decisions taken by management in turn will hinder the effective operation of the business.[45]

3.4.2 Integrated Reporting

The corporate world is experiencing an era of radical transparency which has prompted in a shift in how corporate reporting is perceived.[46] This can be seen in the European Union's Directive on ESG. The traditional reporting system was a revolutionary development when it was instituted, however, there are now higher requirements from regulators and stakeholders as well as a complex regulatory regime. An organisation's reporting is now aimed at reflecting the interconnectedness of its sources of value creation and its relationships with its stakeholders and indicates how its activities affect and are affected in the context in which it operates.[47]

An integrated report is a holistic and integrated representation of the organisation's performance in terms of its finances and its sustainability. An integrated reporting approach takes account of the connectivity and interdependencies between the ranges of factors that affect an organisation's ability to create long-term value. Integrated reporting is in line with the idea of an inclusive, sustainable capital market system and should communicate the current position (business model, performance), where it is going (future outlook) and how it intends to get there (strategy). It tells us the organisation's value creation story in an easily understandable way. By its very nature integrated reporting is not just a reporting by-product, it must be central to the organisation. It needs to flow from the heart of the organisation and it should be the organisation's primary report to stakeholders.[48] This kind of transformation requires a collaborative effort from all parts of

---

[42] Search Cloud 'Definition of Data Silo' https://searchcloudapplications.techtarget.com/definition/data–silo.

[43] Search Cloud (n 42 above).

[44] Search Cloud (n 42 above).

[45] A Shuja 'Silo-Ed Report: Leadership and Supplier Management' (2013) available at https://blog.learningtree.com/silo–ed–reporting–leadership–and–supplier–management/ (accessed on 29 September 2019).

[46] *King IV Report* (n 22 above).

[47] Integrated Reporting (2012) available at https://integratedreporting.org/news/press–release–businesses–believe–integrated–reporting–helps–to–break–down–silos/ (accessed on 30 May 2018).

[48] See Professor Mervyn King's Foreword in IRCSA 2011.

the organisation,[49] as the collaborative effort would break down silos between teams and lead to better connected departments.[50]

Integrated reporting is more than reporting, it emanates from integrated thinking. Reporting and thinking are two sides of the same coin, both necessary to enhance connectivity in an organisation and enhanced communication on value creation.[51] Thinking of integrated reporting from an integrated thinking perspective highlights the fact that there are multiple entry points to integrated thinking and it is a constant process of improvement, through systems, people, behaviours and governance.[52]

This concept requires organisations to factor decisions, trade-offs, and sacrifices into their business model. For example, an organisation may have to decide between reserving its financial capital in the short term or expending same to increase profit in the long term. These decisions, if important, should be set out in an integrated report and defined in the organisation's value creation objectives.[53]

3.4.3 Benefits of Integrated Reporting

The benefits of integrated reporting are remarkable. Making a conscious and coordinated effort to connect the organisation's strategy to its governance and performance unleashes the compelling and durable internal and external benefits of integrated reporting. The more integrated reporting through integrated thinking is assumed into an organisations strategy, the more easily information would flow in management reporting and decision-making. It can also lead to improved integration of the information systems that support internal and external reporting and communication, including preparation of the integrated report.[54] A series of benefits arising from integrated reporting are summarised by research houses for the International Integrated Reporting Council (IIRC) as follows:

- better alignment of reported information with investor needs;
- availability of more accurate non-financial information for data vendors;

---

[49] F Ribeiro, A Giacoman & M Trantham 'Dealing with Market Disruption Seven Strategies For Breaking Down Silos' (2016) available at https://www.strategyand.pwc.com/report/dealing-market-disruption (accessed on 30 May 2018).

[50] Blacksun Plc *Understanding Transformation: Building the Business Case for Integrated Reporting* (2012).

[51] Integrated Reporting 'Creating Value The Cyclical Power of Integrated Thinking and Reporting' available at http://integratedreporting.org/wp-content/uploads/2017/05/CreatingValue_IntegratedThinkingK1.pdf (accessed on 30 May 2018).

[52] Integrated Reporting (n 51 above).

[53] KPMG 'Performance Insight Through Better Business Reporting' available at https://assets.kpmg/content/dam/kpmg/pdf/2011/10/Integrated-Reporting-ENG.pdf (accessed on 30 May 2018).

[54] KPMG (n 53 above).

☑   higher levels of trust with key stakeholders;
☑   better resource allocation decisions, including cost reductions;
☑   enhanced risk management;
☑   better identification of opportunities;
☑   greater engagement with investors and other stakeholders, including current and prospective employees, which improves attraction and retention of skills;
☑   lower reputational risk;
☑   lower cost of, and better access to, capital because of improved disclosure; and
☑   development of a common language and greater collaboration across different functions within the organisation.[55]

3.4.4 Integrated Reporting and Corporate Governance

The origin of integrated reporting lies in corporate governance, as a solution to demands on corporate leadership regarding the sustainability, strategy, performance, and risks facing the organisation. The global financial crisis, the increased incidence of environmental disasters and myriad accounting scandals have motivated an increased focus on corporate governance and integrated reporting. Against this background, stakeholders, investors, and regulators have changed the requirements for corporate reporting and as a result, business reporting has become similarly complex. Modern information needs from investors and other key stakeholders are in a state of continual flux.

The value of a company now extends beyond the historical financial aspects, rather business partners, managers, investors, and other stakeholders nowadays have an increasing need for the complete picture of a company's health in order to gain a clear understanding of the company's global performance and to make better decisions. Based on these factors, companies are being forced to report their financial information and non-financial information to stakeholders, as clearly, concisely, and transparently as possible. Also, corporate reporting has evolved markedly from its traditional iteration as more of a strictly financial report, to its contemporary format where it must include additional matters which would give stakeholders the information they need to value their investments. Integrated reporting then comes into play as traditional financial reporting cannot provide a full picture of corporate-activity elements such as sustainability issues embedded into strategy, information on environmental activities, carbon emissions, health and labour rights, supply chain issues and integration of internal functional units.

---

[55] KPMG (n 53 above).

Corporate governance as part of integrated reporting has been developed to rebuild the trust of stakeholders and to create a feeling that the interest of management is in line with the long-term health of the company. Furthermore, integrated reporting can enhance corporate governance because integrated reporting equips those responsible within the organisation to make better decisions, better actions and better capital and resource allocation to create and sustain long-term sustainable value. Integrated reporting can also help to identify opportunities and risks for the organisation to facilitate better risk management and provides information which is better aligned with investor needs. Above all, integrated reporting is a good tool for improved corporate governance.[56]

3.4.5   How Is Integrated Reporting Structured?

Many people discussing integrated reporting for the first time want to 'see' an example of an integrated report. However, there is no standard format for an integrated report and no specific disclosure requirements. Instead, the Discussion Paper issued by the IIRC sets out five Guiding Principles and six Content Elements for an integrated report. The Guiding Principles are:

1.   strategic focus;
2.   future orientation;
3.   connectivity of information;
4.   responsiveness and stakeholder inclusiveness; and
5.   conciseness, reliability, and materiality.

The Content Elements are:

- *Organisation overview and business model,* which focuses on how organisations can create and sustain short, medium- and long-term value.
- *Operation context, including risks and opportunities*, which entails key resources and relationship on which a corporation depends on, including the key risks and opportunities faced.
- *Strategic objectives*, which focuses on a set out strategic plan to achieve goals.
- *Governance and remuneration*, which relates to the organisations' governance structure, how the governance supports the strategic objectives of the organisation and how it relates to the organisation's approach to remuneration.
- *Performance*, which relates to how the organisation performed in respect to its strategic objectives and related strategies.
- *Future outlook*, which relates to what opportunities, challenges and

---

[56] B Roxana–Iona 'University Anna Stefea Petru, Integrated Reporting for God Corporate Governance (2018) 17 *Economic Sciences.*

uncertainties the organisation would possibly encounter while achieving its objective and the implication for its future performance.

To help users and drafters understand how integrated reporting differs from
traditional corporate reporting, the IIRC also contrasts eight differences
between corporate and integrated reporting. Importantly, integrated reporting addresses financial, manufactured, human, intellectual, natural, and
social resources (referred to as capitals) which the business consumes and
creates. The table below illustrates some of these differences:

Table 3.1

Feature	Current reporting	Integrated reporting
Trust	Narrow Disclosures	Greater transparency
Stewardship	Financial	All forms of capital
Thinking	Isolated	Integrated
FOCUS	Past, financial	Past and future; connected; strategic
Timeframe	Short term	Short, medium, and long term
Adaptive	Rule bound	Responsive to individual circumstances
Concise	Long and complex	Concise and material
Technology-enabled	Paper-based	Technology-enabled

3.5 TECHNOLOGY GOVERNANCE

Technology plays an important role in modern corporate governance,
particularly as a result of its potential to revolutionise, transform product
service and improve and automate the compliance process in the post
corporate governance reforms era.[57] Technology governance itself is the
process of management and control of technology service in alignment with
the needs of a business. Technology has become indispensable to an
organisation s performance; its fast-increasing sophistication and connectivity is used in the production process, supply chains, and to coordinate the
work of employees. At the same time, data has become an ever-important
asset class, creating both the potential to create value and, if security is
mishandled, a potential reputational risk.[58]

In recognition of the undeniable impact of technology governance in
twenty-first-century organisations, the European Commission in 2017
unveiled a directive on corporate governance which in part promotes the use

[57] Z Rezaee 'Globalization, technology, and corporate governance' in *Corporate Governance Post–Sarbanes–Oxley Regulations, Requirements, and Integrated Processes* (2015) ch 13, 457–83.
[58] J Armour 'Corporate Governance and Technological Risks' (University of Oxford Law Blog, February 2017) available at https://www.law.ox.ac.uk/research–and–subject–groups/research–collec-tion–law–and–technology/blog/2017/02/corporate–governance (accessed on 12 September 2018).

of new technologies in the corporate governance of companies. At the European Union Corporate Governance in XXI Century: Shareholder Rights Directive II and Beyond 2017 Conference in Brussels, the benefits of using new technologies in the field of corporate governance were identified and it was noted that technology has the potential to improve interaction between stakeholders globally and in a safe, fast, and low-cost manner.[59]

Technology has become so woven into the DNA of organisational structures, that it has become common place to use technology to store and protect data, increase productivity of employees, promote the business brand (through social media) and to promote sustainability (by allowing organisations to pursue greener initiatives through for example going paperless). However, most organisations, particularly those in emerging markets, are yet to explore technology to achieve two major goals:

☑ improve the role of the board of directors; and
☑ facilitate the relationship between corporate actors using Blockchain Technology.

The above benefits of technology governance will be the focus of the next section.

3.5.1 Improving the Role of Boards of Directors Through Technology

The emergence of board solutions in the form of board portals or applications have been crucial in simplifying board functions and increasing efficiency. Board portals generally offer boards a digital platform in which they can manage meetings, distribute, annotate, and store documents. Many of the applications go further to allow boards electronically vote on decisions, assign and monitor actions, record minutes and input essential data.[60] The software solutions inbuilt in the applications can further track changes in discussions that clearly demonstrate how boards arrived at their decisions.[61] The major advantage of technology board solutions is that they simplify the process of auditing and compliance as they create a permanent record for regulators and shareholders to review. The data and analysis by which decisions are reached by the board members are made available and this aids in transparency and accountability.[62]

---

[59] C Alvarez 'New Technologies Accelerate the Digital Transformation of Corporate Governance' (BBVA, 2017) available at https://www.bbva.com/en/new–technologies–accelerate–digital–transformation–corporate–governance/ (accessed 13 September 2018).

[60] BoardPacks, 'The Changing View and Roles of Technology in Corporate Governance' available at https://eshare.net/wp–content/uploads/2017/07/changing–view–and–roles–of–technology–in–corporate–governance.pdf (accessed 13 September 2018).

[61] NJ Price 'Boardroom Technology: Achieving Strong Corporate Governance through Technology' (Diligent, 2018) available at https://diligent.com/blog/corporate–governance–technology (accessed on 13 September 2018).

[62] Price (n 61 above).

The security of such applications is usually ensured using two-factor authentications and the data within them is encrypted.[63] This also reduces the risk present with printed board packs and materials and directors can easily access their pre-meeting materials on the secured portals. The most important and most unrecognised benefit of technology in this regard is that such applications not only improve efficiency and security, but they also aid in ensuring transparency and accountability. The information and data used to make decisions are clearly made available and can be subject to review by regulators, shareholders, auditors, and future directors.

3.5.2 Facilitating the Relationship Between Corporate Actors Using Blockchain Technology

The latest development in technology solutions is Blockchain Technology which is mostly used in the world of virtual/cryptocurrencies. However, Blockchain Technology can also offer solutions for classical inefficiencies in the corporate field. A blockchain is essentially a decentralised peer-to-peer network of transaction confirmations; it operates as a decentralised ledger that can securely record transactions between parties in an immutable way and within a fraction of a second.[64]

The AGM of Shareholders is the age-long tool that provides the shareholders with a monitoring capacity, however most shareholders especially institutional and short-term investors have become uninterested in the platform. If a private blockchain, managed by the company and only accessible to shareholders is made available, the company can use such a platform to present information to shareholders who may then exercise their voting rights through the same platform.[65] The OECD Directorate for Financial Enterprise Affairs Corporate Governance Committee released a paper in June, 2018 titled *Blockchain Technology and Corporate Governance*. the paper identified that an AGM under a blockchain design will have several material benefits such as easier voting (not mere electronic but digital voting), certainty in the tabulation of votes and making it harder to manipulate board elections. More importantly, the paper identified that Blockchain Technology can eradicate all intermediaries in the relationship between shareholder and company, thereby fostering allegiance and accountability and reducing costs. The paper notes that:

---

[63] Price (n 61 above).

[64] V Akgiray 'Blockchain Technology and Corporate Governance: Technology, Markets, Regulation and Corporate Governance' (Organisation for Economic Co–operation and Development, Directorate for Financial and Enterprise Affairs Corporate Governance Committee, 2018) available at http://www.oecd.org/officialdocuments/publicdisplaydocumentpdf/?cote=DAF/CA/CG/RD(2018)1/REV1&docLanguage=En (assessed 10 September 2018).

[65] A Lafarre & C van Der Elst 'Block Chain Technology Corporate Governance and Shareholder Activism' (ecgi news, April 9, 2018) available at https://ecgi.global/news/blockchain–technology–corporate–governance–and–shareholder–activism (assessed 10 September 2018).

The inefficiency and ineffectiveness of corporate governance systems, in turn, is largely due to the current complexity of the investment chain with an ever increasing number of intermediaries. The distance between households (owners of money) and corporations (user of money) has increased to untraceable measures because of a complex web of intermediaries (managers of money). Since block-chain technology's biggest promise is the elimination of some or all intermediaries, it offers a great opportunity for better corporate governance. Block chain works perfectly for such a need as it is able to provide a cutoff point, calculate majority requirements and shareholders can verify their own transactions. This not only decreases the decision making time but can also decrease organisation's costs.[66]

3.5.3 Corporate Security in Relation to Risk Management

Globalisation is taking companies to riskier places and, as a result, the security risks of organisations have become more complex. Many of the risks, such as terrorism, organised crime, cyberattacks, and information security are asymmetric and networked hence making them more difficult to manage. There is now a greater appreciation of the interdependence between a company's risk portfolio and the way it does business.[67]

Risk management is the process of identifying, comprehending, and managing risks that an organisation will inevitably face in the process of achieving its corporate objectives.[68] The aspect of risk management that has gained the most attention in recent years is corporate security. The responsibility of the security department has widened to include shared responsibility for things such as corporate governance, regulation, CSR, and information assurance.[69] Companies have become increasingly aware of the interdependence between security risks and operating practice, security, and corporate governance.

Corporate governance is one of that main factors that has changed the nature of corporate security by giving it a wider range of responsibility including fraud, corruption, negligence, information security, money laundering, business continuity planning, regulation, employee conduct and proper response to major events including natural and man-made disasters that could result in data loss.[70] Furthermore, the corporate security

---

[66] Lafarre & Van der Elst (n 65 above).

[67] R Briggs & C Edwards 'The Business of Resilience: Corporate Security For The 21st Century' (Demos, 2006) available at https://www.demos.co.uk/files/thebusinessofresilience.pdf (assessed 12 September 2018).

[68] R Lutui & T Ahokovi 'Financial Fraud Risk Management and Corporate Governance' (2017) (Edith Cowan University Research Online, Australian Information Security Management Conference', 2017) available at http://ro.ecu.edu.au/cgi/viewcontent.cgi?article=1200&context=ism (assessed 9 September 2018).

[69] Briggs & Edwards (n 67 above).

[70] BA Hamilton 'Convergence of Enterprise Security Organizations' (The Alliance for Enterprise Security Risk Management, 2005) available at https://pdfs.semanticscholar.org/9cb9/fe2450502b4e8bb4923978d9afc7198eab0b.pdf (assessed 9 September 2018).

community has taken steps to align security with the business so that doing business and security go hand in hand.

A study conducted over the space of one year on multinational companies found that only a handful of these companies appeared to be doing so successfully and what they all had in common were six characteristics:[71]

1.   The organisations understood that security is achieved through the everyday actions of employees right across the company and is not the sole function of the security department.

2.   They recognised the limitations of command and control approaches to change management as change management is a continuing process and not a once-off project. Corporate security departments must therefore build social networks that place increased emphasis on people, management and social skills by being inclusive and not authoritarian in their ways.

3.   They understood that their role is to help the company face risks head-on rather than eliminate them and to have structures that mini-mise damage when things go wrong. Risk taking is essential to the success of any business and the security department can contribute to expanding the frontiers of a business. An example is the business practice of offshoring (opening up affiliates or branches across borders), corporate security aids in ensuring that such offshore businesses are run in an integrated manner but hazard-free manner.

4.   They embraced and contributed towards their company's key business concerns and as a result are expanding the security portfolio significantly. Corporate security departments in such organisations are not seen in the traditional sense of them being an external assisting organ of the company but are seen as a department of the company that shares the business's objectives and policies.

5.   They drew a clear a distinction between the strategic and operational aspects of security management.

6.   The corporate security departments that are leading have abandoned old assumptions about where their power and legitimacy come from in the sense that although the organisation requires their knowledge and skills, they must still compete on the same terms as every other function of the company by incorporating business acumen, people skills, management and communication in carrying out their duties.[72]

3.5.4 Internal Audit and Assurance

In recent times there has been a major focus on internal auditing as a corporate governance mechanism. This is because internal auditing

---

[71] Briggs & Edwards (n 67 above).
[72] Briggs & Edwards (n 67 above).

provides assurance by assessing and reporting on the effectiveness of risk management and control structures in place to assist an organisation to achieve its strategic, operational, financial, and compliance objectives.[73] This increased focus on the role of internal auditing has also been attributed to the dramatic changes in regulations, corporate governance standards, and the focus on tightening the internal controls of organisations.[74]

Al-jabili et al define internal audit to mean:

> Independent activity objectively, confirmatory, and consultant determined to add value and improve the organisation's operations, and in helping them achieve their objectives through a systematic and disciplined method to evaluate and improve the effectiveness of risk management and control processes and governance.[75]

Corporate governance involves the use of multi-layer systems of controls whereas internal audit is the layer that gives the board and management the assurance that the internal measures are sufficient.[76] Internal audit is a key tool for every organisation as it enables a third and objective party to objectively study and report on the organisation's governance. As risks continue to grow and become more complex, the role of internal audit has also expanded to areas such as risk governance, culture and behaviour, sustainability, and other non-financial reporting measures.[77]

It has been argued that an effective internal audit function enables the board to better execute its corporate governance duties. The internal audit function has been described as one of the four cornerstones of corporate governance which plays an important role in assisting the board to monitor the effectiveness of its governance.[78] The exact functions of auditors are discussed in the later chapters of this book. It is important to differentiate an internal audit from an external audit; while they share similar characteristics, they have very different objectives. Internal audit plays a more active role in aiding corporate governance. These differences are explained in the following table:[79]

---

[73] The Institute of Internal Auditors USA' Position Paper on Internal Auditing's Role in Corporate Governance' (2018) available at https://na.theiia.org/about–ia/PublicDocuments/Internal–Auditings–Role–in–Corporate–Governance.pdf (assessed 9 September 2018)

[74] C Holm & PB Laursen 'Risk and control developments in corporate governance: Changing the role of the external auditor' (2007) 15 *Corporate Governance: An International Review* 322–33.

[75] M Al–jabili, O Abdalmanam & K Ziadat 'Middle Eastern Finance and Economics' (ISSN: 1450–2889 Issue 11 161–176).

[76] A Gamal 'The Evolving Role of Internal Audit in Corporate Governance' (Internal Auditor – Middle East, 2015) available at http://www.internalauditor.me/article/the–evolving–role–of–internal–audit–in–corporate–governance/ (accessed on 10 September 2018).

[77] Gamal (n 76 above).

[78] AA Gramling, MJ Maletta, A Schneider & BK Church 'The role of the internal audit function in corporate governance: A synthesis of the extant internal auditing literature and directions for future research' (2004) 23 *Journal of Accounting Literature* 194–244.

[79] Chartered Institute of Internal Auditors website https://www.iia.org.uk/about–us/what–is–internal–audit/ assessed September 12, 2018.

Table 3.2

	Internal Audit	*External Audit*
Report to	The audit committee.	The company and shareholders in general meetings.
Objectives	To improve the effectiveness of governance, risk management and control processes. This provides members of the board and senior management with the adequate information necessary to fulfil their duties to the organisation with greater comfort.	Adds credibility and reliability to financial reports from the organisation.
Coverage	All categories of risk, how such risks are management and also report on the risks.	Financial reports and financial reporting risks.
Responsibility for improvement	Improvement is central to internal auditing. This is done by providing advice and facilitating while ensuring not to undermine the responsibility of management.	There is only a duty to report problems.

3.5.5 Internal Audit and Corporate Governance

The relationship between corporate governance and internal audit *and* to what extent this relationship contributes to business performance has been relatively under-researched. Ideally, an organisation with an effective system of internal control is expected to achieve its goals effective and achieve good corporate governance while an organisation with a weak system of internal control will experience bad corporate governance.[80] Also, the lack of internal controls and measure and their deficient operation makes companies open to risks such as improper recording of accounting transactions, fraud, etcetera. all these have a significant impact on financial performance and competitiveness.[81]

Empirically, researchers have found a positive relationship between internal audit and corporate governance, Mensah for example in his study, found that in Ghana, effective internal control measure improved good

[80] ZO Bilal & OI Twafik 'The influence of internal auditing on effective corporate governance in the banking sector in Oman' (2018) 14 *European Scientific Journal* 257–71.

[81] D Mihaela & S Iulian 'Internal control and the impact on corporate governance, in Romanian listed companies' 2012 *Journal of Eastern Europe Research in Business & Economics* 1–10.

governance practices and decreased corruption.[82] The same discovery was found by a study conducted on state-owned enterprises in West Java Indonesia.[83]

Nila and Viviyanti also found that this positive relationship at state-owned enterprises in West Java Indonesia. A study conducted on the Bucharest Stock Exchange also found that an effective internal control led to a fair presentation of the financial statements and thus increases stakeholders' confidence in them.[84]

3.6 EVOLUTION TOWARDS OUTCOMES-BASED GOVERNANCE

This is the King of all the emerging trends, *primus inter pares*; the concept of governance outcomes, while not revolutionary, is far from mainstream. This approach is still new and in most jurisdictions, it remains largely untested. It is however not without precedent. The 2016 *King Report on Corporate Governance (King IV)* in South Africa addresses governance outcomes explicitly, representing what the authors cite as the 'original intellectual thinking of the King Committee'.[85]

Outcomes-based governance entails considering the positive effects and benefits that an organisation can reap if the underlying principles of good governance (such as leadership, stewardship, independence, transparency, and accountability) are applied properly and fully achieved. This trend fosters the idea that there is a need to consider the potential benefits that result from the implantation of positive corporate governance outputs relating to board structure, the governance process and boardroom dynamics.

It is the trend to encourage businesses to consider this holistic approach to corporate governance by putting its focus on intended outcomes, rather than on isolated actions, details, or procedures. An outcome-focused framework requires companies to think independently about how to apply the principles to achieve this outcome.[86]

It is one thing to discuss the meaning of outcomes-based governance, but

---

[82] ML Mensah 'The effect of audit quality on earnings management' (2003) 15 *Contemporary Accounting Research* 1–21.

[83] N Vafeas 'Board Meeting Frequency and Firm Performance' (1999) 53 *Journal of Financial Economics* 113–42.

[84] Miheala (n 81 above).

[85] J Dinner 'Assessing board performance, an outcomes-based approach' (2018) available at http://csj.hkics.org.hk/site/2018/01/16/assessing-board-performance-an-outcomes-based-approach/ (assessed 10 September 2018).

[86] UL Corporate Governance Code must focus on principles and outcomes say ACCA – ACCA GlobL News An outcome-focused framework requires companies to think independently about how to apply the principles to achieve this outcome.

it is more important to consider the actual benefits of applying good corporate governance principles, some of which include:

- ☑ confidence in the board and management on the part of key stakeholders;
- ☑ reputational respect; and
- ☑ increased organisational value.[87]

For a corporation to holistically adopt and reap the benefits of an outcomes-based corporate governance approach, such an organisation must be willing to disregard traditional governance and organisational principles and move towards implementing the emerging trends that have been introduced and discussed in this chapter.

---

[87] Ibid

Chapter 4

OUTCOMES-BASED GOVERNANCE

4.1 DEFINITION OF OUTCOMES-BASED CORPORATE GOVERNANCE

The principle of outcomes-based governance requires the applicable code of corporate governance to clearly state the intended outcomes. The principle projects the view that the Code need not prescribe to the level of specific practices and that it is up to each company in each situation to decide what these should be in order to achieve some basic principles of governance. Essentially, the Code is there to set the expected outcome that companies should achieve by complying with the principles.

The principle of outcomes-based governance can be further understood by considering the *King IV Report* which is arguably the leading source on outcomes-based governance. Firstly, the Report is principle-based and outcomes-based as opposed to rule-based in line with international require-ments of greater accountability and transparency.[1] It is the goal that the application of the Report should contribute to the performance and health (sustainability) of the company.[2]

The *King IV Report* highlights the desired governance outcome per *chapter* and then proceeds to contextualise each *principle* and provides recommended practices. The principles and intended outcomes are phrased in the Report and are to be applicable to organisations. The recommended practices are to be adapted based on the size, resources, and complexity of strategic objectives and operations of the organisation in question.[3] In other words, the apposite for that particular company.

4.1.1 Definition of Terms

Understanding the relationship between governance outcomes, principles, and practices, is the key to the mindful application of the *King IV Report*. The definition of certain key terms central to the understanding of outco-mes-based corporate governance will be useful at this juncture and are provided in the King IV Code as follows:[4]

Corporate Governance: For the purpose of *King IV*, corporate gover-nance is defined as the exercise of ethical and effective leadership by the

---
[1] IODSA *King IV Report on Corporate Governance* (2016).
[2] *King IV Report* (n 1 above).
[3] *King IV Report* (n 1 above).
[4] *King IV Report* (n 1 above).

governing body towards the achievement of the following governance outcomes: ethical culture, superior performance, effective control and legitimacy.[5]

Outcomes: The Code defines outcomes as the benefits that organisations could realise if the underlying principles- and ultimately, good governance are achieved. These governance outcomes are: ethical culture, good performance, effective control, and legitimacy.

Principles: Conversely, principles embody the aspirations of the journey towards good corporate governance. They provide guidance on what organisations should strive to achieve by the application of governance practices.

Practices: Practices are associated with a particular principle and should be applied if apposite for that business so that they support and give effect to the aspiration expressed by that principle. That is why the regimen in *King IV* was changed from apply or explain to apply the principles and explain the practices undertaken to achieve the principles.

Below is a schedule of the chapters, principles, and governance outcomes of the *King IV Report*.[6]

Table 4.1

Chapters and Principles	Governance outcome
CHAPTER 1: LEADERSHIP, ETHICS AND CORPORATE CITIZENSHIP **Ethical leadership:** **Principle 1.1: the governing body should set the tone and lead ethically and effectively.** **Organisation values, ethics, and culture** **Principle 1.2: the governing body should ensure that the organisation's ethics is managed effectively.** **Responsible corporate citizenship** **Principle 1.3: the governing body should ensure that the organisation is a responsible corporate citizen.**	Ethical Culture

---

    [5] *King IV Report* (n 1 above).
    [6] Strauss Daly 'King IV Report at a Glance' available at https://www.straussdaly.co.za/wp–content/uploads/2016/07/King–Code–IV–At–a–Glance.pdf (accessed on 28 May 2018).

Chapters and Principles	Governance outcome
CHAPTER 2: PERFORMANCE AND REPORTING Strategy, Implementation, performance **Principle 2.1: the governing body should lead the value creation process by appreciating that strategy, risk and opportunity, performance and sustainable development are inseparable elements.** Reports and disclosure **Principle 2.2: the governing body should ensure that reports and other disclosures enable stakeholders to make an informed assessment of the performance of the organisation and its ability to create value in a sustainable manner.**	Performance and value creation
CHAPTER 3: GOVERNING STRUCTURES AND DELEGATION Role of the governing body **Principle 3.1: the governing body should serve as the focal point and custodian of corporate governance in the organisation.** Composition of the governing body **Principle 3.2: the governing body should ensure that in its composition it comprises a balance of the skills, experience, diversity, independence and knowledge needed to discharge its role and responsibilities.** Committees of the governing body **Principle 3.3: the governing body should consider creating additional governing structures to assist with the balancing of power and the effective discharge of responsibilities, but without abdicating accountability.** Delegation to management **Principle 3.4: the governing body should ensure that the appointment of, and delegation to, competent executive management contributes to an effective arrangement by which authority and responsibilities are exercised.**	Adequate and effective control

Chapters and Principles	Governance outcome
Performance evaluations **Principle 3.5: the governing body should ensure that the performance evaluations of the governing body, its structures, its chairs and members, the CEO and the company secretary or corporate governance professional result in continues improved performance and effectiveness.**	
CHAPTER 4: GOVERNANCE FUNCTIONAL AREAS Risk and opportunity governance **Principle 4.1: the governing body should govern risk and opportunity in a way that supports the organisation in defining core purpose and to set and achieve strategic objectives.** Technology and information governance **Principle 4.2: the governing body should govern technology and information in a way that supports the organisation in defining core purpose and to set and achieve strategic objectives.** Compliance governance **Principle 4.3: the governing body should govern compliance with laws and ensure consideration of adherence to non-binding rules, codes, and standards.** Remuneration governance: **Principle 4.4: the governing body should ensure that the organisation remunerates fairly, responsibly and transparently so as to promote the creation of value in a sustainable manner.** Assurance: **Principle 4.5: the governing body should ensure that assurance results in an adequate and effective control environment and integrity of reports for better decision-making.**	Adequate and effective control

Chapters and Principles	Governance outcome
CHAPTER 5: STAKEHOLDER RELATIONSHIPS Stakeholders **Principle 5.1: as part of its decision –making in the best interests of the organisation, the governing body should ensure that a stakeholder-inclusive approach is adopted, which considers and balances their legitimate and reasonable needs, interests and expectations.**	Trust, good reputation and legitimacy.
Applies to financial institutions **Principle 5.2: the governing body of an institutional investor should ensure that the organisation responsibly exercises its rights, obligations, legitimate and reasonable needs, interests and expectations, as holder of beneficial interest in the securities of a company.**	Responsible investment

4.2 UNDERSTANDING THE CHAPTERS, PRINCIPLES AND OUTCOMES OF THE KING IV CODE OF CORPORATE GOVERNANCE 2016

As is evident from the above table, the *King IV Code* is divided into chapters. Each chapter contains several principles geared towards achieving a particular outcome.

Chapter One – Leadership, Ethics and Corporate Citizenship

Leadership

The first chapter relates to leadership, ethics, and corporate citizenship. With respect to leadership, the Report prescribes that the guiding principle should be for the governing body of the corporate entity to lead ethically and effectively. The Report also recommends a number of practices as follows:

1. Members of the governing body should individually and collectively cultivate a number of characteristics and exhibit them in their conduct. Some of these characteristics include integrity, competence, responsibility, accountability, fairness, and transparency.[7]

---

[7] *King IV Report* (n 1 above).

2.   The governing body should embody the above ethical characteristics in order to offer effective leadership that results in achieving strategic objectives and positive outcomes over time.[8]

3.   The arrangements by which the members of the governing body are being held to account for ethical and effective leadership should be disclosed. These arrangements would include, but are not limited to, codes of conduct and performance evaluations of the governing body and its members.[9]

Organisational Ethics

In respect of organisational ethics, the principle states that, 'the governing body should govern the ethics of the organisation in a way that supports the establishment of an ethical culture'.[10] It goes ahead to inter-alia recommend the following practices:

1.   The governing body should assume responsibility for the governance of ethics by setting the direction for how the issue of ethics should be approached and addressed by the organisation.[11]

2.   The governing body should approve codes of conduct and ethics policies that articulate and give effect to its direction on organisational ethics.[12]

3.   The governing body should delegate to management, the responsibility for implementation and execution of the codes of conduct and ethics policies.[13]

4.   The following should be disclosed in relation to organisational ethics:
      a.   An overview of the arrangements for governing and managing ethics
      b.   Key areas of focus during the reporting period
      c.   Measures taken to monitor organisation ethics and how the outcomes were addressed
      d.   Planned areas of future focus

Corporate Citizenship

The applicable principle in respect of responsible corporate citizenship states that 'the governing body should ensure that the organisation is and is seen to be a responsible corporate citizen'. The Report recommends the following practices amongst others in this regard:

1.   The governing body should assume responsibility for corporate

---

[8]   *King IV Report* (n 1 above).
[9]   *King IV Report* (n 1 above).
[10] *King IV Report* (n 1 above).
[11] *King IV Report* (n 1 above).
[12] *King IV Report* (n 1 above).
[13] *King IV Report* (n 1 above).

citizenship by setting out the direction for how it should be approached and addressed by the organisation.

2.   The governing body should ensure that the organisation's responsible corporate citizenship efforts include compliance with the Constitution of the host country, the law, leading standards, and adherence to its own codes of conduct and policies.

3.   The governing body should oversee and take steps to ensure that the organisation's core purpose and values, strategy and conduct are congruent with being a responsible citizen.

4.   The governing body should oversee and monitor, on an ongoing basis, how the consequences of the organisation's activities and outputs affect its status as a responsible citizen.[14]

The following disclosures are required in relation to corporate citizenship:

a.   An overview of the arrangements for governing and managing responsible corporate citizenship

b.   Key areas of focus during the reporting period

c.   Measures taken to monitor corporate citizenship and how the outcomes were addressed

d.   Planned areas of future focus[15]

Chapter Two – Strategy, Performance and Reporting

The second chapter relates to strategy, performance, and reporting.

Strategy and Performance

The Report prescribes the principle that, 'the governing body should appreciate that the organisation's core purpose, its risks and opportunities, strategy, business model, performance and sustainable development are all inseparable elements of the value creation process'.[16]

The Report recommends certain practices in relation to strategy and performance some of which are:

1.   The governing body should assume responsibility for organisational performance by steering the company in the right direction for the realisation of the organisation's core purpose and values through its strategy.

2.   The governing body should delegate to management, the formulation and development of the organisation's short, medium, and long-term strategy.

3.   The governing body should oversee that the organisation continually assesses, and responsibly responds to the negative consequences of its

---

[14]   *King IV Report* (n 1 above).

[15]   *King IV Report* (n 1 above).

[16]   *King IV Report* (n 1 above).

activities and outputs on the triple context in which it operates, and the capitals which it uses and effects.[17]

Reporting

The Report's principle on reporting states that, 'the governing body should ensure that reports issued by the organisation enable stakeholders to make informed assessments of the organisation's performance, and its short, medium and long-term prospects'.

Some of the practices recommended by the Report are as follows:

1. The governing body should assume responsibility for the organisation's reporting by setting the direction for how it should be approached and conducted.
2. The governing body should oversee that reports such as the annual financial statements, sustainability reports, social and ethics committee reports, or other online or printed information or reports are issued, as is necessary, to comply with legal requirements and/or to meet the legitimate and reasonable information needs of material stakeholders.
3. The governing body should approve management's determination of the reporting frameworks (including reporting standards) to be used, considering legal requirements and the intended audience and purpose of each report.

Chapter Three – Governing Structures and Delegation

Primary Role and Responsibilities of the Governing Body

The principle stated in the Code holds thus, 'the governing body should serve as the focal point and custodian of corporate governance in the organisation'. The following practices amongst others are recommended:

1. The governing body should ensure that its role, responsibilities, membership requirements and procedural conduct are documented in a charter which is reviewed regularly to guide its effective functioning.
2. The governing body should approve the protocol to be followed in the event that it or any of its members or committees needs to obtain independent, external professional advice at the cost of the organisation on matters within the scope of their duties.

Composition of the Governing Body

In respect of this subject, the *King IV Report* prescribes a principle that states that 'the governing body should comprise the appropriate balance of knowledge, skills, experience, diversity and independence for it to discharge its governance role and responsibilities objectively and effectively'.

The Report also recommends the following practices:

---

[17] *King IV Report* (n 1 above).

1. The governing body should assume responsibility for its composition by setting the direction and approving the processes for it to attain the appropriate balance of knowledge, skills, experience, diversity, and independence to objectively discharge its governance role and responsibilities.
2. The nomination of candidates for election as members of the governing body should be approved by the governing body as a whole.
3. The processes for nomination, election and ultimately, the appointment of members to the governing body should be formal and transparent.

Committees of the Governing Body

The Report's principle on this subject states that 'the governing body should ensure that its arrangements for delegation within its own structures promote independent judgment and assist with balance of power and the effective discharge of its duties'. The Report recommends the following practices:

1. The governing body should determine if and when to delegate particular roles and responsibilities to an individual member or members of the governing body, or to standing or ad hoc committees. The exercise of judgment by the governing body in this regard, is subject to legal requirements and should be guided by what is appropriate for the organisation and for achieving the objectives of delegation.

Evaluations of the Performance of the Governing Body

The Report's principle in this regard is that 'the governing body should ensure that the evaluation of its own performance and that of its committees, its chair and its individual members, support continued improvement in its performance and effectiveness'.

The Code proceeds to make several useful recommendations including:

1. The governing body should assume responsibility for the evaluation of its own performance and that of its chair and its individual members by determining how it should be approached and conducted.
2. A formal process, either externally facilitated or not in accordance with methodology approved by the governing body, should be followed for evaluating the performance of the governing body, its committees and members as a whole.

Appointment and Delegation to Management

The Code's principle on this subject states that, 'the governing body should ensure that the appointment of, and delegation to, management contribute to role clarity and the effective exercise of authority and responsibilities'.

The Code also recommends a number of practices including:

1. The governing body should appoint the CEO.

2.   The CEO should be responsible for leading the implementation and execution of approved strategy, policy, and operational planning, and should serve as the chief link between management and the governing body.
3.   The CEO should be accountable and report to the governing body.
4.   The governing body should set the direction and parameters for the powers which are to be reserved for itself, and those that are to be delegated to management via the CEO.
5.   The governing body should approve a delegation of authority framework that articulates its set direction on reservation and delegation of power.

Chapter Four – Governance Functional Areas

Risk Governance

The Report's principle in this regard states that, 'the governing body should govern risk in a way that supports the organisation in setting and achieving its strategic objectives'. It recommends the following practices:
1.   The governing body should assume responsibility for the governance of risk by setting the direction for how risk should be approached and addressed in the organisation.
2.   The governing body should treat risk as integral to the way it makes decisions and executes its duties.
3.   The governing body should approve policy that articulates and gives effect to its set direction on risk.

Technology and Information Governance

The applicable principle here is to the effect that 'the governing body should govern technology and information in a way that supports the organisation setting and achieving its strategic objectives'. Some of the Report's recommended practices are as follows:
1.   The governing body should assume responsibility for the governance of technology and information by setting the direction for how technology and information should be approached and addressed in the organisation.
2.   The government body should delegate to management the responsibility to implement and execute effective technology and information management.

Compliance Governance

The Report's principle on this subject states that 'the governing body should govern compliance with applicable laws and adopt, non-binding rules, codes and standards in a way that supports the organisation being ethical and a good corporate citizen'. The Report recommends inter-alia, the following practices:

1.   The governing body should assume responsibility of compliance with applicable laws and adopt non-binding rules, codes, and standards by setting the direction for how compliance should be approached and addressed in the organisation.
2.   Material or repeated regulatory penalties, sanctions, or fines for contraventions of, or non-compliance with statutory obligations, whether imposed on the organisation or on members of the governing body or officers.

Remuneration Governance

The Report stipulates the principle that, 'the governing body should ensure that the organisation remunerates fairly, responsibly and transparently so as to promote the achievement of strategic objectives and positive outcomes in the short, medium and long term'. The Report also recommends the following practices:
1.   The governing body should assume responsibility for the governance of remuneration by setting the direction for how remuneration should be approached and addressed on an organisation-wide basis.
2.   The remuneration policy and the implementation report should be tabled every year for separate non-binding advisory votes by shareholders at the AGM.

Assurance

The Code stipulates the principle that 'the governing body should ensure that assurance services and functions enable an effective control environment, which supports the integrity of information for internal decision-making and of the organisation's external reports'. The Code suggests the following practices amongst others:
1.   The governing body should satisfy itself that a combined assurance model is applied which incorporates and optimises the various assurance services and functions so that, taken as a whole, these support the objectives for assurance.
2.   The governing body should ensure that internal audit provides an overall statement annually as to the effectiveness of the organisation's governance, risk management and control processes.
3.   The governing body should obtain confirmation annually from the Chief Audit Executive that internal audit conforms to a recognised industry code of ethics.

Chapter Five – Stakeholder Relationships

Stakeholders

The principle relating to stakeholders as prescribed in the Report is that 'in the execution of its governance role and responsibilities, the governing body should adopt a stakeholder-inclusive approach that balances the needs, interests and expectations of material stakeholders in the best interests of the organisation over time'. The Code recommends several practices, some of which are:

1.   The governing body should assume responsibility for the governance of stakeholder relationships by setting the direction for how stakeholder relationships should be approached and conducted in the organisation.
2.   The governing body should approve policy that articulates and gives effect to its direction on stakeholder relationships.

Responsibilities of Institutional Investors

The principle on this subject prescribes that 'the governing body of an institutional organisation should ensure that responsible investment is practiced by the organisation to promote the good governance and the creation of value by the companies in which it invests'. The Report also recommends a number of practices which include:

1.   The governing body of an institutional investor should assume responsibility for determining responsible investing by setting the direction for how it should be approached and conducted by the organisation.
2.   The governing body should delegate to management, if in place, or alternatively, to the outsourced service provider if investment decisions and investment activities are outsourced, the responsibility to implement and execute its policy on responsible investment.
3.   The responsible investment code adopted by the institutional investor and the application of its principles and practices should be disclosed.

4.3   FUNDAMENTAL ELEMENTS OF OUTCOMES-BASED CORPORATE GOVERNANCE – THE KING IV REPORT ON CORPORATE GOVERNANCE 2016

(i)   Apply and Explain

With respect to the disclosure requirement on the application of King IV, the *King IV Report* adopts an 'apply and explain' regime which replaces the 'apply or explain' contained in King III.[18] The apply principle entails that all principles are phrased as aspirations and ideals that organisations should

---

[18] *King IV Report* (n 1 above) at note 4

strive for in their journey towards good governance and realising the governance outcomes. The principles are basic and fundamental to good governance, and application thereof is therefore assumed.[19]

Conversely, the explain practices stipulate that an explanation should be provided in the form of a narrative account, with reference to practices that demonstrate the application of the principle. The application should demonstrate which recommended or other practices have been implemented and how these achieve and give effect to the principle.[20] This suggests that the application of all the principles is assumed and companies should explain the practices that have been implemented to give effect to each principle. The *King IV Report* applies a principle-and-outcome based approach and moves away from a tick-box approach.

The 75 King III principles have been consolidated into 16 principles, each linked to very distinct outcomes. The focus of King IV is clearly on ensuring that the application of the principles achieves specifically identified outcomes. Each principle is supported by a limited number of recommended practices and requires an explanation of the practices used to achieve or striving to achieve those principles.[21] It is important to note that the legal status of King IV, as with its predecessors, is that it remains a set of voluntary principles and good practices.[22] If a conflict between legislation and King IV exists, the law prevails.

The King Code is non-legislative and is based on principles and practices. Although the code is not enforced through legislation, due to evolutions in South African law many of the principles are now embodied as law in the Companies Act 71 of 2008. The philosophy of the code consists of the three key elements of leadership, sustainability, and good corporate citizenship. It views good governance as essentially being effective and ethical leadership.[23]

Application of all 16 principles are required to substantiate a claim that good governance is being practised. The explanation is 'outcomes-based' – HOW was the principle applied and WHAT was the outcome.[24] The explanation allows stakeholders to make an informed decision as to whether good governance outcomes have been achieved. King IV contains the following elements: practices, principles, and governance outcomes. The practices are recommended at an optimum level of corporate governance

---

[19] *King IV Report* (n 1 above).

[20] *King IV Report* (n 1 above).

[21] EOH Legal Services 'New King IV Report will boost corporate governance in South Africa' available at <http://www.eohlegalservices.co.za/corporate–governance–south–africa/> (accessed on 23 May 2018).

[22] EOH Legal Services (n 21 above).

[23] Nexia SAB&T 'King IV Report' available at https://www.nexia–sabt.co.za/wp–content/uploads/2016/11/SABTip_October_2016_KingIV.pdf (accessed on 22 May 2018).

[24] *King IV Report* (n 1 above).

and should be adapted by each organisation to achieve the principle. The governance outcome is the positive effect or benefits of good corporate governance for the organisation and includes ethical culture, performance and value creation, adequate and effective control and trust, good reputation, and legitimacy.[25]

The new version has built on the King III principles but is more principle-based and follows an outcome-based rather than rule-based approach. This is in line with current international sentiment which promotes greater accountability and transparency. There have been significant corporate governance and regulatory developments, locally and internationally, since King III was issued. Although South African listed companies have generally been applying King III, other entities have experienced challenges in interpreting and adapting the Code to their particular circumstances.

King IV defines corporate governance as the exercise of ethical and effective leadership by the governing body and comprises of three elements: practices, principles, and governance outcomes.[26] Each of which is interrelated and cannot and will not successfully exist without the existence of the other. Practices are measures recommended to be implemented by an organisation or sector. The implementation of a practice achieves the principle. The principle thus serves as a guide to direct organisations on what they should set out to achieve by implementing a practice. Governance outcomes are the positive effects and benefits that an organisation can reap if the principles are properly applied and fully achieved. These benefits include ethical culture, performance and value creation, adequate and effective control and trust, good reputation, and legitimacy.[27] The principles contained in King IV are drafted and formulated in a manner whereby which each principle reinforces and enhances one another.

Jo Iwasaki,[28] in a submission to the Financial Reporting Council's public consultation on proposed changes to the UK Corporate Governance Code and Guidance on Board Effectiveness, stated that there is a need to put in place an outcome-focused framework which requires companies to think independently about how to apply the principles to achieve these outcome – and therefore encourages a more meaningful exercise. Iwasaki also believes that the role of the board is much broader than wealth maximisation and that today's best performing companies bring together all of their internal and

---

[25] *King IV Report* (n 1 above).
[26] *King IV Report* (n 1 above) at note 4.
[27] *King IV Report* (n 1 above) at note 7.
[28] Jo Iwasaki, the Head, Corporate Governance at ACCA (the Association of Chartered Certified Accountants).

external stakeholders, the entire workforce included, to align with their purpose and create optimal value. She adds thus:[29]

> The Code can most effectively encourage business to consider this holistic approach to corporate governance by putting its focus on intended outcomes, rather than isolated actions, details or procedures. What matters is not simply what companies have done, but more so what they have achieved by doing it. An outcome-focused framework requires companies to think independently about how to apply the principles to achieve this outcome – and therefore encourages a more meaningful exercise.

4.4 CONCLUSION

In conclusion, the words of Mervyn E King SC, (Chair of the King Committee) are apt:[30]

> The principles contained in the King IV Code can be applied by any organisation and all are required to substantiate a claim that good corporate governance is being practiced. The required substantiation allows stakeholders to make an informed decision as to whether or not the organisation is achieving the four corporate governance outcomes required by King IV. The explanation also helps to encourage organisations to see corporate governance not as an act of mindless compliance but something that would yield results only if it is practiced mindfully, with due consideration of the organisa-tion's circumstances.

In all, there is a need for countries across the world to key into this newly developed principle called, 'outcomes-based corporate governance'. The implementation of this Report by corporate entities the world over, has the potential to transform the value inherent in corporate governance itself.

---

[29] ACCA 'UK Corporate Governance Code Must Focus On Principles And Outcomes, Says ACCA' available at http://www.accaglobal.com/uk/en/news/2018/march/corporate–governance–co-de.html (accessed on 24 May 2018).
[30] ACCA (n 29 above) at note 8.

Chapter 5

THE ROLE OF THE BOARD OF DIRECTORS UNDER THE OUTCOMES-BASED GOVERNANCE MODEL

A board of directors is appointed or elected by the shareholders steer companies. The board of directors can be said to be the most important organ of a company responsible for strategy, governance, and oversight.[1]

This must mean that an efficient, effective and accountable board of directors is not only essential to every company but is also demanded by every standard of corporate governance principles. A board must act responsibly in ensuring an effective performance of the management to protect and enhance long-term value creation and to understand the needs, interests, and expectations of the company's stakeholders. Hence, a board must be effective in its composition, the performance of its duties, in its strategy and delegation of functions. This chapter seeks to break down the board of directors, from their composition to roles and even to how boards should delegate their functions.[2]

5.1 COMPOSITION OF THE BOARD OF DIRECTORS

A board's effectiveness is largely dependent on its size and composition. On a general note, the composition of the board should be relative to the scale and complexity of the company's operations and the Board is to be composed in such a way as to ensure diversity of experience without compromising independence, compatibility, and integrity. The board must not be too big as to become unwieldy and uncontrollable which will result in time waste before simple decisions would be arrived at, or too small that will exclude the necessary knowledge, skills, and experience to make effective decisions.[3]

The right mix of the executive and non-executive directors is very important. Executive directors have a better knowledge of issues because of their coalface experience. A proper and proportionate balance of the executive and non-executive directors will bring proper and genuine growth, and quality decisions backed by experience. In an ideal world, all

---

[1] K Aina 'Board of Directors and Corporate Governance in Nigeria' 2013 *International Journal of Business and Finance Management* 21–34.

[2] Aina (n 1 above).

[3] Aina (n 1 above).

boards of directors would comprise a diverse group of experienced and talented individuals all of whom would practice the characteristics and values of good commercial sense, courage, openness, and integrity.

In England, Principle A3 of the Combined Code states that the board should include a balance of executive and non-executive directors, (or in particular independent non-executive directors) such that the individual or a small group of individuals cannot dominate the board of directors' decision-taking. In Nigeria, the SEC's Code provides that the majority of the board members should be non-executive directors and at least one of them should be an independent director.

In South Africa the *King IV Code* notes that in determining the requisite number of members of the governing body certain factors must be considered including the 'appropriate mix of knowledge, skills and experience, including the business, commercial and industry experience, needed to govern the organisation' and the 'appropriate mix of executive, non-executive and independent non-executive members and 'diversity targets relating to the composition of the governing body'.

The following factors which contribute to the composition of the board of directors will be discussed in the next sections.

5.1.1 Size of the Board

The appropriate size of board is not a one-size-fits-all situation; different studies conducted over the last several years have come up with different numbers that are considered optimum, ranging from 5 to 8.[4] However it is not as simple as that, there are a number of factors that aid in determining board size; one such factor is the depth as well as the complexity of the issues facing the corporation. It is usually recommended that small to medium-sized corporations with relatively simple operations should have no more than five directors.[5] As a company grows in size and complexity it is likely that the board will also grow, for instance it was found that the complexities of the new regulatory environment created after the Sarbanes Oxley legislation in 2002 enacted by the US congress tended to trigger an increase in average board size.[6]

It is important to know that studies have shown effective decision-making decreases as the group expands.[7] GMI's Ratings report prepared for the *Wall Street Journal* showed that smaller boards consistently produced stronger

---

[4] Dorger Consulting 'Size Matters: Right Sizing Your Board of Directors' (2018) available at http://dorgerconsulting.com/2011/07/20/size–matters–right–sizing–your–board–of–directors/ (accessed on 20 October 2018).

[5] Dorger Consulting (n 4 above).

[6] AL Boone, LC Field, JM Karpoff & CG Raheja 'Determinants of Corporate Board Size and Composition: An Empirical Analysis' (2007) 85(1) *Journal of Financial Economics* (JFE).

[7] Dorger Consulting (n 4 above).

returns between 2011 and 2014. The study showed that small boards with an average of 9.5 board directors outperformed larger boards and produced better returns for shareholders by 8.5 per cent. In contrast, larger boards with an average of 11.2 directors underperformed by 10.85 per cent.[8] A major reason for this could be that smaller board sizes support a collaborative environment as directors are more likely to contribute and less likely to dominate. The chair may also be able to identify those who are side-lined and solicit their participation. Furthermore, board members are more likely to enjoy themselves and in turn naturally give extra effort.[9] Smaller boards are easier to manage and allow for better coordination unlike bigger board which may be harder to manage given the size.[10] However, it is important to state that there is no specific number that will guarantee a well-functioning board. The board must exercise its collective mind in concluding about what its optimal number of members should be. [11] No two companies are the same and their boards must reflect an organisation's uniqueness, needs and the context in which it operates. [12]

5.1.2 The Mix Between Executive and Independent Directors

Independent boards are considered optimal safeguards of shareholder value by closely monitoring the management team and by providing strategic advice and business contacts. This is why there has been a call for boards to consist of independent directors.[13] Independent directors (otherwise known as outside directors) are directors other an executive officer or employee of a company or any other individual having a relationship which would interfere in the exercise of independent judgment.[14] What is important is that they have no operational responsibilities within the company and have not engaged in business or professional activities associated with the firm.

Although their actual impact on board effectiveness is a subject of debate, recent corporate governance literature emphasises the importance of outside directors' monitoring role and their independence, this is because independent

---

[8] NJ Price 'Bes Practices: Board Size and Corporate Governance' (Diligent, 2017) https://diligent.com/blog/board–size–corporate–governance (accessed on 20 October 2018).

[9] Price (n 8 above).

[10] Institute of Directors Southern Africa 'What is The Ideal Board Size? (2018) available at https://www.iodsa.co.za/news/392547/What–is–the–ideal–board–size.htm (accessed on 20 October 2018).

[11] Institute of Directors Southern Africa (n 10 above).

[12] R Barker 'What Makes a Balanced Board of Directors' (Real Business, 2014) available at https://realbusiness.co.uk/what–makes–a–balanced–board–of–directors/ (accessed on 19 October 2018).

[13] P de Andres, L Arranz–Aperte & JA Rodriguez–Sanz 'Independent versus non–independent outside directors in European companies: Who Has a say on CEO compensation?' (2018) 20 *Business Research Quarterly* 79–95.

[14] Donald C. Clarke 'Three Concepts of The Independent Director' (32 Del. J. Corp. L. 73 (2007) pp. 73–111.

directors are said to perform an oversight and monitoring role since they have no other affiliation with the company; they are also said to improve firm value as a result of the skill and expertise they bring.[15] Independent directors are usually academics, retired executives and private investors amongst others, so they bring their expertise and 'a breath of fresh air' to the board.[16]

5.1.3 Diversity of the Board

Traditionally the reason for board diversity tended to be moral, however, in recent times the trend has shifted towards economic and legal justifications.[17] These economic justifications also tend to have moral rationales ties to them. As with many elements of corporate governance, there is diverse evidence as to whether board diversity translated into actual benefits.[18] Some studies show that board diversity translated to improved financial performance and others depict a negative relationship or none at all.[19]

One study found that board diversity can have positive economic effects under some conditions and negative effects under others.[20] Another study found that 'the process through which gender and ethnic diversity impacts financial performance is subtle and complex'.[21]

Perhaps, each company must analyse the company's peculiar circumstanced and create a board diversity plan to suits its needs and goals. Boards must re-examine their diversity policies annually, perhaps at the same time the board reviews its committee charters and governance guidelines.[22]

5.2 THE ROLE OF THE BOARD OF DIRECTORS IN OUTCOMES-BASED GOVERNANCE

The *King IV Code* summarised that the role and responsibilities of the board of directors as follows:

> to steer the organisation and set its strategic direction, on the basis of which management will develop the strategy which is to be approved by the governing body. To give

---

[15] SW Joh & JY Jung 'Effects of Independent and Friendly Outside Directors' (College of Business Administration Seoul National University, Korea available at http://aicg.org/_res/aicg/etc/Effects_of_Independent_and_Friendly_Outside_Directors.pdf (accessed on 20 October 2018).

[16] Joh & Jung (n 15 above).

[17] LM Fairfax 'Revisiting Justifications for Board Diversity' The Conference Board *Director Notes*, Nov. 2011.

[18] DA Katz, L Wachtell, Rosen & Katz 'Analyzing Aspects of Board Composition – Harvard Law School' available at https://corpgov.law.harvard.edu/2012/02/20/analyzing-aspects-of-board-composition/ (accessed on 20 October 2018).

[19] Fairfax (n 17 above)

[20] DA Carter 'Corporate governance, board diversity and firm value' (2003) 38 *The Financial Review.*

[21] Carter (n 20 above).

[22] Katz et al (n 18 above).

effect to the organisation's strategy, management formulates policy and operational plans, also to be approved by the governing body. Management then implements and executes strategy in accordance with policy and plans which are overseen and supervised by the governing body. The governing body finally ensures that there is accountability for organisational performance through, among others, reporting and disclosure. The latter in turn forms the basis for reviewing strategic direction which starts the business cycle anew.[23]

In summary, the role of the board in corporate governance is to:

- ☑ Steer and set strategic direction;
- ☑ Approve policy and planning;
- ☑ Oversee and monitor; and
- ☑ Ensure accountability.

A major role of the board of directors when considering taking the first step in building an outcomes-based governance system, which this book will explore, is establishing culture, values and ethics. The board must lead by example and ensure that good standards of behaviour permeate through all levels of the organisation. In recent times, investors have placed an increased importance on delivering long-term business and economic success, in order to achieve these there must be the development of an appropriate corporate vision, ethics and working culture in the company so that at all times, the company can be relied upon to maintain a resilient performance.[24]

A performance management and reward system are necessary to encourage behaviour that is consistent with the business' strategy model and values and the board is responsible for explaining this approach to shareholders and other stakeholders. The board can however delegate this to a remuneration committee who in turn reports to the board.[25] The board and executive management must ensure that the decisions around value creation and the company's value system and culture are fully integrated. The board must also ensure that the corporate governance culture embedded in the organisation must have a degree of flexibility to enable the company to adapt to changing patterns within the business world.[26] Once a board is able to establish policy with regards to culture, values and ethics, such a

---

[23] IODSA *King IV Report on Corporate Governance* (2016).

[24] M Kelly 'The Role of Board of Directors in Corporate Governance' (CPA Ireland, 2017) available at http://www.cpaireland.ie/docs/default–source/Students/exam–related–articles–2017/p1–corp–governance–the–role–of–the–board–of–directors.pdf?sfvrsn=2 (accessed on 20 October 2018).

[25] Kelly (n 24 above).

[26] Kelly (n 24 above).

company can then go on to implement corporate governance principles based on those values and ethics.

5.2.1 Delegation of Functions by the Board of Directors

Undeniably the board of directors is the primary organ charged with the oversight of management and the development of a company, however as we have just seen, a board has multifaceted and complex roles and in order to carry out their functions adequately, there must be delegation of power and responsibility. Delegation is important because it allows for quick decision-making, empowers employees, reduces red tape, and increases organisational efficiency and performance.[27] However having delegation without accountability controls and regular monitoring can allow behavioural issues to go undetected. For successful monitoring, the board must be prepared to establish necessary controls for the delegation framework and there must be transparency, accountability, and an effective flow of information.[28]

The board must determine when it is appropriate to delegate responsibility, bearing in mind it is not absolved from the performance or any liability resulting from the same. Furthermore, the exercise of judgment by the governing body in this regard, is subject to legal requirements and the articles of association and should be guided by what is appropriate for the organisation in achieving its objectives. A board may delegate matters to the following entities: [29]

- ☑ A Board Sub-Committee;
- ☑ Any board member;
- ☑ The CEO or Managing Director; or
- ☑ Members of staff. [30]

It must be borne in mind that a board may delegate but it cannot abdicate responsibility.

5.2.2 Reducing Risks Associated with Delegation

Good corporate governance includes devolution of authority and maintaining control over that process. It must however be determined how to

---

[27] Katz et al (n 18 above).

[28] P Steele & S Bennet 'Delegations and corporate risk management – how do they intersect' available at https://www.sibenco.com/delegations-and-corporate-risk-management-how-do-they-intersect/ (accessed on 20 October 2018).

[29] NCOSS 'Board Delegations' available at https://www.ncoss.org.au/sites/default/files/public/resources/Board%20Delegations.pdf (accessed on 20 October 2018).

[30] BREFI Group 'Delegate Authority to Management' available at https://www.brefigroup.co.uk/directors/e-course/delegation/delegate_authority_to_management.html (accessed on 20 October 2018).

minimise the risks that come with delegating powers. The mix of a well-designed corporate risk management framework and appropriate delegations framework and policy should result in increased organisational efficiency and performance.[31] The following steps are necessary for a board to consider delegating matters to sub-committees:

- ☑ Delegation to staff members and individual members of the board should be recorded in writing and approved by the governing body and should set out the nature and extent of the responsibility delegated.[32]

- ☑ Delegations should be exercised under authorised policies and procedures of the organisation with particular attention to the company's articles of association.[33]

- ☑ Delegation to committees must be formal in terms of reference approved and reviewed annually by the board. The terms of reference should at a minimum deal with the composition of the committee, committee's role, delegated authority with respect to decision-making, tenure, chain of reporting, meeting procedures, access to resources and information and arrangement for evaluation.[34]

- ☑ There must be a delegation framework that clearly identifies boundaries and accounting structures linked to a policy framework.[35]

- ☑ There must be available and readily accessible policies and procedure that articulate clearly the corporate cultures, expectations, and obligations.[36]

- ☑ There must be a framework of regular reporting to the board on specified decision-making which corresponds to the organisation's risk matrix and appetite.[37]

- ☑ Regular monitoring of the delegations framework.[38]

- ☑ Encouragement and protection of whistle-blowers.[39]

5.3 BOARD COMMITTEES

Board committees are essential to the corporate governance process. They should be established with clear reporting procedures and written defini-

---

[31] Steele & Bennet (n 28 above)
[32] *King IV Report* (n 23 above).
[33] *King IV Report* (n 23 above).
[34] *King IV Report* (n 23 above).
[35] Steele & Bennet (n 28 above).
[36] Steele & Bennet (n 28 above).
[37] Steele & Bennet (n 28 above).
[38] Steele & Bennet (n 28 above).
[39] Steele & Bennet (n 28 above).

tions of their authority and responsibilities.[40] The committees should have comprehensive charters that define roles and responsibilities, limits, composition, and tenure.

The *King IV Code* notes that for board committees to work, there must be effective collaboration among committees with reduced overlap and fragmentation of duties as well as distribution of power. The code recognises the following committees:

5.3.1 Audit Committee

The audit committee is a key governance structure charged with oversight of financial reporting and disclosure.[41] In the last two decades, an audit committee has become a common mechanism of corporate governance.[42] Government authorities, regulators and international bodies worldwide have indicated that they view an audit committee a powerful tool with the ability to enhance the transparency and accuracy of financial information.[43] In many jurisdictions it has even become compulsory, for example the United States Sarbanes-Oxley Act 2002 requires that all publicly traded companies establish an independent audit committee. There is an overwhelming number of studies indicating that the establishment of an audit committee results in the following substantial benefits:[44]

- ☑ Enhances third-party perceptions of auditor independence;
- ☑ Enhances earnings quality and over-statements of earnings are less likely in organisations with an audit committee; and
- ☑ Is associated with higher quality audits and associated with fewer shareholding lawsuits alleging fraud.[45]

Even studies that question whether an audit committee is actually beneficial still seem to recognise that factors such as size and independence of the audit committee do have significant impact on certain aspects of financial reporting.[46]

---

[40] Deloitte 'Board Committee' (2014) available at https://www2.deloitte.com/content/dam/Deloitte/za/Documents/governance–risk–compliance/ZA_BoardCommittees_24032014.pdf (accessed on 21 October 2018).

[41] DCSL Corporate Services Limited 'The Role of The Audit Committee in Corporate Governance' (DCSL Blog, 2015) available at http://blog.dcsl.com.ng/blog/2015/09/07/the–role–of–the–audit–committee–in–corporate–governance–2/ (accessed on 21 October 2018).

[42] ML Bhasin 'Audit committee mechanism to improve corporate governance: Evidence from a developing country' (2012) 3 *Modern Economy* 856–72.

[43] Bhasin (n 42 above).

[44] Bhasin (n 42 above).

[45] DA McMullen 'Audit committee performance: An investigation of the consequences associated with audit committee' (1996) 15 *Auditing: A Journal of Practice & Theory* 87–103.

[46] See, eg the study of MC Pucheta–Martinez & C de Fuentes 'The impact of audit committee characteristics on the enhancement of the quality of financial reporting: An empirical study in the Spanish context' (2007) 15 *Corporate Governance: An International Review* 1394– 412

There are debates on the accurate composition of the membership of audit committee.[47] Prentice and Space argue that independent directors should make up the audit committee as that would improve reporting,[48] while Romano argues that an audit committee composed solely of independent directors does not in itself limit the occurrence of accounting improprieties.

The duties of an audit committee often include recommending the appointment, removal and remuneration of external auditors, authorising internal auditors to carry out investigations, reviewing the corporation's financial statements, acting on items raised by the auditors, leading communication between auditors and management, and advising on significant findings in the external and internal audit investigations.[49]

To be effective, audit committees should have a charter that clearly defines responsibilities and modus operandi. Meetings should be well organised, efficient, and convened often enough to allow for discussions on relevant issues. The committee should also enjoy external and internal support and resources. In terms of composition there should be a good mix of members whose skills complement one another in terms of financial literacy and knowledge of the company's business and industry as well as applicable laws and regulations affecting the company. New board members should also be oriented adequately in this regard.[50]

In recent times of corporate governance failures, the role of audit committees has evolved and has become more relevant in enhancing confidence in the integrity of an organisation's processes and procedures relating to internal control and corporate and financing reporting.[51] A Deloitte Report released in 2018,[52] notes that that audit committees in addition to their oversight of financial reporting can also take responsibility in the two following areas:

a.   **Cyber Risk** – Cyber risk is often at the top of the agenda for management and boards of companies of all sizes and industries. Cyber risk increases concerns regarding the safety financial information and internal controls in place as well as other risks including the reputational risks that can result from a cyber-incident. An

---

[47] Bhasin (n 42 above).

[48] RA Prentice & DB Space 'Sarbanes–Oxley as quack corporate governance: How wise is the received wisdom?' (2007) 95 *Georgetown Law Journal* 1843–909.

[49] J Caskey, V Nagar & P Petacchi 'Reporting Bias with an Audit Committee' (2010) 85 *The Accounting Review* 447–81.

[50] DCSL (n 41 above).

[51] DCSL (n 41 above).

[52] Deloitte 'The Role of the Audit Committee (2018) available at https://www2.deloitte.com/content/dam/Deloitte/us/Documents/center–for–board–effectiveness/us–audit–committee–resource–guide–section–2.pdf (accessed on 21 October 2018).

effective cyber risk management programme requires proactive engagement and is mostly the responsibility of the board. In some organisations, a level of oversight may be delegated to a risk committee or the audit committee. The audit committee may be asked to play a strong role in monitoring management's preparation for and response to cyber threats, coordinate cyber management initiatives and policies. There must be regular dialogue with the chief information officer, chief information security officer and other technology-focused leaders who can help the committee determine where attention should be focused. The audit committee chairperson can be a particularly effective liaison with other groups in enforcing and communicating expectations regarding cyber and financial risk mitigation.[53]

b.   **Mergers and Acquisition** – Audit committees can play an important role in mergers and acquisition both before and after a transaction

c.   **Before the transaction** – 'Due Diligence' – Due diligence is the responsibility of the board, but the audit committee can perform a closer oversight function with regards to risk analysis and internal controls. In the absence of strong internal control systems

Audit committees must ensure that due diligence is thorough and the board is fully informed of the risks associated with every action or transaction they approve. Due diligence also prevents weak internal control system which can create organisational burdens.[54] A due diligence today does not consist only of a financial one. There should be a due diligence of the intangible assets which are not reflected in a balance sheet according to financial reporting standards.

d.   **Post transaction** – 'Integration Oversight' – One area an audit committee is useful is for the melding of internal control systems and processes, so they are stable and so that the systems integrate and complement one another.[55]

5.3.2 Nominations Committee

The spirit of most codes of corporate governance is that the search, selection process and recommendation to the board of prospective candidates should be the duty of the nominations committee. The role of the nominations

---

[53] Deloitte (n 52 above).
[54] Deloitte (n 52 above).
[55] Deloitte (n 52 above).

committee is to regularly review board composition and improve on lacking skills and experience.[56] Another key consideration for nominations committees is to ensure effective succession plan which can mitigate the harsh effects that losing a board member may presents, most especially non-executive directors who may be harder to replace as opposed to executive directors who have usually follow a defined career path through the management of the company.[57] The nominations committee should be comprised of non-executive directors to ensure a greater level of objectivity, transparency, and independence.[58]

A nominations committee also has a role in board evaluation and can aid in ensuring that the evaluation process is not a box ticking exercise but a means of realigning the board's focus and activities in line with the organisation's strategy. It also should assist in ensuring a formal induction programme for new directors and that directors are on an ongoing basis trained and developed.

The ultimate responsibility for appointing directors rests with the shareholders, however, this does not detract from the need for the board of directors through the nomination committee to define the selection criteria and identify the skill required to improve the effectiveness of the board of directors. The board of directors still has a responsibility to ensure that the nominated persons are minimum standards of law and have the relevant skills and experience required to meet the company's needs.

5.3.3   Risk Governance Committee

The responsibility for ensuring that the risks are adequately managed is usually not acknowledged by organisations or is not adequately delegated to the audit committee. The role of the risk governance committee is to provide oversight functions by analysing the company's risk policy and guidelines, determine the company's risk appetite. The risk governance committee must also ensure that regular risk assessments are performed and that internal and external assurances are provided.

When it comes to risk management and strategy, it is important to note that it is not a one-size-fits-all situation and some organisations may not require a separate standalone committee for risk management.[59]

---

[56] Deloitte (n 52 above).

[57] Deloitte (n 52 above).

[58] Deloitte (n 52 above).

[59] D McAvoy & JC Partigan 'The Role and Construction of Risk Committees' (Nixon Peabody, 2010) available at https://www.nixonpeabody.com/en/ideas/articles/2010/08/11/the–role–and–cons-truction–of–risk–committees (accessed on 21 October 2018).

5.3.4 The Interplay Between Risk Committees, the Board and Management

The establishment of a risk committee would not sufficient for the oversight of a corporation's risks and management of same if a framework is not put in place to ensure effective communication of the organisation's risks to the risk committee. Furthermore, lines of communication must be established between the risk committee, the board, other committees of the board and management to ensure that risks considerations are given at every stage. There must also be the establishment of the committee structure and charter to ensure that the risk committee performs its functions within the context of the rest of the board and management, and to ensure that there is no significant overlapping of duties between the risk committee and the other board committees.

It is recommended that one member of the risk committee is also on the audit committee and one member who is on the remuneration committee as certain responsibilities of the committees will inevitably overlap, especially with respect to risks concerning compensation policies. Members of the risk committee should ideally also be independent but there must be established lines of open communication between the committee, board, chief risk officer and management. The committee should also organise executive sessions with risk management employees, in the same way as most audit committees would have executive sessions with the company's independent outside auditors.[60]

5.3.5 Remuneration Committee

Director remuneration is one of the most sensitive and topical issues facing boards today and hence is a crucial element of good corporate governance to establish a committee to handle this.[61] The main role of the Remuneration Committee is to assist and advise the board of directors on matters relating to the remuneration of the board of directors and senior management, in order to motivate and retain executives and also to ensure that the Company is able to attract the best talents in the market in order to maximise value creation.[62] A major responsibility of the committee is to remain informed on the appropriate levels, structuring methods and types of remuneration in the

---

[60] McAvoy & Partigan (n 59 above).

[61] Deloitte (n 52 above).

[62] China Resources Power Holding Company Limited 'Remuneration Committee, Terms of Reference' (2014) available at http://www.cr–power.com/en/InvestorRelations/CorporateGovernance/BoardCommittees/201312/P020141216643862411311.pdf (accessed on 21 October 2018).

environment in which the company operates.[63] The committee is responsible for establishing a formal and transparent procedure for the remuneration of directors and senior management and determination of compensation payments and benefits. When considering same, it should take into consideration salaries paid by comparable companies and responsibilities of directors and it should have access to professional advice, if necessary.[64] There must be good balance between recommending competitive remuneration and remuneration which does not attract the desired quality of board members.[65] Variable remuneration should be seriously considered, that is, a salary considering the gap between remuneration for the top executives and those employees at the bottom of the corporate ladder. Bonus determined by the positive and negative impacts of the company's activities on the economy, society, and the environment. Reward for positive impacts on society and the environment are more palatable to stakeholders than positive financial results but with a negative impact on people and the planet.

5.3.6 Social and Ethics Committee

The social and ethics committee's key role is to be the social conscience of the business. The committee must ensure that the organisation is a responsible corporate citizen in all aspects of its business including its business activities, its sustainability, environmental and community impact, relationship with investors and stakeholders including employees, etcetera.[66] For the social and ethics committee must ensure that there are open communication channels with other committees such as the audit, risk, executive, nomination, remuneration and sustainability committees because the decisions of those committees are to be carried out in a social and ethical manner. There must also be open communication because there might be an overlap with the issues dealt with the various committees in this regard particularly the audit, risk, and sustainability committees. The committee must understand and determine their roles and functions vis-à-vis the other board committees.[67] The Social and Ethics Committee in some jurisdictions must report to shareholders at the AGM.[68]

---

[63] Deloitte (n 52 above).

[64] Deloitte Solutions 'Audit, Remuneration and Nomination Committees' available at https://www2.deloitte.com/cn/en/pages/risk/solutions/cg–audit–and–remuneration–committees.html (accessed on 21 October 2018).

[65] Deloitte Solutions (n 64 above).

[66] Deloitte 'The Companies Act The Social and Ethics Committee and The Management of the Ethics Performance of The Company' available at https://www2.deloitte.com/content/dam/Deloitte/za/Documents/governance–risk–compliance/ZA_SocialAndEthicsCommitteeAndTheManagementOfTheEthicsPerformance_24032014.pdf (accessed on 21 October 2018).

[67] Deloitte 'The Social and Ethic Committee and the Management of The Ethics Performance of The Company' (2014) available at https://www2.deloitte.com/content/dam/Deloitte/za/Documents/

In some jurisdictions the establishment of a social and ethics committee is statutorily required.[69] The governing body of any organisation not so obliged should consider allocating oversight of and reporting of organisational ethics, responsible corporate citizenship, sustainable development and stakeholder relationships to a committee because it is accepted in business today that it is not only financial matters that are critical to the success and sustainability of a company and that there are many so called 'soft issues' covered by the S&E Committee which could have a serious impact on a company's reputation and ultimate success.[70]

5.3.7 Mechanisms for Evaluating the Performance of Directors

One responsibility of a board is to put in place a formal and rigorous process for bi-annually reviewing its overall performance as well as performance of individual directors and committees. Board evaluation is not simply a control mechanism over board members but is a tool to identify areas of governance improvement.[71] It provides the board a chance to reflect on and assess its areas of strength and weaknesses and provides the board with an invaluable yardstick by which it can prioritise its activities for the future. It is also an avenue for accountability to investors, the public, etcetera[72] Annual reports shall include the in-depth disclosure of the complete mechanism adopted and the approaches and techniques used in the performance evaluation process.[73]

In most companies globally, board evaluation is an annual exercise tailored to the requirements of the company and the corporate structure, board structure, etcetera hence there is no common format for performance of board evaluation.[74] The company must determine the objective of board evaluation. It is not enough for the company to want to meet regulatory

---

governance–risk–compliance/ZA_SocialAndEthicsCommitteeAndTheManagementOfEthics Performance_04042014.pdf (accessed on 22 October 2018).

[68] Deloitte (n 64 above).

[69] Section 72 of the Companies Act read with the Companies Regulations.

[70] KMPG 'The oversight role of the social and ethics committee' (2016) available at https://assets.kpmg.com/content/dam/kpmg/pdf/2016/07/Oversight–role–of–social–and–ethics–committee.pdf (accessed on 22 October 2018).

[71] MJ Larson & C Pierce 'Board Evaluations: Insights from India and Beyond' (2015) available at http://www.sbp.org.pk/bprd/2016/C11–Annx–A.pdf (accessed on 22 October 2018).

[72] B Cropp 'Evaluating Board Performance' (University of Wisconsin Center for Cooperatives, 1996) available at http://www.uwcc.wisc.edu/issues/Governance/board.html (accessed on 29 October 2018).

[73] Companies Circle: Board Evaluation Working Group 'Board Evaluation Practices Experiences from the Latin American Companies Circle' (2017) available at https://www.ifc.org/wps/wcm/connect/fbd48a42-b6c2-481d-b61d-80605c4df938/Latin_American_Companies_Circle_Fact_Sheet.pdf?MOD=AJPERES&CVID=msgK 3r (accessed on 29 October 2018).

[74] Deloitte 'Performance Evaluation of Boards and Directors' (March, 2014) available at https://www2.deloitte.com/content/dam/Deloitte/in/Documents/risk/Corporate%20Governance/in–cg–performance–evaluation–of–boards–and–directors–noexp.pdf (accessed on 29 October 2018).

requirements, the primary goal should be the need to ensure a build a high-performing board, well-suited to meets the company's needs and challenges. Boards are steadily moving away from a 'check-the-box' evaluation mentality to ensuring that board evaluation is aligned with the company's long-term strategy.[75] The method and approach of board evaluation adopted must be determined along the line of the company's objectives and strategy.[76]

A Deloitte report notes that the effectiveness of a board depends on various factors including:

☑   board structure;
☑   dynamics and functioning of the board;
☑   business strategy governance; and
☑   financial reporting process, internal audit and internal control and risk management.[77]

There are several questions that come up in determining the structure of board evaluation from who should conduct it, to the methodology, frequency, and even disclosure of findings. It is also important to mention that bi-annual reviews are becoming the norm to give the board a year to correct the deficiencies highlighted by the review.

5.4 APPROACHES FOR PERFORMANCE EVALUATION

5.4.1 In-house Evaluation

These have the advantage of causing fewer concerns to boards that are reluctant to conduct board evaluations and it is also simple and easy to perform.[78] However the issue of conflict of interest arises and directors may overlook sensitive issues thus eroding the true picture;[79] a way to remedy this is for there to be an evaluation committee, generally responsible for the selection and appointment of board members, furthermore the company secretary can play a huge role in assisting the committee in ensuring transparency of the process.[80]

5.4.2 External Evaluation

Many companies engage the services of an external consultant/evaluator, who brings an objective view by providing a best practice perspective. To

---

[75] K Kastiel 'Board Evaluation – A Window into the Boardroom' (Harvard Law School Forum on Corporate Governance and Financial Regulation' (2013) available at https://corpgov.law.harvard.edu/2013/05/31/board–evaluation–a–window–into–the–boardroom/ (accessed on 29 October 2018).

[76] Kastiel (n 75 above).

[77] Deloitte (n 52 above).

[78] Kastiel (n 75 above).

[79] State Bank of Pakistan Guidelines on Performance Evaluation of Board of Directors http://www.sbp.org.pk/bprd/2016/C11–Annx–A.pdf.

[80] State Bank of Pakistan (n 79 above).

avoid conflicts, the external evaluator should neither have an ongoing nor recent relationship with the company.[81] External evaluation provides assurance to stakeholders that the evaluation is objective and thorough, however another issue becomes the process of the selection of the external evaluator in terms of a cost/benefit analysis and determination of who selects such an evaluator. [82]

5.4.3 Hybrid Evaluation

In large international corporations, board evaluations are usually conducted by the governance and nomination committee with the help of outside experts.[83] The involvement of such an external party in the process can have several advantages as it could provide independent advice to the board throughout the process or simply act as a facilitator.[84]

5.4.4 Techniques for Performance Evaluation

Whether the evaluation is conducted internally, externally or by a combination of the two, the methodology broadly remains the same and can be either of the following:

- **Quantitative**: This sort of evaluation is administered face to face, using portals or emails. It can consist of surveys, questionnaires and similar methods; general comments are also solicited.
- **Qualitative**: This method of evaluation includes an in-depth analysis of responses through interview, observations appraisals, and so forth.[85]

Good evaluations have both qualitative and quantitative parts and usually the latter informs the former with rich data which brings greater objectivity to the evaluation exercise.[86]

5.4.5 Result/Outcome

Board assessments by themselves are not a remedy to board or governance problem because there is no guarantee that a board will implement needed changes.[87] Board evaluation should be a thought-provoking-process for the board to reflect on its strengths and weaknesses as well as opportunity to improve its functioning and performance. Boards will be able to effectively address any limits or weaknesses only when they acknowledge what these

---

[81] Kastiel (n 75 above).
[82] Kastiel (n 75 above).
[83] Deloitte (n 52 above).
[84] Kastiel (n 75 above).
[85] State Bank of Pakistan (n 79 above).
[86] Deloitte (n 52 above).
[87] Kastiel (n 75 above).

limitations are.[88] An effective board must be willing to proactively consider the findings of the evaluation, hold open discussion of the findings, identify issues for improvement and enactment of same. Communicating the outcome of the board assessment process is an important means for the follow-up implementation and for enhancing dialogue with the stakeholders on board matters.[89] The result or outcome of the performance evaluation should include a:

a)   performance report of overall board;
b)   performance report of individual board members; and
c)   performance report of committees.

The task of implementing the outcome of board evaluations is heavily placed on the chair. The chair should discuss the results/findings collectively with each individual board member and have feedback sessions. The chair should also dedicate adequate time to discuss the results of the board evaluation and same should constitute a major input for consideration for re-appointment of board members.[90] Following the evaluation process, identified issues, weaknesses and challenges need to be addressed adequately through a proper action plan. The chair or the concerned board committee responsible for the performance evaluation process should also formulate the requisite strategies and action plans to address the identified challenges/issues.[91]

---

[88] Kastiel (n 75 above).
[89] Kastiel (n 75 above).
[90] State Bank of Pakistan (n 79 above).
[91] State Bank of Pakistan (n 79 above).

Chapter 6

OTHER KEY OFFICERS AND THEIR ROLES UNDER OUTCOMES-BASED GOVERNANCE MODEL

This book has focused mainly on the evolving role of the board of directors in relation to an outcome-based governance model and in this chapter we discuss the composition of the board of directors as well as what their specific role ought to be in enforcing corporate governance. However, it is important to note that to achieve best corporate governance standards, all individuals associated with the functioning of a corporation have their respective crucial role to play[1] This chapter of the book focuses on other key personnel who perform an increased corporate governance role in recent times. These are the company secretary, the corporate stakeholder relationship manager, auditors, and institutional investors.

6.1 THE COMPANY SECRETARY

The interaction between the board and the company is the main work of the company secretary.[2] Traditionally, when we imagine a company secretary, we think of a person who assists the board. The stereotype is the picture of a person who is scurrying around and doing things like taking notes and setting up meeting.[3] The existence of the company secretary is built on a company's statutory duties and requirements. The law shapes the role of a company secretary and the regulations create a framework for the scope of actions carried out by the company secretary.[4]

The importance of the company secretary has often been underestimated in research and practice. The majority of publications that cover the company secretary's role do not include the updated duties and responsibilities of company secretaries in line with developments in statutory and regulatory requirements; hence there are very few empirical studies which

---

[1] 'Company Secretary in Good Corporate Governance' available at https://www.lawteacher.net/free–law–essays/business–law/company–secretary–in–good–corporate–governance–business–law–essay.php (accessed on 30 September 2019).

[2] A Filiz *The Company Secretary Within The Corporate Governance Framework*' (unpublished dissertation, University of St. Gallen, School of Management, Economics, Law, Social Studies and International Affairs, 2013).

[3] N Price 'The Evolving Role of The Company Secretary in Today's Corporate World' (Board Effect, 2017) https://www.boardeffect.com/blog/evolving–role–company–secretary–todays–corporate–world/ (accessed on 12 October 2018).

[4] Filiz (n 2 above).

cover the company secretary's specific role.[5] However, as a result of recent advances in corporate governance, today's corporate secretary holds the responsibility for all that and much more.[6] The role of a company secretary is evolving from being a support assistant to one of the key governance positions within a corporation.[7] Professor Mervyn King, suggests that there could be a whole new future awaiting company secretaries and it is an exciting one.[8]

A company secretary office is built on independence and trust, and the company secretary is a key to the achievement of best corporate governance practice. While it is undisputed that the ultimate responsibility for corporate governance compliance rests with the board of directors, it is the duty of the company secretary to assist the board and management in implementing an enduring corporate governance culture.[9] The company secretary is now regarded as the guardian of a company following with laws, regulations, corporate governance and ethics.[10]

6.1.1 The Role of a Company Secretary

The evolved role of the corporate secretary covers a multitude of tasks and responsibilities. One of the roles is at the heart of the governance systems of companies and is receiving greater focus.[11] The role of a company secretary has become multifaceted. In this regard, the International Finance Corporation's (IFC) Corporate Secretary Toolkit, succinctly describes the role of a corporate secretary as someone who:

1. manages the company's corporate governance framework;
2. ensures compliance with governance procedures;
3. oversees and conducts induction trainings for newly elected directors;
4. is the officer of the company;
5. is the conscience of the company;
6. communicates with directors;
7. communicates between the board and managements; and
8. fosters shareholders relations and manages shareholders meetings.[12]

---

[5] Filiz (n 2 above).

[6] Price (n 3 above).

[7] Price (n 3 above).

[8] CSJ 'Stakeholder Relationship Officers – Coming To Your Company' (2013) available at http://csj.hkics.org.hk/site/2013/09/05/stakeholder–relationship–officers–coming–to–your–company/

[9] Global Business Journal 'The Role of The Company Secretary' available at http://govandbusinessjournal.com.ng/the–role–of–the–company–secretary–in–corporate–governance–compliance/ (accessed on 30 September 2019).

[10] Global Business Journal (n 9 above).

[11] International Finance Corporation 'The Corporate Secretary: The Governance Professional' (IFC's Corporate Governance Group, 2016) available at https://www.ifc.org/wps/wcm/connect/2c2a9f57–3e3d–43b2–be9f–beaed1d47fff/CG_CoSec_June_2016.pdf?MOD=AJPERES (accessed on 12 October 2018).

[12] IFC Corporate Secretary Toolkit, 2013. Slide 5 from IFC's Corporate Secretary Toolkit, Part 1 Module 1/The Corporate Secretary: The Governance Professional Presentation.

In its working paper on *The Corporate Secretary: The Governance Professional*,[13] the IFC lists out the new and multifaceted roles of a company secretary as follows:

6.1.2 Company Secretary as a Governance Professional

A company secretary has a valuable role as a bridge for information communication, advice and arbitration between the board and management and the organisation and its stakeholders. Beyond the compliance role, a company secretary can manage people to create the appropriate cultures and thereby enable the corporate governance structures, policies, and procedures to work effectively. In this regard a company secretary has the responsibility to:

☑ identify which governance practices should be adopted by the organisation;

☑ implement within the organisation best practices through the creation and maintenance of cultures and relationships;

☑ facilitate communication between board members, the board and management, the company and its shareholders and the company and its stakeholders; and

☑ be commercially minded by understanding how the organisation makes money, what the organisation needs, understanding the organisation's competitive advantage and keeping up to date with the industry or sector within which that the organisation operates, in order to advise the board on governance. issues.[14]

6.1.3 Company Secretary's Role in Board Management

A company secretary plays a huge role in managing the board's activities, particularly with respect to the following:

(i) *Role before, during and after meetings*

A company secretary is expected to prepare for board meetings and most importantly must ensure that the board members all receive information in a format that is easily digestible before meetings. During the meeting the company secretary must ensure that a quorum is present and continues to be present, and that the meeting complies with the company's constitutions, policies and procedures, laws, regulations, standards, and codes of best practice. After the meeting, a company secretary must communicate board

---

[13] International Finance Corporation (n 12 above).
[14] International Finance Corporation (n 12 above).

decisions, follow up on actions and organise independent professional advice if required.[15]

(ii) Role in Board Composition and Succession Planning

A company secretary also advises the board on its composition, tenure, selection and appointment. The company secretary must advise on the requirements for a balanced board, ensure that the requirements for independence are met and maintained, and advise on the most effective board size for the organisation. The secretary also plays a huge role in refreshing a board through an organised succession plan that has been drafted in advance, most especially for the positions of the chair and CEO. To do so, the secretary must identify board capability gap and create a matrix of skills and experience for the board. Such skills included in the matrix could be skills relating to financial expertise, industry experience, legal expertise, diversity in terms of age, gender, culture, character traits, etcetera.[16]

6.1.4 Advice in Director Management

A company secretary's role is also to aid directors in their management of the company's affairs and in the execution of their duties. Hence a company secretary must advise the board on actual or potential conflict of interest, coordinate drafting, implementation, and enforcement of policy on related-party transactions and most importantly, advise directors on their rights and liabilities.

6.1.5 Role of Company Secretary to Shareholders

The duties of a corporate secretary to a company's shareholders are often overlooked. A company secretary must do the following:

☑   Ensure that shareholders interests are registered;
☑   Organise the transfer or transmission of shares from one shareholder to another;
☑   Drafting of shareholder agreements;
☑   Protection of powers and rights of shareholders (such as the appointment and removal of directors, appointing auditors, remuneration of directors, amending articles, etc.);
☑   Preparation and circulation of agenda/materials of meetings; and
☑   Provide advice on the content of shareholder agreements.[17]

---

[15] International Finance Corporation (n 12 above).
[16] International Finance Corporation (n 12 above).
[17] International Finance Corporation (n 12 above).

6.1.6 Role in Strategy Risk and Good Corporate Citizenship

As the primary facilitator of the board, a company secretary can aid in managing risk, determining strategy, and ensuring good corporate citizenship by:

☑ ensuring that strategic discussions are listed on the agenda of board meetings;

☑ advising the board on compliance with the organisation s objectives;

☑ ensuring an effective and structured monitoring of progress against strategic objectives;

☑ advising on disclosure requirements and issues relating to reputational risk;

☑ ensuring that risk is considered on the board s agenda;

☑ educating the board on its responsibilities for risk management;

☑ assisting the board with assessment of the effectiveness of the risk management system and internal controls;

☑ developing board guidelines for risk that reflect the board s decision on the risk appetite for the company;

☑ managing (identifying, assessing, mitigating and monitoring) risks within the areas of the corporate secretary s responsibilities;

☑ identifying the reputational risk associated with the decisions, actions taken, or inaction by the board;

☑ advising the board on business continuity planning;

☑ ensuring that the laws, regulations, standards, and codes applicable to the organisation have been identified and are being complied with;

☑ advising the board and where possible, provide inspiration for the inclusion of good corporate citizenship activities in the organisation's strategy and business continuity planning; and

☑ drafting integrated or stand-alone sustainability reports.

6.1.7 Role in Financial Oversight and Reporting

Corporate governance has given the company secretary an increased role in ensuring accountability and transparency in financial systems of a corporation and ensuring that financial reporting systems comply with legal and other stakeholder requirements.[18] A company secretary is now called upon to do the following:

☑ interpret in non-financial terms the financial performance and results of the organisation for ease of understanding;

☑ advise the board on the implications and the potential reputational risks of the financial performance and results for the organisation, the shareholders, and other stakeholders;

---

[18] International Finance Corporation (n 12 above).

☑   advise and assist the board in its financial oversight role;

☑   advise the board on the appropriateness of delegating the financial oversight role to an audit committee;

☑   advise the board on its responsibilities regarding risk management and internal controls;

☑   coordinate with internal and external auditors;

☑   provide oversight, on behalf of the board, for the preparation of the annual report and accounts; and

☑   advise the board on applicable laws, regulations, standards, and codes relating to reporting of non-financial information.[19]

6.1.8 Role in Building Ethical Cultures

A company secretary is usually referred to as the conscience of the company and as such they have the duties of:

☑   ensuring that ethical business standards are set by the board and an ethical culture is built, as well as notifying the board when these standards are breached;

☑   developing a code of conduct;

☑   communicating the expected standards of ethical behaviour;

☑   ensuring compliance with the values and the code of ethics;

☑   ensuring that ethical values and the code of ethics are reviewed from time to time; and

☑   ensuring that the board approves and monitors implementation of whistleblowing policies and procedures.

6.1.9 Competing Roles of the Company Secretary

The company secretary's evolving role and functions may vary from company to company. In connection with this variation, characteristics such as duties and responsibilities may vary according to the degree of alternation within the role and its extended functions. Although the company secretary's sphere of activities embraces variation, this characteristic often results in blurred boundaries between the role and its additional functions. The company secretary's sphere of activities embraces variations.[20]

An example of company secretaries and the blurred boundaries between their role and additional functions is the fact that in many companies, the company secretary also doubles as in-house-counsel.[21] This dual role usually tasks the independence of the company secretary and as such there

---

[19] International Finance Corporation (n 12 above).

[20] Filiz (n 2 above).

[21] A Bisi 'The Role of The Company Secretary in Corporate Governance Compliance' (GBJ, 2007) available at http://govandbusinessjournal.com.ng/the–role–of–the–company–secretary–in–corporate–governance–compliance/ (accessed on 13 October 2018).

is a need to avoid potential situations of conflict of interest where the performance of one role may conflict with the responsibilities required of the other.[22]

Companies must ensure that the roles of the company secretary as the conscience of the company is not jeopardised.[23] For instance, a general counsel who doubles as company secretary will have to take sides in his or her legal role to represent the particular interests of the company.[24] Although he or she may be complying with the letter of the law and in the interests of management, he or she may not be acting in the best long-term interests of the company. This would be inconsistent with the corporate secretary's governance role, which requires impartiality when advising on governance issues. It may also prevent a corporate secretary from speaking out against bad governance or unethical practices.[25] Hence, company secretaries who take up other executive duties ensure that the multiples and interests of the roles are considered and disclosed.[26]

6.1.10 Reporting Lines

Reporting line must be set to ensure that the company secretary discharges his/her role efficiently.[27]

Usually, the appointment and removal of the Company Secretary is a matter for the board (for instance section 296 of Nigeria's Companies and Allied Matters Act Cap and section 8.5 of Nigeria's SEC Code gives the board the powers of appointment and removal over a company secretary), the same goes for the UK Combined Code of 2003 which requires that 'both the appointment and removal of the company secretary should be a matter for the board as a whole'.

The company secretary is to act in the interests of the company and is accountable to the board in doing so. It is although not feasible or desirable to expect the company secretary to report to the directors daily. It is therefore important that the reporting lines are established in such a way that the principle and practicality are well-balanced.[28] Section 8.3 of the Nigerian Securities and Exchange Code provides that the company secretary shall report directly to the CEO/MD but also have a direct channel of communication to the chair. Hence, it is expedient to establish dual

---

[22] Bisi (n 21 above).

[23] Bisi (n 21 above).

[24] Guidance Note – Chartered Secretaries. https://www.hkics.org.hk/media/publication/attach-ment/2026_GN4–Reporting%20lines.pdf

[25] International Finance Corporation (n 12 above).

[26] The Hong Kong Institute of Chartered Secretaries 'Guidance Note: A Practical Guide to Corporate Governance' (June 2007) available at https://www.hkics.org.hk/media/publication/attach-ment/2026_GN4–Reporting%20lines.pdf (accessed on 13 October 2018).

[27] Hong Kong Institute of Chartered Secretaries (n 26 above).

[28] Hong Kong Institute of Chartered Secretaries (n 26 above).

reporting lines to allow the company secretary report to the chair directly on matters which concern the board (setting an agenda for board meetings, running of board meetings, information flow within the board, etc.) and to the CEO, on matters which relate to management.[29] Furthermore, as the role of a company secretary increases and becomes more complex, multiple reporting lines should be established between the company, the secretary and the board.[30] However, it is important to note that a company secretary is not accountable to any individual directors but to the board as a whole, accordingly, no individual director is to unfetter discretion over the appointment, removal, remuneration and benefits of a company secretary so as to reduce any undue influence which underpins the impartiality and independence of the company secretary.[31]

6.1.11 Outsourcing the Role of the Company Secretary

The shift from employing a company secretary to outsourcing one from corporate secretarial services firms has gained great momentum over the years, mostly as a result of the expertise they provide and the reduced costs of recruitment and training. Outsourcing corporate secretarial services allows smaller and mid-sized companies to effectively implement the corporate governance best practices that are now common among larger corporations.[32] In addition to governance expertise and know-how, corporate secretary service providers bring knowledge of tools that can be used to improve efficiency and effectiveness of governance.[33] Furthermore, because corporate secretarial services firms are solely focused on the corporate secretarial function, they possess the technical know-how and experience. They deal with numerous companies and have learnt from their experiences.[34] However, some argue that an external company secretary cannot be as effective as an internal company secretary as a result of the multifaceted and interconnected role of the company secretary.

An in-house company secretary acquires an in-depth knowledge and understanding of the workings of the company and of the board and management. Furthermore an in-house secretary can be relied on to main-

---

[29] DCSL 'Who Does The Company Secretary Report To?' (2014) available at http://blog.dcsl.com.ng/blog/2014/03/24/who–does–the–company–secretary–report–to/ (accessed on 13 October 2018).

[30] DCSL (n 29 above).

[31] Hong Kong Institute of Chartered Secretaries (n 26 above).

[32] Hong Kong Institute of Chartered Secretaries (n 26 above).

[33] BoardBookit 'Outsourcing Corporate Secretarial Services and Board Portals' available at https://boardbookit.com/blog/outsourcing–corporate–secretarial–services/ (accessed on 13 October 2018).

[34] Reliance Consulting: '5 Reasons Outsourcing A Corporate Secretary is More Efficient' (2016) available at https://www.corporateservicessingapore.com/5–reasons–outsourcing–a–corporate–secretary–is–more–efficient/ (accessed on 13 October 2018).

tain confidentiality and can easily be held liable for any breaches of same, whereas this may be problematic in cases of an outsourced service.[35] This should place a sense of duty on company secretarial firms to raise their standards and improve their knowledge of the day to day affairs of the company, their presence must be felt daily in the affairs of the company.

6.1.12 Corporate Stakeholder Relationship Officer/ Public Relations Manager

Stakeholder expectations of companies are ever-changing and have become multifaceted in the twenty-first century.[36] In order to determine the expectation of stakeholders, management must maintain a close, continual relationship with those stakeholders. Some organisations have taken the proactive step of appointing a specialist Corporate Stakeholder Relationship Officer (CSRO) whose responsibility is to communicate with stakeholders and relay information to management of stakeholders' legitimate and reasonable needs, interests and expectations and even the expectations that may not seem legitimate.[37]

It has been suggested that if a company is not inclined to appoint a CSRO, a company secretary is particularly well-placed to carry out the function of a CSRO. This is largely because modern day corporate governance trends have called for company secretaries to play a more active role in corporate governance and management. Company secretaries are now expected to know the capital resources being used by the company and to be able to identify the key stakeholders of the business since they attend board and executive meetings and are aware of the strategic long-term thinking of the company.[38] The issue with this approach is that it places an additional burden on the company secretary and might require the strengthening of the secretarial department by the addition of a general counsel.[39]

Considering the sensitivity of what is required of a CSRO, it is suggested that an existing company position that best fits this description is the public relations manager. This is because the role of public relations management is to establish and maintain lines of communication, understanding, acceptance and operation between an organisation and its public.[40] The two major functions of public relations (to know the environment better and let the environment know you better) not only fit clearly into the scope of a stakeholder relationship manager but also make a distinctive contribution to

---

[35] International Finance Corporation (n 12 above).
[36] CSJ (n 8 above).
[37] IODSA *King IV Report on Corporate Governance* (2016).
[38] CSJ (n 8 above).
[39] CSJ (n 8 above).
[40] ZBA Vural 'The Role of Public Relations on Corporate Governance' (2015) 1 *The Online Journal of Communication and Media.*

the realisation of corporate governance principles such as openness, transparency, clarity, responsibility and accountability.[41] The main aim of a public relations manager in carrying out the role of stakeholder relationship management would be to maintain positive relations and a constructive dialogue between a corporation and its stakeholders through a balanced information flow.

6.1.13 What Is Expected of a Corporate Stakeholder Relationship Officer?

As earlier noted, the key function of a CSRO is to communicate with stakeholders and inform management of their legitimate expectations. To achieve this, a CSRO would be expected to do the following.

- ☑ Create and maintain a highly comprehensive, robust and reliable stakeholder database.[42]
- ☑ Develop various stakeholder engagement strategies and approaches.[43]
- ☑ Develop processes to monitor relevant networking opportunities and foster relationships with stakeholders.[44]
- ☑ Conduct regular monitoring and assessment of activities to measure the effectiveness of corporate outreach activities.[45]

6.1.14 Auditors

Auditors of the company play an important role because they are the eyes and ears of external stakeholders. They instil confidence and provide a true and fair account of the company by being objective, undeniably an auditor is a necessity. [46] Excellent corporate governance needs to include effective internal control systems, policies procedures and group direct management to serve the needs of all stakeholders. An external auditor's role is to check transparency, integrity and accountability of the management.[47] External auditors' primary role is to give an opinion as to whether or not the financial statements adhere to the financial reporting standards applicable to the

---

[41] Vural (n 40 above).

[42] Devex Website (advert for the role of Stakeholder Relations Officer) available at https://www.devex.com/jobs/zaaap–stakeholder–relations–officer–522253 (accessed on 13 October 2018).

[43] Innovation.CA (advert for the role of Stakeholder Relations Officer) available at https://www.innovation.ca/sites/default/files/Careers/senior_officer_stakeholder_relations_jan_2017_eng_0.pdf (accessed on 13 October 2018).

[44] Innovation.CA (n 43 above).

[45] Innovation.CA (n 43 above).

[46] S Navajyoti & D Tirthankar 'Role of auditors in Corporate Governance' (2009) available at https://papers.ssrn.com/sol3/papers.cfm?abstract_id=1487050 (accessed on 15 October 2018).

[47] S Ray 'Auditors' role in corporate governance of India's business perspective' (2012) 2 *Public Policy and Administration Research*.

company, such as International Financial Reporting Standards (IFRS) in Nigeria.[48]

Internal auditors are to introduce measures and policies designed to compel accountability in the workplace.[49] They also help promote corporate governance by conducting periodic risk assessments. Internal auditors review the security measures that a company has in place against corporate fraud or corruption. They can also analyse the overall risk tolerance of the company as well as the efforts the company has made towards mitigating risks. Internal auditors ensure good corporate governance by implementing an efficient crisis-management plan to be used in the event of allegations of fraud or corruption thus, if the company becomes embroiled in financial crises, there must be an active plan in place to implement and sustain confidence among investors.[50]

Another important but largely unexplored role which an external auditor can play in corporate governance is fostering a good relationship between the corporation and its regulators. Most regulators are supportive of companies that appear to have transparent operations; and regulators are more likely to trust company disclosures after an auditor attests to them. [51]

6.1.15 Institutional Investors

Institutional investors are financial institutions that accept funds from third parties, for investment in their own name but on such parties' behalf.[52] Institutional investors include pension funds, mutual funds and insurance companies.[53] Institutional investors as at 2009 had managed an estimated USD53 trillion of assets in the OECD area, including USD22 trillion in equity.[54] Given the size of their shareholding, the power of the institutional investor cannot be doubted, Hirschman, identified the exercise of institutio-nal power within an exit and voice framework, arguing that dissatisfaction may be expressed directly to management, which is known as the voice option, or by selling of their shareholding, which is known as the exit option. The exit option is not often viable for many institutional investors given the size of their holding or policy of holding a balanced portfolio.[55]

---

[48] K Harow 'Role of an external auditor in corporate governance' (Chron, 2018) available at https://work.chron.com/role–external–auditor–corporate–governance–27754.html (accessed on 15 October 2018).

[49] Harow (n 48 above).

[50] Harow (n 48 above).

[51] Harow (n 48 above).

[52] OECD 'The Role of Institutional Investors in Promoting Good Corporate Governance' (2011) *Corporate Governance* OECD Publishing available at https://www.oecd.org/daf/ca/49081553.pdf (accessed 18 August 2019).

[53] Ibid (n 52 above).

[54] Ibid (n 52 above).

[55] Dialogue with companies' institutional shareholders should .... available at https://www.coursehero.com/file/p1eqc3d/Dialogue–with–companies–institutional–shareholders–should–enter–into–a–dialogue/ (accessed on 15 October 2018).

The latter is notoften viable for many institutional investors given the size of their holding or policy of holding a balanced portfolio.[56]

A fiduciary relationship exists between institutional investors and the beneficial owners of the investment. Institutional investors also have a duty to derive a positive return on investment.[57] Accordingly, institutional investments traditionally tended focused on profitable investments. While this remains the case, governments and pressure groups have raised the question of how these profits are achieved. Now institutional investors are more concerned with the governance of companies and the respective company's relationship with other stakeholder groups.[58]

The Cadbury Committee[59] viewed institutional investors as having a special responsibility to try to ensure that their recommendations were adopted by companies, stating that 'we look to the institution in particular to ensure that the companies in which they have invested comply with best standards of corporate governance'.[60] Codes of corporate have started to recognise this influence. The UK Combined Code, in relation to institutional shareholders, notes the following:

Institutional investors should follow the UN's principles of responsible investment.

6.1.16 Dialogue with Companies

Institutional shareholders should dialogue with companies based on mutual understanding of objectives

6.1.17 Evaluation of Governance Disclosures

Institutional investors must ensure that governance disclosure requirements are drawn to their attention and that they carefully consider them and all factors drawn to their attention. Most especially those relating to issues such as board composition.

6.1.18 Shareholder Voting

Institutional shareholders have a responsibility to their beneficiaries to make considered use of their votes. Academics have also identified certain tools for institutional investor participation in corporate governance which include the following:

---

[56] C Mallin 'The Role of Institutional Investors in Corporate Governance' (runall.tex, 2006) available at https://www.kantakji.com/media/3426/xx7.pdf (accessed on 15 October 2018).

[57] Role of Institutional Investors (n 52 above).

[58] Role of Institutional Investors (n 52 above).

[59] The Cadbury Report (Financial Aspects of Corporate Governance) issued by The Committee on the Financial Aspects of Corporate Governance in 1992.

[60] Ibid.

☑ One on one meetings between companies and their institutional investors.

☑ Voting rights.

☑ Keeping focus lists – Institutional investors tend to keep a list of underperforming companies.

☑ Corporate governance rating systems – it is ideal that institutional investors invest in companies who have high corporate governance and good citizenship ratings. This would encourage companies to work towards having good corporate governance mechanisms in place.[61]

6.1.19 Government Agencies and Regulators

Good corporate governance is important for overall economic stability and national credibility. The collapse of companies due to poor corporate ethics and poor board oversight can lead to financial disruption and result in job loss. In developing countries such as Nigeria, a lapse in corporate culture can be devastating for reputational capital which cannot easily be repaired and its financial costs not easily determined or absorbed. The maintenance of effective corporate governance structures at every level of our society (government, government parastatals, regulators, etc.) is imperative for the continued wellbeing of any economy. Hence, there is an important role for a regulator as a standard setter in corporate governance.[62]

Furthermore, recent corporate scandals have led to public pressure to reform business practices and increase regulations, these have also brought into question the challenge of who should regulate. Currently the government in most jurisdictions shares regulatory authority and oversight with various non-governmental, self-regulatory institutions. Another challenge is deciding how to regulate; most regulators face a choice between principles and rules. Should regulatory standards articulate board objectives through by adherence to general principles? or should regulations be specific and mandate what is acceptable and unacceptable? Finally, regulators also face the challenge of how to enforce rules or principles they have adopted; is more aggressive enforcement needed? Should enforcement target individual perpetrators or should they also go after the corporations in which misconduct occurs.[63] This was the subject of a report released by the Regulatory Policy Program, Centre for Business and Government at Harvard University. The report considered the subject of the role of the government and

---

[61] Ibid

[62] Address by Julian W. Francis, Governor of the Central Bank of Bahamas to the Bahamas Director's Forum on Corporate Governance, 'The Role of the Regulator in Corporate Governance'. (24 February 2004).

[63] C Coglianese, TJ Healey, EK Keating & ML Michael 'The Role of Government in Corporate Governance,' Regulatory Policy Program Report RPP–08 (2004), Cambridge, MA: Center for Business and Government, John F. Kennedy School of Government, Harvard University.

regulators in corporate governance in three parts (self-regulation, rules versus principles and enforcement) which is discussed below.[64]

6.1.20 Government Regulation Versus Self-Regulation by Industries

The report explained the advantages and disadvantages of self-regulation as follows in the diagram below:

Table 6.1

	Advantages	Disadvantages
1.	**Proximity** – Industry regulators have more information about the industry than the government tends to have.	**Conflict of interest** – The very proximity which is an advantage can be a disadvantage, knowing an industry better does not mean that the regulator has the proper incentives to regulate it more effectively. Rather such a regulator may use its role to simply keep put market entrants.
2	**Flexibility** – Self-regulators are not subject to the same kinds of procedures and due process hurdles that government does.	**Inadequate Sanctions**: The greater flexibility afforded such bodies may result in the meeting out only modest sanctions against violators.
3.	**Compliance** – the greater the involvement of industry in setting the rules, the more those rules may appear reasonable to corporations.	**Under-enforcement** – A self-regulator's conflict of interests and flexibility may also make it more likely that compliance with rules will be insufficiently monitored.
4.	**Collective interests of the industry** – Self-regulation can harness the collective interests of the industry.	**Global competition**: Foreign markets may not be equally burdened with regulation; thus, aggressive self-regulation could put domestic companies at a serious disadvantage providing yet another reason to question whether self-regulators will make socially optimal decisions.

---

[64] Coglianese et al (n 63 above).

5.	**Resources** – Self-regulators may have a better ability to secure needed resources within the industry in which they operate.	**Insufficient resources**: although funding of self-regulatory bodies may not be susceptible to the whims of legislature, there may be underlying conflicts of interest which would leave self-regulatory bodies with less than sufficient funding. [65]

It can be seen that the major disadvantage of self-regulation is conflict of interest. An example can be seen in the Nigerian Petroleum Industry; in recent times there have been complaints by operators in the industry that certain regulators of the industry have also been involved in the importation of fuel and this has had a negative impact on the financial performance of operators in the industry. For instance, the Nigerian National Petroleum Corporation is a regulator as well as an operator and this may mean that they will not play fair in the industry.[66] Regardless, self-regulation has both advantages and disadvantages. The challenge lies in finding the circumstances in which self-regulation or government regulation is the most appropriate model and if self-regulation is ideal, the challenge is to find optimal ways of designing self-regulatory institutions and how much government oversight they should have.[67]

6.1.21 Rules versus Principles

The decision of applying either rules or principles is one that every government regulator or self-regulator must make. The norm seems to be with principles, and this is in a bid to not interfere with the activities of corporations as private entities and to afford them the liberty to govern as they deem fit. However, rules are generally perceived as being simpler and easier to follow than principles as they reduce discretion on the part of management, making it less likely that their judgment is motivated by personal gain at the expense of investors and other stakeholders.

On the other hand, rules can be more complex than principles, as lawmakers try to address every conceivable eventuality, the rule book becomes harder to understand and even simple and clear rules can be manipulated.[68] Rules and principles also have pros and cons; regulators are

---

[65] Coglianese et al (n 63 above).

[66] Vanguard 'Regulators Defy Corporate Governance – Mikail' (July 2, 2018) available at https://www.vanguardngr.com/2018/07/regulators–defy–corporate–governance–principle–mikail/ (accessed on 15 October 2018).

[67] Coglianese et al (n 63 above).

[68] Coglianese et al (n 63 above).

advised to try and combine both to create a hybrid system of regulation, where there is clarity but also freedom on the part of corporations.

6.1.22 Enforcement

Enforcement affects the overall credibility of a regulatory system and sends a message to the broader public. Stricter enforcement is however not always better because it can negatively affect valuable risk-taking. Regulators must ensure a balance and know in what means to pursue enforcement actions, particularly criminal prosecutions.[69] Regulatory enforcement is a complicated enterprise because of the existence of multiple enforcers. Competition among enforcement jurisdictions may increase deterrence, hence there should be continued efforts to coordinate enforcement amongst regulators to ensure that the limited enforcement resources are adequately and consistency applied across board.[70]

6.1.23 What Should the Government Be Doing?

Regardless of the discussions of who should regulate and how, it is clear that the heart of good corporate governance is in the court of the board, therefore any regulator should concern itself with the issue of directors' responsibility and accountability. An important element of corporate governance is also the issue of disclosure requirements and accounting standards. Hence regulatory bodies must take this into account.[71]

The role of the government in corporate governance goes beyond the crafting of rules and regulations but also the active involvement in evaluating whether these regulations are actually encouraging economic growth and promoting the protection of investors and the society at large.[72] The government has to ensure that it restores public confidence in the economy by taking effective action through reformed regulatory systems, improved auditing and effective enforcement mechanisms.[73] Most importantly there needs to be the creation of an enabling environment for businesses to thrive.[74]

The government should provide relevant infrastructure and basic services that companies can utilise in carrying out their businesses, lack of which negatively affects the establishment and growth of businesses without these adequate services and infrastructure, businesses are forced to provide for

[69] Coglianese et al (n 63 above).
[70] Coglianese et al (n 63 above).
[71] Francis (n 62 above).
[72] The Herald 'The Role of Government in Corporate Governance (2016) available at https://www.herald.co.zw/role–of–govt–in–corporate–governance/ (accessed on 17 October 2018).
[73] The Herald (n 72 above).
[74] The Herald (n 72 above).

them out of pocket and this affects their investment in proper corporate governance systems and in turn overall business performance.[75] Furthermore, the government must demonstrate the good values and ethics through the companies it has controlling stakes in so that private players can emulate the same. This would also give the government credibility when it assesses the compliance level of other corporations and can easily press companies to provide adequate explanations for non-compliance. Responses to corporate failures must also be effective and corporate leaders' involvement in scandals must be investigated adequately and fairly.[76]

---

[75] The Herald (n 62 above).
[76] The Herald (n 62 above).

Chapter 7

RELATIONSHIP MANAGEMENT UNDER THE OUTCOMES-BASED GOVERNANCE MODEL

For corporate governance to be effective, the mechanisms put in place in the organisation must take into consideration that no company can exist as an island; rather organisations must maintain and foster relationships between their internal components and third parties. For instance, the board needs to learn and appreciate the NIEs of its employees at all levels. The board as a collective, needs to take account of these NIE's in making business judgement calls. The more employees buy into long-term strategy the more successful the company will be.

This chapter evaluates the key relationships that are crucial for a company to maintain in order to increase its prospects for long-term sustainability and profitability. This chapter further delves into conflict management and the strategies that the board and management must put in place to ensure that key relationships are maintained for the benefit of the organisation.

7.1 EMPLOYEES ROLE IN WHISTLEBLOWING

Whistleblowing is a mechanism through which anyone can report dishonest or illegal activities and misconduct in the company. The alleged misconduct may include the likes of fraud, rules violation, gross misconduct or mismanagement, abuse of authority, and so forth. Whistleblowing can be internal (reported to the appropriate authorities within the organisation) or external (reported to third parties such as the media or law enforcement authorities). In principle, employees are likely to have increased expertise and be more keenly interested in monitoring senior management.[1] Employees are the limbs of the organisation and are involved in both management and the complete working of the company. They are, therefore, ideally placed to observe and detect ethical or illicit activities. Employees may choose to either ignore such illicit activities or bring it to the attention of the relevant authorities. For an employee to choose to do the latter, there must be put in place structures to protect such an employee from discrimination by co-workers.[2] Organisations must put in place a safety net that

---

[1] MLP Lower 'Employee Participation in Corporate Governance: An Ethical Analysis' (The Chinese University of Hong Kong, 2018).

[2] Lower (n 1 above).

protects the confidentiality of employees who decide to blow the whistle. For example, an external consultant, whose duty it is to receive reports from willing employees and inform the board and management of the complaints while protecting the identity of the employee, could manage the whistle blowing structure.

7.2 EMPLOYEE REPRESENTATION AT BOARD LEVEL

This can be useful because employee representatives can provide information about the economic condition and strategy of the firm and as earlier noted can act as whistleblowers and raise an early warning about management proposals that have the potential of harming employee interest. Employees could add a new dimension to board discussions by pointing out difficulties or strategies that management has not considered. It can also be used as a further tool for monitoring board performance similar to the use of outside directors. It builds a participative company where there is worker involvement in the implementation of policy and improvement of work processes.

7.3 STAKEHOLDER RELATIONSHIPS

The number one goal concerning stakeholder relationships is for an organisation to strike an appropriate balance between its various stakeholder groupings.[3] This is necessary because different groups of stakeholders play different roles in relation to the company and as such, can be classified according to their importance for the company's performance.[4] The board should identify key aspects such as communication guidelines mechanisms and processes to support stakeholder engagement and interaction, a means for dispute resolution and then delegate to management these aspects maintaining an oversight function.[5]

Communication and trust are the main sources with which to create a lasting relationship between stakeholders.[6] Janci has developed a model of exchange and communication with the company's stakeholders which he based on relationship marketing. He emphasises the wide range of relationships in which a company will likely be involved and govern at the same time. According to Janci, the organisation must adopt different levels of

---

[3] Candour Governance Specialists 'Stakeholder Relationships' available at http://www.candorsolutions.co.za/king–iii/chapter–8–stakeholder–relationships/ (accessed on 31 October 2018).

[4] C Ljubojevic & G Ljubojevic, 'Improving the Stakeholder Satisfaction by Corporate Governance Quality' (Skola biznisa Broj 1/2011).

[5] Ljubojevic & Ljubojevic (n 4 above).

[6] Ljubojevic & Ljubojevic (n 4 above).

exchange in its communication activities to foster good relationships with its numerous stakeholders.[7]

However, before establishing communication and trust, an organisation must first identify all its stakeholders, understand their needs, prioritise their needs, satisfy these needs and monitor the engagement efforts, which should be the duty of the corporate stakeholder relationship manager discussed previously.

7.3.1 Relationship Between Board and Management

A relationship of trust and understanding between the board and management is critical for good governance and organisational effectiveness. However, in reality, this is difficult to achieve.[8] Common challenges that may arise between boards and management include:

☑ an inadequate framework for the implementation of policies, monitoring, and feedback;
☑ the board attempting to act as a top layer of management;
☑ boards taking a reactive approach rather than a proactive one;
☑ the board attempting to encroach the role of management; and
☑ conflicts of interest which may arise.[9]

Central to their relationship is a clear mutual understanding of roles, delegations, and boundaries which allows each to respect and acknowledge the others responsibilities, contributions, and expectation[10] To be effective the board and management must work together, and their relationship must comprise of:

☑ a two-way flow of information;
☑ constructive debate;
☑ commitment to strategic direction; and
☑ a clear understanding of the organisation's mission, strategic business plans, implementations plans and understanding boundaries. [11]

Management must accept the board's role in monitoring, probing, seeking clarity and offering insight, knowledge, and experience. Similarly, the board

[7] Ljubojevic & Ljubojevic (n 4 above).

[8] Australian Institute of Company Directors 'Relationship Between The Board and Management: Governance Relations' available at https://aicd.companydirectors.com.au/–/media/cd2/resources/director–resources/director–tools/pdf/05446–3–10–mem–director–gr–rel–board–management_a4–web.ashx (accessed on 31 October 2018).

[9] Chapter II – The Relationship Between Board and Management available at http://worldanimal.net/documents/Professional_APSM_Online_Book/Chapter_2_Board_and_Management.pdf (accessed on 1 November 2018).

[10] Australian Institute of Company Directors (n 8 above).

[11] Effective Governance, HopgoodGanim Advisory Group, 'Improving Board–Management Relations' https://www.effectivegovernance.com.au/improving–board–management–relations/ (accessed on 1 November 2018).

must trust management to implement strategy and deliver outcomes without undue interference. Management must also ensure the timely and relevant flow of information and reporting and in turn the board should signal the standards of discipline and rigour expected of management by challenging and asking the hard questions. Management must further exert its critical role in effective board decision-making by reporting relevant material information to the board and stimulating board discussion on emerging issues, while still keeping the board well informed of changing risks and so forth.[12]

7.3.2 Relationship Between the Chair and Chief Executive Officer

A business relationship must always be maintained between the chairperson and the CEO. The relationship should be one of trust, respect, unity, and mutual support; the chair should be a mentor to the CEO. At the same time, there must be frankness and candour behind the scenes.[13]

7.3.3 Relationship Between Respective Board Members and Executive Management

The statement of the Australian Institute of Company Directors on the relationship between individual board members and executive management is apt:

> Individual board members have no inherent authority or executive power. Enquiries by board members of management and by management of individual board members should primarily be channeled via the chair and CEO. Where there is any direct material contact between individual board members and executive management, the chair and CEO should be kept informed by way of courtesy. Where there is strength of mutual respect and confidence that the chair's and CEO's authority will not be undermined, communications between executive management and board members may be freer. There may also be expectations of freer communication between the chairs of the audit and risk committees and the relevant executives responsible for those functions, on matters within the scope of those functions.[14]

7.3.4 Relationships Within Group of Companies

Regardless of whether a company exists within a group structure, corporate law and regulations in most companies focus on the duty of directors to the

---

[12] Australian Institute of Company Directors (n 8 above).
[13] Australian Institute of Company Directors (n 8 above).
[14] Australian Institute of Company Directors 'Relationship Between The Board and Management, Governance Relations available at available at https://aicd.companydirectors.com.au/~/media/cd2/resources/director–resources/director–tools/pdf/05446–3–10–mem–director–gr–rel–board–management_a4–web.ashx (accessed on 1 November 2018).

company as a separate legal entity and not in relation to the group.[15] Companies establish separate legal entities to address certain business needs ranging from diversification of assets to bifurcation of business services as well as tax efficiency and expansion into a new geographical market.[16] As companies grow and diversify their operations, the number of subsidiaries tend to increase, and the structures of the companies become more complex. This creation of different entities under one umbrella give rise to challenges as it becomes difficult for the parent company to supervise and perform an oversight function over all its subsidiaries.[17] These challenges include inter alia numerous decision-making levels, challenges in relation to the implementation of strategic objectives, monitoring and maintenance of corporate culture and risks as well as reporting.[18] A lack of regulatory attention to governance of group entities, of course, heightens these challenges. This statement by the academic advisor on governance policy to firms and regulators in the UK succinctly explains this issue as follows:

> This is a neglected area of corporate governance amongst academics, practitioners and policy makers. Group entities pose a challenge to traditional concepts of governance. Company law in most jurisdictions typically expects the boards of such entities to define the best interests of their companies in an independent and objective manner. And yet the ownership structure of such entities – and the constraints that such ownership places on directors and boards – means that such independence is very difficult to achieve in practice. The interests of the parent company typically override those of the group entities. This places the directors of such entities in a legally ambiguous and potentially vulnerable position.[19]

The above challenges may result in corporate failures and although the corporate veil is rarely pierced to establish liability of directors of the parent company, the parent company may find itself financially liable to the failures of a company under its umbrella and may also suffer reputational damage.[20]

---

[15] MY Teen & C Bennett 'Governance of Company Groups' (The Iclif Leadership & Governance Centre, CPA Australia, 2014) available at http://www.iclifgovernance.org/file/files/governance–co–groups.pdf (accessed on 1 November 2018).

[16] Deloitte 'Governance of Subsidiaries: A Survey of Global Companies' (2013) available at https://www2.deloitte.com/content/dam/Deloitte/in/Documents/risk/Corporate%20Governance/in–gc–governance-of-subsidiaries–a–survey–of–global–companies–noexp.pdf (accessed on 1 November 2018).

[17] Teen & Bennett (n 15 above).

[18] Latin American Companies Circle 'Corporate Governance Recommendations for Company Groups' (OECD, 2014) available at https://www.oecd.org/daf/ca/2014LatinAmericaCorporate GovernanceRoundtableRecommendationsCompanyGroups.pdf (accessed on 1 November 2018).

[19] Teen & Bennett (n 15 above).

[20] Teen & Bennett (n 15 above).

7.4 GOVERNANCE FRAMEWORK

A proactive approach to the governance of group entities is thus required to minimise the risk of governance failures in group entities that may cause significant financial and reputational harm to the entire group. This governance framework must be established to allow for the general integration of the business objectives in line with the group's business model. It should also allow for operational efficiency, proper reporting and enforcement of best practices across the group and at the same time preserve the decisions-making autonomy of the individual company.[21]

The board of the parent company is ultimately responsible for determining the approach which should be adopted to govern entities within the group.[22] The CEO of the holding company or parent company is usually responsible for effective organisation within the group through the establishment of management guidelines from the board of directors as well as dissemination, implementation, and monitoring of the global strategy.[23] The board of the parent company then need to determine the specific governance measures which should be adopted for different entities within the group. Five broad categories of specific governance measures must be included: formal group governance programmes, learning and communication, group polices on audit, internal controls and reporting, and open and effective communication. Some of the measures that can be implemented to supervise subsidiaries and enforce governance include:

- establishing a general strategy for the group and ensure that it is effectively communicated.
- establishing an information management system and a reporting framework;
- ensuring risk management practices are established;
- ensuring that all the group companies consider sustainable governance issues such as social and environmental concerns in decision-making;
- establishing group-wide policies on branding, internal control, compliance, and accounting.
- preserving shareholders right to approve sensitive issues;
- establishing monitoring frameworks; for example, meetings between representatives of the participants of the group as well as a framework for implementing directives and evaluating performance;
- setting a corporate-wide independent internal audit function; and
- ensuring that related party transactions, which present potential for abuse, are entered into at an arm s length basis.[24]

---

[21] Latin American Companies Circle (n 18 above).
[22] Latin American Companies Circle (n 18 above).
[23] Teen & Bennett (n 15 above).
[24] Latin American Companies Circle (n 18 above).

Another common practice adopted by parent companies to ensure control over its subsidiaries is appointing directors or senior management officers from the holding company to the subsidiaries as board members of the subsidiary or to executive positions as the CEO or Chief Financial Officer. In addition to the advantage of control and monitoring, this practice ensures a higher degree of communication. The directors of a subsidiary, however, owe their duties of loyalty and care to the subsidiary company. The issue with this approach, is that although the replication of the parent company's board on the subsidiaries board would ensure an alignment of the group's objective, appointing a diverse board would enable the board of each company be directly suited to its needs in terms of industry experience and knowledge. It would also offer an external perspective and critical analysis of the subsidiary's management.[25]

7.5 IMPLEMENTING THE FRAMEWORK

Following the establishment of a group governance framework, the said framework must be implemented. For this framework to be effective, there must be group-wide participation. The board of directors of the parent company must also be willing to address the concerns of the board of the group of entities. Gaining the support of the entities within the group is essential for the framework of governance of company groups to succeed.[26]

Technology plays a key role in ensuring the implementation of the group framework. Technology systems can be configured to assist the governance framework for example, by automating approval processes and providing clear audit trails for decision-making purposes.[27]

7.6 THE KING IV PRACTICE NOTE ON GROUP GOVERNANCE, 2019

The King Committee in South Africa issued a Practice Note on Group Governance in March 2019.[28] The Practice Note explains the challenge in this regard as follows:

---

[25] Latin American Companies Circle (n 18 above).

[26] Teen & Bennett (n 15 above).

[27] PWC 'Subsidiary Governance: An Unappreciated Risk (2013) available at https://www.pwc.com/gx/en/legal/entity–governance–compliance/publications/assets/subsidiary–governance.pdf (accessed on 2 November 2018).

[28] King IV Practice Notes 'Group Governance' (Institute of Directors South Africa, January 2019) available at <https://cdn.ymaws.com/www.iodsa.co.za/resource/collection/562ED5CF–02E8–4957–97C8– D3F0C66A7245/Group_Governance_Framework_Practice_Note.pdf> (accessed on 27 March 2018).

[S]ubsidiaries within group structures tend to expose the group and holding company to increased risk, inappropriate/excessive oversight by the holding company over subsidiaries, dilution of accountability at the subsidiary board level and lack of strategic and governance alignment between the holding company and its subsidiaries.[29]

To address this challenge, the Practice Note provides that 'a fine balance is thus needed to ensure that there is alignment between the holding company's strategic direction and the implementation of appropriate group governance'. The Practice Note further provides a minimum framework for group governance as follows:

Role Clarity:

Leadership and governance: The holding company should determine priorities for achieving group objectives and then provide direction on how the relationships and exercise of power within the group should be structured to achieve these. This includes direction on what should be centrally or locally driven.

Ethical culture: The holding company has a special responsibility to shape the culture and values of the entire group.

Strategy and performance: There should be clarity regarding both accountability, and the process, for strategy development and target setting.

Group corporate governance:

Monitory and oversight: The holding company should reach an agreement with its subsidiaries regarding key governance outcomes and specific governance issues relevant or specific to the subsidiary.

Group policies: There should be clarity about the nature and extent to which policies, structures and processes will be centralised or devolved to the subsidiary level, taking into account the risks a subsidiary represents, in light of its governance maturity and effectiveness.

Authority and reserved powers:

Reserved Powers: Matters that the holding company wishes to reserve for its decisions-making (shareholder-reserved matters) should be clearly set out in the constitutive documents (memorandum of incorporation ('MOI') or equivalent) of the subsidiary and should be limited to what is reasonably necessary.

Operating across jurisdictions:

Global policies need to be modified for local use to ensure that they are locally relevant and compliant with local laws.[30]

Importantly, the Practice Note states that there is:

No one-size-fits-all model. Consequently, an effective Famework has to be tailored to the relevant subsidiary's needs, as well as to the requirements of the holding company, by taking into account the nature and role of each of the entities within the group.[31]

---

[29] King IV Practice Notes (n 21 above).
[30] IODSA *King IV Report on Corporate Governance* (2016) at 3–4.
[31] Ibid.

Chapter 8

OUTCOMES-BASED GOVERNANCE IN AFRICA

8.1 APPLYING OUTCOMES-BASED GOVERNANCE TO SMALL AND MEDIUM-SIZED ENTERPRISES

There is no agreed definition of what SMEs are; the definitions of SMEs vary across countries and sectors but are usually based on the number of employees, assets, or a combination of the two. The OECD in its policy briefing titled *Small and Medium-Sized Enterprises: Local Strength, Global Reach* defined SME as non-subsidiary, independent firms which employ fewer than a given number of employees, which number varies across nations. The most frequent upper limit is 250 employees in the European Union and 500 in the US. SMEs, however, generally employ fewer than 50 employees, while micro-enterprises employ at most ten workers. SMEs can also be considered from a turnover perspective. In the European Union, to qualify as an SMEs, the enterprise must have an annual turnover of 40 million or less and/or a balance sheet valuation not exceeding 27 million.[1]

Traditionally, adopting corporate governance principles was associated with larger companies. In recent times however, there has been a global concern for the application of good corporate governance to SMEs. This is because of the importance of corporate governance in growing companies and strengthening the foundation of society.[2] It is also because SMEs comprise the majority of businesses in the private sector worldwide. For example, a study conducted in Egypt showed that SMEs accounted for 80 per cent of the total value added by the private sector and that 13 per cent of adults in Egypt are reportedly in the process of starting a business or own a young enterprise.[3] However, it seems that the corporate governance sector tends to overlook SMEs. A study conducted on SMEs in Ghana showed a very low rate of corporate governance practice amongst SMEs in Ghana.[4]

---

[1] OECD Policy Brief 'Small and Medium–sized Enterprises: Local Strength, Global Reach' (2000) available at http://www.oecd.org/cfe/leed/1918307.pdf (accessed on 15 November 2018).

[2] J Abor & CKD Adjasi 'Corporate governance and the small and medium enterprises sector: Theory and implications' (2007) 7 *Corporate Governance: The International Journal of Business in Society* 111–22.

[3] OECD Corporate Governance of Small and Medium Sized Enterprises (SMEs), Cairo, Egypt (2010) available at http://www.oecd.org/daf/ca/corporategovernanceofstate–ownedenterprises/corpo-rategovernanceofsmallandmedium–sizedenterprisessmes.htm (accessed on 15 November 2018).

[4] D Dzigba 'Corporate Governance Practice among Small and Medium Scale Enterprises (SMEs) in Ghana; Impact on Access to Credit (School of Management, 2015) available at https://www.diva–portal.org/smash/get/diva2:829172/FULLTEXT01.pdf (accessed on 15 November 2018).

As a result of the United Nation's Principles for Responsible Investment, asset owners and managers are now conducting a due diligence on a listed company's supply chain, inter alia, before investing in the equity of that company. As there are many SMEs in a supply chain, capital providers expect the listed company today to monitor what is happening in its supply chain. This market force is driving SMEs to start adopting good ESG standards. Asset owners and managers have learnt that if there is something socially or environmentally unacceptable in an SME supplier's conduct, such as the use of child labour or deforestation, the ultimate listed company customer will have its market cap severely reduced.

There are strong arguments in favour of SMEs adopting good corporate governance principles, as has already been highlighted in previous chapters. Good corporate governance practices promote growth, sustainability and financial stability, and SMEs are not left out of this equation.[5] Implementing corporate governance principles also attracts investors as an alternative to raising capital than through borrowing from banks at high costs.[6] Furthermore, SMEs may be small in size but the reality is that today's SME could grow to become a big entity in the future. For this reason, it is advantageous for SMEs to adopt corporate governance standards early or else the corporate governance sector will continue to face issues of non-compliance that occur with larger organisations.

In the research carried out on SMEs in Egypt it was further discovered that one-third of SMEs collapse after three years as a result of insufficient planning and a lack of forward-thinking, inadequate leadership and management, an inability to cope with ever-changing business requirement, environment and economic conditions, and inadequate access to technical assistance. These are all components that corporate governance deals with.[7] In summary the major areas in which SMEs can benefit from applying corporate governance are:

- ☑ Growth Patterns – the Association of Chartered Certified Accountants (ACCA s) Anne Kimari notes that SMEs benefit from strong corporate governance and the input of non-executive directors during times of growth. They need assistance to keep up with the growth and during crises points; they need fresh ideas and solutions which a solid board would provide.
- ☑ Stronger controls – a functional board can ensure that performance and management control are in place.

---

[5] Dzigba (n 4 above).

[6] Dzigba (n 4 above).

[7] M Loewe, I Al-Ayouty, A Altpeter, L Borbein, M Chantelauze, M Kern, E Niendorf & M Reda 'Which Factors Determine the Upgrading of Small and Medium-Sized Enterprises (SMEs)? The case of Egypt' (German Development Institute, 2013).

- ☑ Enhanced access to credit.
- ☑ Reduced risk of conflict between family members or other owners who are actively managing the business and those who are not.[8]
- ☑ Increased adaptability to deal with change.
- ☑ Improved succession planning.

8.2 APPLYING OUTCOMES-BASED GOVERNANCE TO EMERGING MARKETS

Emerging markets play an increasingly important role in the global economy.[9] Emerging markets have high growth prospects and improved infrastructures and legal climates. Combined emerging markets account for 40 per cent of global gross domestic product.[10] Emerging markets have, since the dissemination of the borders of developed countries and some merging countries, been quick to adopt and implement some of these corporate governance codes derived from the more developed nations.[11]

Corporate governance in emerging markets is of great importance because effective corporate governance has the potential to compensate for a county's weakness in its overall national governance system. For example, organisations in emerging markets face greater concerns associated with minority exploitation than firms in developed markets; corporate governance structures could therefore aid in equipping investors with protective measures in the face of weak legal enforcement mechanisms.[12] However, in order for these codes or principles to have any positive impact on an economy, it needs more than just copying external models which display a proper functioning in developed economies. Governance arrangements that are optimal in one market may be suboptimal in others. This is coupled with the fact that emerging markets are often riddled with corruption, lack of proper frameworks (legal and institutional) and regulation as well as a lack of support for enterprises. The major issues that emerging market corporations face concern board independence and business group affiliation.

---

[8] ACCA 'UK Corporate Governance Code Must Focus On Principles And Outcomes, Says ACCA' available at "http:// www.accaglobal.com/uk/en/news/2018/march/corporate"http//www.accaglobal.com/uk/en/news/2018/march/corporate-governance-co- de.html (accessed on 24 May 2018).

[9] N Feleaga, L Feleaga, VD Dragomir & AD Bigioi 'Corporate governance in emerging economies: 'The Case of Romani' (2011) 18 *Theoretical and Applied Economics* 5–16.

[10] World Bank Document: Private Sector Opinion 'Corporate Governance in Emerging Markets: Why it Matters to investors– and What They Can Do About It' (International Finance Corporation, 2011) available at https://openknowledge.worldbank.org/bitstream/handle/10986/11071/645880BRI0 Corp00Box0361540B0PUBLIC0.pdf?sequence=1&isAllowed=y (accessed on 15 November 2018).

[11] Feleaga et al (n 9 above).

[12] RV Aguilera & I Haxhi 'Corporate Governance in Emerging Markets' (Harvard Law School Forum on Corporate Governance and Financial Regulation, 2018) available at https://corpgov.law.harvard.edu/2018/08/21/corporate–governance–in–emerging–markets–2/ (accessed on 15 November 2018).

Certain factors have proven to be essential in shaping corporate governance of firms in emerging markets:

☑ **The quality of public governance and law enforcement**: The quality of public governance in a nation can be crucial to the corporate governance of firms, mostly in relation to corruption. Furthermore, where there is adequate enforcement of corporate governance and compliance cannot be avoided through bribes, the corporate governance of firms would be enhanced.[13] However, it is common amongst emerging markets that regulators are laxed or can be easily withered through corruption.

☑ **Product market competition**: Emerging markets tend to have protected sectors where the infiltration of competition is reduced to protect few individuals and this reduces good corporate governance as increased competition is crucial to ensure corporate governance.[14]

☑ **Ownership structures:** The practice in emerging economies is to have controlling family members occupy managerial positions and succession planning is usually focused on family members. Furthermore, the presence of founders on the board is associated with better performance; this is in emerging markets such as Thailand where relationship is crucial and the business elite are closely connected. In other markets such as Republic of Korea the presence of outsiders has a positive effect on performance.[15]

☑ **Practice of State Ownership:** In markets that practice state ownership, it is likely that the governance of such enterprises would be stronger in developed markets as opposed to emerging markets because in emerging markets the incentives and the quality of government officials and regulators would determine corporate behaviour. For example, in China state ownership works while in Turkey it has a negative impact on the economy.[16]

Emerging countries must make the passage from intuitions that are heavily relationship-based to ones that are effectively rules-based.[17] A study conducted on Romania showed that functioning market rules need to exist prior to the implementation of corporate governance codes otherwise they fail in their purpose of ensuring accountability. The research showed that most of the sample companies did not meet the recommendations of the Romanian

---

[13] G Dallas 'Corporate Governance in Emerging Markets' (Havard Law School Forum, August, 2011) available at https://corpgov.law.harvard.edu/2011/08/24/corporate-governance-in-emerging-markets/ (accessed 16 April 2018).

[14] Dallas (n 13 above).

[15] Dallas (n 13 above).

[16] World Bank (n 10 above).

[17] Feleaga et al (n 11 above).

Code of Corporate Governance especially in aspects of independence of directors and audit committee members and the degree of transparency was much less that of European companies.[18]

The initial problem is that there is comparatively little research on emerging markets to guide companies and investors. More country-specific studies could reveal the fundamental differences and areas of target. It is only after such studies are conducted that codes and principles of governance that suit emerging markets can be developed.

The consensus seems to be that while emerging markets wait for the government to become organised and conduct research, investors have a role to play in promoting and fostering corporate governance. Investors can do this by valuing the comparatively few companies in the emerging markets with good governance. Notwithstanding the constraints they face, investors should shape governance practice by informed voting and ongoing engagement with companies and regulators. Voting delivers a message to management about investor concerns. Investors must call for these organisations to deliver a good standard of corporate governance to secure their investments.[19]

---

[18] Feleaga et al (n 11 above).
[19] World Bank (n 10 above).

Bibliography

LITERATURE

Abdullah H & Valentine B 'Fundamental and ethics theories of corporate governance' 2009 *Middle Eastern Finance and Economics Issue* 4.

Abdullah H & Valentine B 'Fundamental and ethics theories of corporate governance' 2009 *Middle Eastern Finance and Economics* 88–96.

Abor J & Adjasi CKD 'Corporate governance and the small and medium enterprises sector: Theory and implications' (2007) 7 *Corporate Governance: The International Journal of Business in Society* 111–122.

Adams R, Hermalin BE & Weisbach MS 'The Role of Boards of Directors in Corporate Governance: A Conceptual Framework and Survey' 2008 *National Bureau of Economic Research.*

Address by Julian W. Francis, Governor of the Central Bank of Bahamas to the Bahamas Director's Forum on Corporate Governance, 'The Role of the Regulator in Corporate Governance' (24th February 2004).

Afza T & Nazir MS 'Theoretical perspective of corporate governance: A review' (2014) 119 *European Journal of Scientific Research* 255–264.

Aguilera RV, Filatotchev I, Gospel H, & Jackson G 'An organizational approach to comparative corporate governance: Costs, contingencies, and complementarities' (2008) 19 *Organization Science* 475–492.

Aina K 'Board of Directors and Corporate Governance in Nigeria' 2013 *International Journal of Business and Finance Management* 21–34.

Ajogwu FI *Corporate Governance & Group Dynamics* (2013).

Ajogwu FI *Corporate Governance in Nigeria: Law and Practice* (2007).

Al–jabali M, Abdalmanam O & Ziadat K 'Middle Eastern Finance and Economics' (ISSN: 1450–2889 Issue 11 pp 161–176).

Allen F & Zhao M *The Corporate Governance Model of Japan: Shareholders Are Not Rulers* (2007).

Armstrong P *Status Report on Corporate Governance Reform in Africa. Prepared on behalf of the Pan–African Consultative Forum on Corporate Governance* (2003).

Armstrong P *The Evolution of Corporate Governance in South Africa.* Speech delivered at the 4th Annual AIG Corporate Governance Seminar on 4 August 2004.

Bebchuk LA 'The case for increasing shareholder power' (2004) 118 *Harvard Law Review* 833–914.

Bebchuk L & Fried J *Pay Without Performance – the Unfulfilled Promise of Executive Compensation* (2004).

Bhasin ML 'Audit committee mechanism to improve corporate governance: Evidence from a developing country' (2012) 3 *Modern Economy* 856–872.

Bilal ZO & OI Twafik 'The influence of internal auditing on effective corporate governance in the banking sector in Oman' (2018) 14 *European Scientific Journal* 257–271.

Blacksun Plc *Understanding Transformation: Building the Business Case for Integrated Reporting* (2012).

Boone AL, Audra L, Laura Casara Field, Jonathan M. Karpoff and Charu G. Raheja, 'Determinants of Corporate Board Size and Composition: An Empirical Analysis (2005)

Bradley M 'The purposes and accountability of the corporation in contemporary society: Corporate governance at a crossroads' (1999) 62 *Law and Contemporary Problems*.

Cadbury A 'Thoughts on corporate governance' 1993 *Corporate Governance* 5–10.

Cadbury A *Report of the Committee on the Financial Aspects of Corporate Governance* (1992).

Cadbury A *Report of the Committee on the Financial service Aspects of Corporate Governance* (1992).

Carter DA 'Corporate governance, board diversity and firm value' (2003) 38 *The Financial Review 33–53*.

Caskey J, Nagar V & Petacchi P 'Reporting Bias with an Audit Committee' (2010) 85 *The Accounting Review* 447–481.

Chairperson: Ira M Millstein, (1998), Corporate Governance, Competitiveness and Access to Capital in Global Markets (a report to the OECD).

Charkham JP *Keeping Good Company* (1995).

Claassen S, Djankov S & Lang LHP 'The separation of ownership and control in East Asian corporations' 2000 *Journal of Financial Economics*.

Coglianese C, Healey TJ, Keating EK & Michael ML 'The Role of Government in Corporate Governance,' Regulatory Policy Program Report RPP–08 (2004), Cambridge, MA: Center for Business and Government, John F Kennedy School of Government, Harvard University.

Crane A & Matten d *Business Ethics: Managing Corporate Citizenship and Sustainability in the Age of Globalization* (2007).

Crawford CJ *The Reform of Corporate Governance: Major Trends in the U.S. Corporate Boardroom, 1977–1997* (unpublished doctoral dissertation, Capella University, 2007).

Davis JH, Schooman FD & Donaldson L 'Toward a stewardship theory of management' (1997) 22 *The Academy of Management Review* 20–47.

Donaldson L, Davis JH 'Stewardship Theory or Agency Theory: CEO governance and shareholder returns' (1991) 16 *Australian Journal of Management* 49–65.

Donaldson T & Preston L 'The stakeholder theory of the corporation: Concepts, evidence, and implications' (1995) 20 *Academy of Management Review* 65–91.

Dowling G *Creating Corporate Reputations: Identity, Image and Performance* (2001).

Eisenhardt KM 'Agency– and institutional – theory explanations: The case of retail sales compensation' (1988) 31 *The Academy of Management Journal* 488–511.

Fairfax LM 'Revisiting Justifications for Board Diversity,' The Conference Board *Director Notes*, Nov. 2011.

Fama EF & Jensen M 'The separation of ownership and control' (1983) 26 *Journal of Law and Economics* 301–325.

Feleaga N, Feleaga L, Dragomir VD & Bigioi AD 'Corporate governance in emerging economies: 'The Case of Romani' (2011) 18 *Theoretical and Applied Economics* 5–16.

Fernando AC *Business Ethics and Corporate Governance* 2 ed (2012).

Filiz A *The Company Secretary Within The Corporate Governance Framework*' (unpublished dissertation, University of St. Gallen, School of Management, Economics, Law, Social Studies and International Affairs (2013).

Foreword by Sir Adrian Cadbury to MR Iskander & N Chamlou *Corporate Governance: A Framework for Implementation* (2000).

Garner BA *Black's Law Dictionary* 7 ed (1999).

Ghula A, Binish K & Zeeshan R & Alia A 'Theoretical perspectives of corporate governance' (2014) 3 *Bulletin of Business and Economics* 166–175.

Gramling AA, Maletta MJ, A Schneider A & Church BK 'The role of the internal audit function in corporate governance: A synthesis of the extant internal auditing literature and directions for future research' (2004) 23 *Journal of Accounting Literature* 194–244.

Harrison FE, Wicks J, Parmer A, De Colle B *Stakeholder Theory. The State of the Art* (2010).

Herzberg F *The Motivation to Work* (1959).

Higgs D *Review of the Role and Effectiveness of Non-Executive Directors* (2003).

Holm C & Laursen PB 'Risk and control developments in corporate governance: Changing the role of the external auditor' (2007) 15 *Corporate Governance: An International Review* 322–333.

IFC Corporate Secretary Toolkit, 2013. Slide 5 from IFC's Corporate Secretary Toolkit, Part 1 Module 1/The Corporate Secretary: The Governance Professional Presentation.

IKnoepfel I 'Dow Jones Sustainability Group Index: A global benchmark for corporate sustainability, corporate environmental strategy' (2001) 8 *Corporate Environmental Strategy* 6–15.

Inyang BJ 'Nurturing corporate governance system: The emerging trends in Nigeria' (2009) 4 *Journal of Business Systems, Governance and Ethics* 1–13.

IODSA *King IV Report on Corporate Governance* (2016).

Jensen MC 'Agency costs of free cash flow, corporate finance and take-overs' (1986) 76 *American Economic Review* (Papers & Proceedings) 323.

Klaus S 'Global Corporate Citizenship: Working with Governments and Civil Society.' (2008) 87 *Foreign Affairs* 107–118.

Krechovska M & Prochazkova PT 'Sustainability and its integration into corporate governance focusing on corporate performance management and reporting' (Elsevier University of West Bohemia, Faculty of Economics Husova 11, Plzeh 306 14, Czech Republic.

Ljubojevic C & Ljubojevic G 'Improving the Stakeholder Satisfaction by Corporate Governance Quality' (Skola biznisa Broj 1/2011)

Marshal JB 'Corporate governance practices: An overview of the evolution of corporate governance codes in Nigeria' (2015) 3 *International Journal of Business & Law Research* 49–65.

Mathiesian H *Managerial Ownership and Financial Performance* (unpublished Ph.D. thesis, Department of International Economics and Management, Copenhagen Business School, 2002).

McaFalls R 'Testing the limits of 'inclusive capitalism': A case study of the South Africa HP i–Community (No 28, is Corporate Citizenship Making a Difference?) 2001 *The Journal of Corporate Citizenship* 85–98.

McMullen DA 'Audit committee performance: An investigation of the consequences associated with audit committee' (1996) 15 *Auditing: A Journal of Practice & Theory* 87–103.

Meier–Schatz CJ 'Corporate governance and legal rules: A transnational look at concepts and problems of internal corporate management control' (1988) 13 *The Journal of Corporation Law* 431–469.

Mensah ML 'The effect of audit quality on earnings management' (2003) 15 *Contemporary Accounting Research* 1–21.

Mihaela D & Iulian S 'Internal control and the impact on corporate governance, in Romanian listed companies' 2012 *Journal of Eastern Europe Research in Business & Economics* 1–10.

MLP Lower 'Employee Participation in Corporate Governance: An Ethical Analysis' (The Chinese University of Hong Kong, 2018).

Morck RK *The Global History of Corporate Governance around the world: Family Business Groups to Professional Managers* (2007)

Nunnenkamp P 'The German model of corporate governance: Basic features, critical issues, and applicability to transition economies' Kiel Working Paper, No 713 (1995) *Institut für Weltwirtschaft* (IfW).

Nworji ID, Adebayo O & Olanrewaju A 'Corporate governance and bank failure in Nigeria: Issues, challenges and opportunities' (2011) 2 *Research Journal of Finance and Accounting.*

O'Donovan G 'Change management: A board culture of corporate governance' (2003) 6 *Corporate Governance International Journal* 28–37.

OECD *Principles of Corporate Governance* (1999).

Prentice RA & Space DB 'Sarbanes–Oxley as quack corporate governance: How wise is the received wisdom?' (2007) 95 *Georgetown Law Journal* 1843–909.

Pucheta–Martinez MC & De Fuentes C 'The impact of audit committee characteristics on the enhancement of the quality of financial reporting: An empirical study in the Spanish context' (2007) 15 *Corporate Governance: An International Review* 1394–1412.

Rajendran V 'Corporate governance practices – Emerging trends' (2012) 1 *TRANS Asian Journal of Marketing & Management Research.*

Ray S 'Auditors' role in corporate governance of India's business perspective' (2012) 2 *Public Policy and Administration Research.*

Rezaee Z 'Globalization, technology, and corporate governance' in *Corporate Governance Post–Sarbanes–Oxley Regulations, Requirements, and Integrated Processes* (2015) 457–483.

Roxana–Iona B 'University Anna Stefea Petru, Integrated Reporting for God Corporate Governance' (2018) 17 *Economic Sciences.*

Ruigrok W, Peck S, Tacheva S, P Greve P & Hu Y 'The determinants and effects of board nomination committees' (2006) 10 *Journal of Management & Governance* 119–148.

Saad NM 'Corporate governance compliance and the effects to capital structure in Malaysia' (2010) 2 *International Journal of Economics and Finance* 105 114.

Salvioni DM, Gennari F & Bosetti L *Sustainability and Convergence: The Future of Corporate Governance System:* Department of Economics and Management, University of Brescia, Contrada Santa Chiara (2016).

Securities and Exchange Commission *Code of Corporate Governance for Public Companies* (2014).

Smerdon R *Cadbury Report on The Financial Aspects of Corporate Governance, A Practical Guide to Corporate Governance*.

Strone LE Jr. 'One fundamental corporate governance question we face: Can corporations be managed for the long term unless their powerful electorates also act and think long term?' (2010) 66 *The Business Lawyer*.

Sundaramurthy C & Lewis M 'Control and collaboration: Paradoxes of governance' (2003) 28 *Academy of Management Review* 397–415.

The Henry Jackson Initiative *Towards A More Inclusive Capitalism* (2012).

The National Code of Corporate Governance (2018).

Thomas C (ed) *Theories of Corporate Governance: The Philosophical Foundations of Corporate Governance* (2004).

Tricker B & The Economist Newspaper Ltd *Essentials for Board Directors: An A–Z Guide* 2 ed (2003, 2009).

Tuengler G 'The Anglo–American board of directors and the German supervisory board – Marionnettes in a puppet theatre of corporate governance or efficient controlling devices?' (2000) 12 *Bond Law Review* 230.

UN Global Compact. Guide to Corporate Sustainability (2015).

Ungureanu M & Cuza AI *Models and Practices of Corporate Governance Worldwide* (CES Working Papers) (2013).

Vafeas N 'Board Meeting Frequency and Firm Performance' (1999) 53 *Journal of Financial Economics* 113–42.

Wrights M, Siegel D, Kasey K & Filatatchey I (eds) *Oxford Handbook of Corporate Governance* (2013) University of Cambridge Faculty of Law Research Paper No 54/2011 ECCGI – Law Working Paper No 184/2012.

Young MN, Peng MW, Ahlstrom D, Bruton GD & Jiang Y, Corporate governance in emerging economic: A review of the principal–principal perspective, (2008) 45 *Journal of Management Studies*.

Yusoff WFW & Alhaji IA 'Insight of corporate governance theories' (2012) 1 *Journal of Business & Management* 52–63

ZBA Vural 'The Role of Public Relations on Corporate Governance' (2015) 1 *The Online Journal of Communication and Media* 30–36.

South Africa

Companies Act 71 of 2008

King I Report of 1994

King II Report of 2002

King III Report of 2009

King IV Practice Note on Group Governance, 2019

King IV Report of 2016

Nigeria

Code of Corporate Governance for Banks and Discount Houses in Nigeria and Guidelines for Whistle

Blowing in the Nigerian Banking Industry 2014

Code of Corporate Governance for Banks Post Consolidation, 2006

Code of Corporate Governance for Licensed Pension Operators 2008

Code of Corporate Governance for Public Companies, 2003

Code of Corporate Governance for Public Companies, 2011

Code of Corporate Governance for Public Companies, 2014

Code of Corporate Governance for the Insurance Industry 2009

Code of Corporate Governance for the Telecommunication Industry 2014

The National Code of Corporate Governance, 2018

Companies Act 1968

Financial Reporting Council of Nigeria Act 2011

Securities and Exchange Commission Code of Corporate Governance for Public Companies 2011

The National Code of Corporate Governance, 2016 (suspended code)

Others

Dubai Code of Corporate Governance for Small and Medium Enterprises, 2011

German Co-Determination Act of 1976 – Germany

German Labor-Management Relations Act of 1952

German Stock Corporation Act of 6 September 1965 (Federal Law Gazette 1, p. 1089) as last amended by Article 9 of the Act of 17 July 2017 (Federal Law Gazette 1 p. 2446) of the United Kingdom

Sarbanes Oxley Act of 2002 enacted by the United States congress

United Kingdom Combined Code on Corporate Governance, 2003

United Kingdom Companies Act 1948 11& 12 Geo. 6. Chapter 38

United Kingdom Corporate Governance Code, 2016

WEBSITES

'Corporate Governance in Germany: A model out of time?' *The Economist* available at http://www.economist.com/node/3600260.
ACCA 'UK Corporate Governance Code Must Focus On Principles And Outcomes, Says ACCA' available at http://www.accaglobal.com/uk/en/news/2018/march/corporate–governance–code.html.
ACCA Global 'Corporate Governance' available at http://www.accaglobal-.com/content/dam/acca/global/PDF-students/2012s/sa_oct12-f1fab_governance.pdf .
Aguilera RV & Haxhi I 'Corporate Governance in Emerging Markets' (Harvard Law School Forum on Corporate Governance and Financial Regulation, 2018) available at https://corpgov.law.harvard.edu/2018/08/21/corporate–governance–in–emerging–markets–2/.
Akgiray V 'Blockchain Technology and Corporate Governance: Technology, Markets, Regulation and Corporate Governance' (Organisation for Economic Co–operation and Development, Directorate for Financial and Enterprise Affairs Corporate Governance Committee, 2018) available at http://www.oecd.org/officialdocuments/publicdisplay documentpdf/?cote=DAF/CA/CG/RD(2018)1/REV1&docLanguage=En.
Alvarez C 'New Technologies Accelerate the Digital Transformation of Corporate Governance' (BBVA, 2017) available at https://www.bbva.com/en/new–technologies–accelerate–digital–transformation–corporate–governance/.
Armour J 'Corporate Governance and Technological Risks' (University of Oxford Law Blog, February 2017) available at https://www.law.ox.a-c.uk/research–and–subject–groups/research–collection–law–and–tech-nology/blog/2017/02/corporate–governance.
Australian Institute of Company Directors 'Relationship Between The Board and Management: Governance Relations' available at https://

aicd.companydirectors.com.au/–/media/cd2/resources/director–resour-
ces/director–tools/pdf/05446–3–10–mem–director–gr–rel–board–
management_a4–web.ashx.

Australian Institute of Company Directors 'Relationship Between The
Board and Management, Governance Relations available at https://
aicd.companydirectors.com.au/~/media/cd2/resources/director–resour-
ces/director–tools/pdf/05446–3–10–mem–director–gr–rel–board–
management_a4–web.ashx.

Barker R 'What Makes a Balanced Board of Directors' (Real Business,
2014) available at https://realbusiness.co.uk/what–makes–a–balanced–
board–of–directors/.

Ben O'Connell Updated September 26, 2017 'Models of Corporate Governance' available at https://bizfluent.com/list–6710522–models–corporate–governance.html.

Bisi A 'The Role of the Company Secretary in Corporate Governance
Compliance' (GBJ, 2007) available at http://govandbusiness
journal.com.ng/the–role–of–the–company–secretary–in–corporate–
governance–compliance/.

BoardBookit 'Outsourcing Corporate Secretarial Services and Board Portals' available at https://boardbookit.com/blog/outsourcing–corporate–
secretarial–services.

BoardPacks, 'The Changing View and Roles of Technology in Corporate
Governance' available at https://eshare.net/wp–content/uploads/2017/
07/changing–view–and–roles–of–technology–in–corporate–governan-
ce.pdf.

Boleat M 'Inclusive Capitalism: Searching for a purpose beyond profit'
2014 *Ethical Business Finance* available at https://www.theguardian-
.com/sustainable–business/inclusive–capitalism–purpose–beyond–
profit.

BREFI Group 'Delegate Authority to Management' available at https://
www.brefigroup.co.uk/directors/e-course/delegation/
delegate_authority_to_management.html.

Briggs R & Edwards C 'The Business of Resilience: Corporate Security for
The 21st Century' (Demos, 2006) available at https://
www.demos.co.uk/files/thebusinessofresilience.pdf.

Businesswire 'Global Private Sector Leaders Make Commitments to Investment and Business Practices That Stimulate Long-Term Value Creation
at the 2016 Conference on Inclusive Capitalism in New York
City' available at https://www.businesswire.com/news/home/
20161010005815/en/Global–Private–Sector–Leaders–Commitments–
Investment–Business.

Candour Governance Specialists Stakeholder Relationships' available at http://www.candorsolutions.co.za/king–iii/chapter–8–stakeholder–relationships/.

Carney DF (ed) *Inclusive capitalism The Pathway to Action*, 'Thoughts form the 2015 Conference on Inclusive Capitalism (London, 26 June 2015) available at http://www.inc–cap.com/wp–content/uploads/2015/07/Book–2.pdf.

Chapter II – The Relationship Between Board and Management available at http://worldanimal.net/documents/Professional_APSM_Online_Book/Chapter_2_Board_and_Management.pdf.

Chartered Institute of Internal Auditors available at https://www.iia.org.uk/about–us/what–is–internal–audit/

China Resources Power Holding Company Limited 'Remuneration Committee, Terms of Reference' (2014) available at http://www.cr–power.com/en/InvestorRelations/CorporateGovernance/BoardCommittees/201312/P020141216643862411311.pdf.

Companies Circle, Board Evaluation Working Group, 'Board Evaluation Practices Experiences from the Latin American Companies Circle (2017) available at https://www.ifc.org/wps/wcm/connect/ebd342804d2020359ce1ddf81ee631cc/Board+Evaluation+–+121018+Final+v11.pdf?MOD=AJPERES&ContentCache=NONE.

Corplaw 'Shareholder and Stakeholder Theories of Corporate Governance available at http://www.corplaw.ie/blog/bid/317212/Shareholder–Stakeholder–Theories–Of–Corporate–Governance.

Cropp B 'Evaluating Board Performance' (University of Wisconsin Center for Cooperatives, 1996) available at http://www.uwcc.wisc.edu/issues/Governance/board.html.

CSJ 'Stakeholder Relationship Officers – Coming To Your Company' (2013) http://csj.hkics.org.hk/site/2013/09/05/stakeholder–relationship–officers–coming–to–your–company/.

Dallas G 'Corporate Governance in Emerging Markets' (Harvard Law School Forum, August, 2011) available at https://corpgov.law.harvard.edu/2011/08/24/corporate–governance–in–emerging–markets/.

DCSL 'Who Does The Company Secretary Report To?' (2014) available at http://blog.dcsl.com.ng/blog/2014/03/24/who–does–the–company–secretary–report–to/.

DCSL Corporate Services Limited 'The Role of The Audit Committee in Corporate Governance' (DCSL Blog, 2015) available at http://blog.dcsl.com.ng/blog/2015/09/07/the–role–of–the–audit–committee–in–corporate–governance–2/.

De Andres P, Arranz–Aperte L & Rodriguez–Sanz JA 'Independent versus non–independent outside directors in European companies: Who Has a say on CEO compensation?' (2018) 20 *Business Research Quarterly* 79–95.

De Rothschild LF & Barton D 'A Case for Inclusive Capitalism' *The Guardian* available at https://www.theguardian.com/commentisfree/2012/may/15/case–for–inclusive–capitalism.

Deloitte 'Board Committee' (2014) available at https://www2.deloitte.com/content/dam/Deloitte/za/Documents/governance–risk–compliance/ZA_BoardCommittees_24032014.pdf.

Deloitte 'Governance of Subsidiaries: A Survey of Global Companies' (2013) available at https://www2.deloitte.com/content/dam/Deloitte/in/Documents/risk/Corporate%20Governance/in–gc–governance–of–subsidiaries–a–survey–of–global–companies–noexp.pdf.

Deloitte 'The Role of the Audit Committee (2018) available at https://www2.deloitte.com/content/dam/Deloitte/us/Documents/center–for–board–effectiveness/us–audit–committee–resource–guide–section–2.pdf.

Deloitte 'The Social and Ethics Committee and the Management of The Ethics Performance of The Company' (2014) available at https://www2.deloitte.com/content/dam/Deloitte/za/Documents/governance–risk–compliance/ZA_SocialAndEthicsCommitteeAndTheManagementOfEthicsPerformance_04042014.pdf.

Deloitte Solutions 'Audit, Remuneration and Nomination Committees' available at https://www2.deloitte.com/cn/en/pages/risk/solutions/cg–audit–and–remuneration–committees.html.

Deloitte, 'Performance Evaluation of Boards and Directors' (March, 2014) available athttps://www2.deloitte.com/content/dam/Deloitte/in/Documents/risk/Corporate%20Governance/in–cg–performance–evaluation–of–boards–and–directors–noexp.pdf.

Devex Website (advert for the role of Stakeholder Relations Officer) available at https://www.devex.com/jobs/zaaap–stakeholder–relations–officer–522253.

Devi N A Brief History of Corporate Governance, Agra University available at https://www.docsity.com/en/a-brief-history-of-corporate-governance-corporate-governence-lecture-slides/81334/.

Dialogue with companies' institutional shareholders should . . . . available at https://www.coursehero.com/file/p1eqc3d/Dialogue–with–companies–institutional–shareholders–should–enter–into–a–dialogue/.

Dinner J 'Assessing board performance, an outcomes-based approach' (2018) available at http://csj.hkics.org.hk/site/2018/01/16/assessing-board-performance-an-outcomes-based-approach/.

Dorger Consulting 'Size Matters: Right Sizing Your Board of Directors' (2018) available at http://dorgerconsulting.com/2011/07/20/size–matters–right–sizing–your–board–of–directors/.

Dzigba D 'Corporate Governance Practice among Small and Medium Scale Enterprises (SMEs) in Ghana; Impact on Access to Credit (School of Management, 2015) available at https://www.diva–portal.org/smash/get/diva2:829172/FULLTEXT01.pdf.

Effective Governance, HopgoodGanim Advisory Group, 'Improving Board–Management Relations' https://www.effectivegovernance.com.au/improving–board–management–relations/.

Emerging Markets ESG 'Three Models of Corporate Governance' available at http://www.emergingmarketsesg.net/esg/wp–content/uploads/2011/01/Three-Models-of-Corporate-Governance-January-2009.pdf.

EOH Legal Services 'New King IV Report will boost corporate governance in South Africa' available at http://www.eohlegalservices.co.za/corporate–governance–south–africa/.

Flynn M & Wallace M 'Corporate governance and sustainability: Who's connecting the dots?' available at https://www.greenbiz.com/article/corporate-governance-and-sustainability-whos-connecting-dots.

Galan IS 'The Meaning of Inclusive Capitalism' *Huffington Post* available at https://www.huffingtonpost.com/inclusive–capitalism/the–meaning–of–inclusive_b_8922230.html.

Gamal A 'The Evolving Role of Internal Audit in Corporate Governance' (Internal Auditor – Middle East, 2015) available at http://www.internalauditor.me/article/the–evolving–role–of–internal–audit–in–corporate–governance/.

Global Business Journal 'The Role of The Company Secretary' http://govandbusinessjournal.com.ng/the–role–of–the–company–secretary–in–corporate–governance–compliance/.

Guidance Note – Chartered Secretaries. https://www.hkics.org.hk/media/publication/attachment/2026_GN4–Reporting%20lines.pdf.

Hamilton BA 'Convergence of Enterprise Security Organizations' (The Alliance for Enterprise Security Risk Management, 2005) available at https://pdfs.semanticscholar.org/9cb9/fe2450502b4e8bb4923978d9afc7198eab0b.pdf.

Harow K 'Role of an external auditor in corporate governance' (Chron, 2018) available at https://work.chron.com/role–external–auditor–corporate–governance–27754.html.

Hsieh L 'Long-term value and shareholder theory of corporate governance, available at http://www.eiuperspectives.economist.com/strategy-leadership/long-term-value-and-shareholder-theory-corporate-governance.

Implicity 'The Anglo–American Model of Corporate Governance– Basic Overview' available at https://implicity.wordpress.com/2009/09/15/the–anglo–american–model–of–corporate–governance–basic–overview/.

Inclusive Capitalism 'About Us' available at https://www.inc–cap.com/about–us/.

Innovation.CA (advert for the role of Stakeholder Relations Officer) available at https://www.innovation.ca/sites/default/files/Careers/senior_officer_stakeholder_relations_jan_2017_eng_0.pdf.

Institute of Directors in New Zealand 'The Future of Governance' available at https://www.iod.org.nz/Portals/0/Branches%20and%20events/Auckland%20branch%20docs/2017%20documents/Rpt%20-%20The%20Future%20of%20Governance%20by%20Prof%20King-csj_2017_july_mervyn.pdf.

Institute of Directors in South Africa, 'What is The Ideal Board Size? (2018) available at https://www.iodsa.co.za/news/392547/What–is–the–ideal–board–size.htm.

Integrated Reporting 'Creating Value The Cyclical Power of Integrated Thinking and Reporting' available at http://integratedreporting.org/wp-content/uploads/2017/05/CreatingValue_IntegratedThinkingK1.pdf.

International Finance Corporation 'The Corporate Secretary: The Governance Professional' (IFC's Corporate Governance Group, 2016) available at https://www.ifc.org/wps/wcm/connect/2c2a9f57–3e3d–43b2–be9f–beaed1d47fff/CG_CoSec_June_2016.pdf?MOD=AJPERES.

Jan S & Sangmi M 'The Role of the Board of Directors in Corporate Governance' 2016 2(5) *Imperial Journal of Interdisciplinary Research (IJIR)* available at https://pdfs.semanticscholar.org/ab6c/60705060fa198a543890d4968925943cc71c.pdf

Joh SW & Jung JY 'Effects of Independent and Friendly Outside Directors' (College of Business Administration Seoul National University, Korea available at http://aicg.org/_res/aicg/etc/Effects_of_Independent_and_Friendly_Outside_Directors.pdf.

Kastiel K 'Board Evaluation – A Window into the Boardroom' (Harvard Law School Forum on Corporate Governance and Financial Regulation' (2013) available at https://corpgov.law.harvard.edu/2013/05/31/board–evaluation–a–window–into–the–boardroom/.

Katz DA, Wachtell L, Rosen & Katz 'Analyzing Aspects of Board Composition – Harvard Law School' available at https://corpgov.law.harvard.edu/2012/02/20/analyzing-aspects-of-board-composition/.

Kelly M 'The Role of Board of Directors in Corporate Governance' (CPA Ireland, 2017) available at http://www.cpaireland.ie/docs/default–source/Students/exam–related–articles–2017/p1–corp–governance–the–role–of–the–board–of–directors.pdf?sfvrsn=2.

King IV Practice Notes 'Group Governance' (Institute of Directors South Africa, January 2019) available at https://cdn.ymaws.com/www.iodsa-.co.za/resource/collection/562ED5CF–02E8–4957–97C8–D3F0C66A7245/Group_Governance_Framework_Practice_Note.pdf.

KPMG 'Performance Insight Through Better Business Reporting' available at https://assets.kpmg/content/dam/kpmg/pdf/2011/10/Integrated-Re porting-ENG.pdf.

Lafarre A & Van Der Elst C 'Block Chain Technology Corporate Governance and Shareholder Activism' (ecgi news, April 9, 2018) available at https://ecgi.global/news/blockchain–technology–corporate–gover nance–and–shareholder–activism.

Larson MJ & Pierce C 'Board Evaluations: Insights from India and Beyond' (2015) available at http://www.sbp.org.pk/bprd/2016/C11–Annx–A.pdf.

Latin American Companies Circle 'Corporate Governance Recommendations for Company Groups' (OECD, 2014) available at https://www.oecd.org/daf/ca/2014LatinAmericaCorporateGovernance RoundtableRecommendationsCompanyGroups.pdf.

Little AD 'The Business Case for Corporate Citizenship' available at http://www.csrwire.com/pdf/Business–Case–for–Corporate–Citzens-hip.pdf.

Lutui R & Ahokovi T 'Financial Fraud Risk Management and Corporate Governance' (2017) (Edith Cowan University Research Online, Australian Information Security Management Conference', 2017) available at http://ro.ecu.edu.au/cgi/viewcontent.cgi?article=1200& context=ism.

Mallin C 'The Role of Institutional Investors in Corporate Governance' (runall.tex, 2006) available at https://www.kantakji.com/media/3426/xx7.pdf.

Mallin CA 'Handbook on International Corporate Governance' available at https://epdf.pub/handbook-on-international-corporate-governanceec28966954d9be3c45a88aada145f00279128.html.

McAvoy D & Partigan JC 'The Role and Construction of Risk Committees' (Nixon Peabody, 2010) available at https://www.nixonpeabody.com/en/ideas/articles/2010/08/11/the–role–and–construction–of–risk–com-mittees.

Navajyoti S & Tirthankar D 'Role of auditors in Corporate Governance' (2009) available at https://papers.ssrn.com/sol3/papers.cfm?abstract_id=1487050.

NCOSS 'Board Delegations' available at https://www.ncoss.org.au/sites/default/files/public/resources/Board%20Delegations.pdf.

Nelson J 'Corporate Citizenship in A Global Context' (2005) Corporate Social Responsibility Working Paper No 13 available at https://

sites.hks.harvard.edu/m–rcbg/CSRI/publications/Workingpaper_
13_nelson.pdf.

Nexia SAB&T 'King IV Report' available at https://www.nexia–sabt.co.za/
wp–content/uploads/2016/11/SABTip_October_2016_KingIV.pdf.

Obi-Chukwu O 'MTN reports N870 billion revenue from Nigeria alone in
2017 HY' available at https://nairametrics.com/mtn-reports-n870-
billion-revenue-from-nigeria-alone-in-2017-hy/.

OECD 'The Role of Institutional Investors in Promoting Good Corporate
Governance' (2011) *Corporate Governance* OECD Publishing available at https://www.oecd.org/daf/ca/49081553.pdf.

OECD 'The Tangible Benefits of Good Governance' available at https://
www.oecd.org/daf/ca/corporategovernanceprinciples/43654500.pdf.

OECD Corporate Governance of Small and Medium-Sized Enterprises
(SMEs), Cairo, Egypt (2010) available at http://www.oecd.org/daf/ca/
corporategovernanceofstate–ownedenterprises/corporategovernan-
ceofsmallandmedium–sizedenterprisessmes.htm.

OECD Policy Brief 'Small and Medium–Sized Enterprises: Local Strength,
Global Reach' (2000) available at http://www.oecd.org/cfe/leed/
1918307.pdf.

Opedia CE 'Anglo–Saxon Model of Corporate Governance' https://ceope-
dia.org/index.php/Anglo–Saxon_model_of_corporate_governance.

Price NJ 'Bes Practices: Board Size and Corporate Governance' (Diligent,
2017) https://diligent.com/blog/board–size–corporate–governance.

Price NJ 'Boardroom Technology: Achieving Strong Corporate Governance
through Technology' (Diligent, 2018) available at https://diligent.com/
blog/corporate–governance–technology.

Price NJ 'The Evolving Role of The Company Secretary in Today's
Corporate World' (Board Effect, 2017) https://www.boardeffect.com/
blog/evolving–role–company–secretary–todays–corporate–world/.

PWC 'Subsidiary Governance: An Unappreciated Risk (2013) available at
https://www.pwc.com/gx/en/legal/entity–governance–compliance/pu
blications/assets/subsidiary–governance.pdf.

Reliance Consulting: '5 Reasons Outsourcing A Corporate Secretary is
More Efficient' (2016) available at https://www.corporateservices
singapore.com/5–reasons–outsourcing–a–corporate–secretary–is–
more–efficient/.

Ribeiro F, Giacoman A & Trantham M 'Dealing with Market Disruption
Seven Strategies For Breaking Down Silos' 2016 available at https://
www.strategyand.pwc.com/report/dealing-market-disruption.

Role of Institutional Investors – Roles of Institutional . . . . available at
https://www.coursehero.com/file/18597475/Role–of–Institutional–
Investors/.

Ross S 'What are different Corporate Governance Systems around the world?' available at https://www.investopedia.com/ask/answers/ 051115/what–are–some–examples–different–corporate–governance– systems–across–world.asp.

Saint DK & Tripathi AN 'The shareholder and stakeholder Theories of Corporate Purpose' available at http://knowledgeworkz.com/ samatvam/newsletter/The%20Shareholder%20and%20Stakeholder %20Theories%20of%20Corporate%20Purpose.pdf.

Sakai H & Asaoka H 'The Japanese Corporate Governance System and Firm Performance: toward sustainable growth' 2003 *Research Center for Policy and Economy.* Mitsubishi Research Institute, Inc. available at http://www.esri.go.jp/jp/prj/int_prj/prj–rc/macro/macro14/05mri1_ t.pdf.

Search Cloud 'Definition of Data Silo' https://searchcloudapplications.tech-target.com/definition/data–silo

Skeet A 'Corporate Governance Continues to Evolve' (2018) Markulla Center for Applied Ethics available at https://www.scu.edu/ethics/ focus–areas/business–ethics/resources/trends–in–corporate– governance/.

Skroupa C 'How Boards of Directors Shaping to Meet New Challenges' *Skytop Strategies* (2017) available at https://skytopstrategies.com/ how-boards-of-directors-are-shaping-to-meet-new-challenges/.

Smith HJ 'The Shareholders vs Stakeholders Debate' available at https:// sloanreview.mit.edu/article/the-shareholders-vs-stakeholders-debate/

State Bank of Pakistan Guidelines on Performance Evaluation of Board of Directors http://www.sbp.org.pk/bprd/2016/C11–Annx–A.pdf.

Steele P & Bennet S 'Delegations and corporate risk management – how do they intersect' available at https://www.sibenco.com/delegations-and-corporate-risk-management-how-do-they-intersect/.

Stout LA Bad and Not–so–Bad Arguments for Shareholder Primacy. https:// scholarship.law.cornell.edu/facpub/448/.

Strauss Daly 'King IV Report at a Glance' available at https://www.strauss-daly.co.za/wp–content/uploads/2016/07/King–Code–IV–At–a–Glan-ce.pdf.

Teen MY & Bennett C 'Governance of Company Groups' (The Iclif Leadership & Governance Centre, CPA Australia, 2014) available at http://www.iclifgovernance.org/file/files/governance–co–groups.pdf.

The Business Professor 'Stakeholder Theory of Corporate Governance' available at https://thebusinessprofessor.com/knowledge–base/ stakeholder–theory–of–corporate–governance/.

The Corporate Prof 'Historical development of Corporate Governance in Nigeria' available at http://thecorporateprof.com/historical-development-of-corporate-governance-in-nigeria/.

The Herald 'The Role of Government in Corporate Governance (2016) available at https://www.herald.co.zw/role–of–govt–in–corporate–governance/.

The Hong Kong Institute of Chartered Secretaries 'Guidance Note: A Practical Guide to Corporate Governance' (June 2007) available at https://www.hkics.org.hk/media/publication/attachment/2026_GN4–Reporting%20lines.pdf.

The Institute of Internal Auditors USA' Position Paper on Internal Auditing's Role in Corporate Governance' (2018) available at https://na.theiia.org/about–ia/PublicDocuments/Internal–Auditings–Role–in–Corporate–Governance.pdf.

Vanguard 'Regulators Defy Corporate Governance – Mikail' (July 2, 2018) available at https://www.vanguardngr.com/2018/07/regulators–defy–corporate–governance–principle–mikail/.

World Bank Document: Private Sector Opinion 'Corporate Governance in Emerging Markets: Why it Matters to investors– and What They Can Do About It' (International Finance Corporation, 2011) available at https://openknowledge.worldbank.org/bitstream/handle/10986/11071/645880BRI0Corp00Box0361540B0PUBLIC0.pdf?sequence=1&isAllowed=y.

FINANCIAL REPORTING COUNCIL OF NIGERIA

Federal Ministry of Industry, Trade and Investment

ADOPTION AND COMPLIANCE WITH NIGERIAN CODE OF CORPORATE GOVERNANCE 2018

[Commencement: January 15, 2019]

In exercise of the powers conferred on me by Section 73 of the Financial Reporting Council of Nigeria Act of 2011, and all other powers enabling me in that behalf and with the advice of the Council, **I, Dr. Okechukwu Enyinnaya Enelamah, Minister for Industry, Trade and Investment** hereby make the following Regulation:

1.   Application

   (1)   From the commencement of this Regulation, the following entities shall adopt and comply with Nigerian Code of Corporate Governance 2018, which is the Schedule to this regulation:

   (a)   all public companies (whether a listed company or not);

   (b)   all private companies that are holding companies of public companies or other regulated entities;

   (c)   all concessioned or privatised companies; and

   (d)   all regulated private companies being private companies that file returns to any regulatory authority other than the Federal Inland Revenue Service (FIRS) and the Corporate Affairs Commission (CAC).

   (2)   These entities shall report on the application of the Code in their annual reports for financial years ending after January 1, 2020 in the form and manner prescribed by the Financial Reporting Council of Nigeria.

2.   Miscellaneous

Words and phrases used in this Regulation bear the same meaning as provided in the Nigerian Code of Corporate Governance, the Schedule to this Regulation.

3.   Short Title

This Regulation may be cited as the Regulation on the Adoption and Compliance with Nigerian Code of Corporate Governance 2018.

Made at Abuja this 15th day of January 2019.

Dr. Okechukwu Enyinnaya Enelamah
Minister for Industry, Trade and Investment

133

Schedule
[Paragraph 1(1)]

NIGERIAN CODE OF CORPORATE GOVERNANCE, 2018

NIGERIAN CODE OF CORPORATE GOVERNANCE 2018

Table of Contents

List of Abbreviations

Board	Board of Directors
CBN	Central Bank of Nigeria
Code	Nigerian Code of Corporate Governance 2018
Chairman	Chairman of the Board of Directors
ED	Executive Director
ESG	Environmental, Social and Governance
FRC, Council	Financial Reporting Council of Nigeria
INED	Independent Non-Executive Director
IAS 24	International Accounting Standard 24 (on Related Party Disclosures)
IT	Information Technology
MD/CEO	Managing Director/ Chief Executive Officer
NAICOM	National Insurance Commission
NED	Non-Executive Director
PenCom	National Pension Commission
SEC	Securities and Exchange Commission

Introduction

A. Authority of the Code

Sections 11c and 51c of the Financial Reporting Council of Nigeria Act confer upon the Council, the powers to ensure good corporate governance practices in the public and private sectors of the Nigerian economy and to issue the code of corporate governance and guidelines. The Nigerian Code of Corporate Governance 2018 was approved by the Council pursuant to this authority and commended to the Minister for issuance in accordance with Section 73 of the Act.

B. Aims and Objectives

Corporate Governance is a key driver of corporate accountability and business prosperity. In response to challenges in their respective sectors, a number of industry regulators developed corporate governance codes for companies operating in their sectors. The sectoral codes are:

1. Code of Corporate Governance for the Telecommunication Industry 2016, issued by the Nigerian Communications Commission (replaced 2014 NCC Code);
2. Code of Corporate Governance for Banks and Discount Houses in Nigeria 2014 issued by the Central Bank of Nigeria (replaced 2006 CBN Code);
3. Code of Corporate Governance for Public Companies in Nigeria 2011 issued by the Securities and Exchange Commission (replaced 2003 SEC Code);
4. Code of Good Corporate Governance for Insurance Industry in Nigeria 2009 issued by the National Insurance Commission; and
5. Code of Corporate Governance for Licensed Pension Fund Operators 2008 issued by the National Pension Commission.

The Nigerian Code of Corporate Governance 2018 seeks to institutionalise corporate governance best practices in Nigerian companies. The Code is also to promote public awareness of essential corporate values and ethical practices that will enhance the integrity of the business environment. By institutionalising high corporate governance standards, the Code will rebuild public trust and confidence in the Nigerian economy, thus facilitating increased trade and investment.

Companies with effective boards and competent management that act with integrity and that are engaged with shareholders and other stakeholders are better placed to achieve their business goals and contribute positively to society. In such well managed organisations, the interests of the Board and management are aligned with those of the shareholders and other stakeholders.

By adhering to the principles articulated in this Code, companies will demonstrate a commitment to good governance practices and increase their levels of transparency, trust and integrity, and create an environment for sustainable business operations.

C. Code Philosophy

The Code is aimed at companies of varying sizes and complexities across industries. Consequently, flexibility – the ability to apply the Code in a wide range of circumstances, and scalability – the ability to apply to companies of differing sizes, are of utmost importance for successful implementation. Accordingly, the Code adopts a principle-based approach in specifying minimum standards of practice that companies should adopt.

Where so required, companies should adopt the "Apply and Explain" approach in reporting on compliance with this Code. The '**Apply and Explain**' approach which assumes application of all principles and requires entities to explain how the principles are applied. This requires companies to demonstrate how the specific activities they have undertaken best achieve the outcomes intended by the corporate governance principles specified in the Code. This will help to prevent a 'box ticking' exercise as companies deliberately consider how they have (or have not) achieved the intended outcomes. Although the Code recommends practices to enable companies apply the principles, it recognises that these practices can be tailored to meet industry or company needs. The Code is thus scalable to suit the type, size and growth phase of each company while still achieving the outcomes envisaged by the principles.

D. Monitoring the Implementation of the Code

The implementation of this Code will be monitored by the FRC through the sectoral regulators and registered exchanges who are empowered to impose appropriate sanctions based on the specific deviation noted and the company in question. Additionally, the FRC may conduct reviews on the implementation of the Code where deviations from the Code recur. Other monitoring mechanisms adopted by the FRC will be based on its review of the level of implementation of the Code.

In consonance with the relevant regulatory agencies of the Federal Government of Nigeria, the Council will subsequently issue corporate governance guidelines to assist implementation as may be required to respond to prudential considerations in different sectors of the economy.

E. Structure of the Code

The Code consists of seven (7) parts and twenty-eight (28) principles together with practices recommended by the Code for the implementation of each principle. The highlights of the twenty-eight (28) principles are shown below:

Part	Principle Number	Definition of Principle
A: Board of Directors and Officers of the Board	Principle 1	A successful Company is headed by an effective Board which is responsible for providing entrepreneurial and strategic leadership as well as promoting ethical culture and responsible corporate citizenship. As a link between stakeholders and the Company, the Board is to exercise oversight and control to ensure that management acts in the best interest of the shareholders and other stakeholders while sustaining the prosperity of the Company.
	Principle 2	The effective discharge of the responsibilities of the Board and its committees is assured by an appropriate balance of skills and diversity (including experience and gender) without compromising competence, independence and integrity.
	Principle 3	The Chairman is responsible for providing overall leadership of the Company and the Board, and eliciting the constructive participation of all Directors to facilitate effective direction of the Board.
	Principle 4	The Managing Director/Chief Executive Officer is the head of management delegated by the Board to run the affairs of the Company to achieve its strategic objectives for sustainable corporate performance.
A: Board of Directors and Officers of the Board	Principle 5	Executive Directors support the Managing Director/Chief Executive Officer in the operations and management of the Company.
	Principle 6	Non-Executive Directors bring to bear their knowledge, expertise and independent judgment on issues of strategy and

Part	Principle Number	Definition of Principle
		performance on the Board.
	Principle 7	Independent Non-Executive Directors bring a high degree of objectivity to the Board for sustaining stakeholder trust and confidence.
	Principle 8	The Company Secretary plays an important role in supporting the effectiveness of the Board by assisting the Board and management to develop good corporate governance practices and culture within the Company.
	Principle 9	Directors are sometimes required to make decisions of a technical and complex nature that may require independent external expertise.
	Principle 10	Meetings are the principal vehicle for conducting the business of the Board and successfully fulfilling the strategic objectives of the Company.
	Principle 11	To ensure efficiency and effectiveness, the Board delegates some of its functions, duties and responsibilities to well-structured committees, without abdicating its responsibilities.
	Principle 12	A written, clearly defined, rigorous, formal and transparent procedure serves as a guide for the selection of Directors to ensure the appointment of high quality individuals to the Board.
A: Board of Directors and Officers of the Board	Principle 13	A formal induction programme on joining the Board as well as regular training assists Directors to effectively discharge their duties to the Company.
	Principle 14	Annual Board evaluation assesses how each Director, the committees of the Board and the Board are committed to their roles, work together and continue to contribute effectively to the achievement of the

Part	Principle Number	Definition of Principle
		Company's objectives.
	Principle 15	Institutionalising a system for evaluating the Company's corporate governance practices ensures that its governance standards, practices and processes are adequate and effective.
	Principle 16	The Board ensures that the Company remunerates fairly, responsibly and transparently so as to promote the achievement of strategic objectives and positive outcomes in the short, medium and long term.
B: Assurance	**Principle 17**	A sound framework for managing risk and ensuring an effective internal control system is essential for achieving the strategic objectives of the Company.
	Principle 18	An effective internal audit function provides assurance to the Board on the effectiveness of the governance, risk management and internal control systems.
	Principle 19	An effective whistle-blowing framework for reporting any illegal or unethical behaviour minimises the Company's exposure and prevents recurrence.
	Principle 20	An external auditor is appointed to provide an independent opinion on the true and fair view of the financial statements of the Company to give assurance to stakeholders on the reliability of the financial statements.
C: Relationship with Shareholders	**Principle 21**	General Meetings are important platforms for the Board to engage shareholders to facilitate greater understanding of the Company's business, governance and performance. They provide shareholders with an opportunity to exercise their ownership rights and express their views to the Board on any areas of

Part	Principle Number	Definition of Principle
		interest.
	Principle 22	The establishment of a system of regular dialogue with shareholders balances their needs, interests and expectations with the objectives of the Company.
	Principle 23	Equitable treatment of shareholders and the protection of their statutory and general rights, particularly the interest of minority shareholders, promote good governance.
D: Business Conduct with Ethics	Principle 24	The establishment of professional business and ethical standards underscores the values for the protection and enhancement of the reputation of the Company while promoting good conduct and investor confidence.
	Principle 25	The establishment of policies and mechanisms for monitoring insider trading, related party transactions, conflict of interest and other corrupt activities, mitigates the adverse effects of these abuses on the Company and promotes good ethical conduct and investor confidence.
E: Sustainability	Principle 26	Paying adequate attention to sustainability issues including environment, social, occupational and community health and safety ensures successful long term business performance and projects the Company as a responsible corporate citizen contributing to economic development.
F: Transparency	Principle 27	Communicating and interacting with stakeholders keeps them conversant with the activities of the Company and assists them in making informed decisions.

Part	Principle Number	Definition of Principle
	Principle 28	Full and comprehensive disclosure of all matters material to investors and stakeholders, and of matters set out in this Code, ensures proper monitoring of its implementation which engenders good corporate governance practice.

NIGERIAN CODE OF
CORPORATE
GOVERNANCE 2018

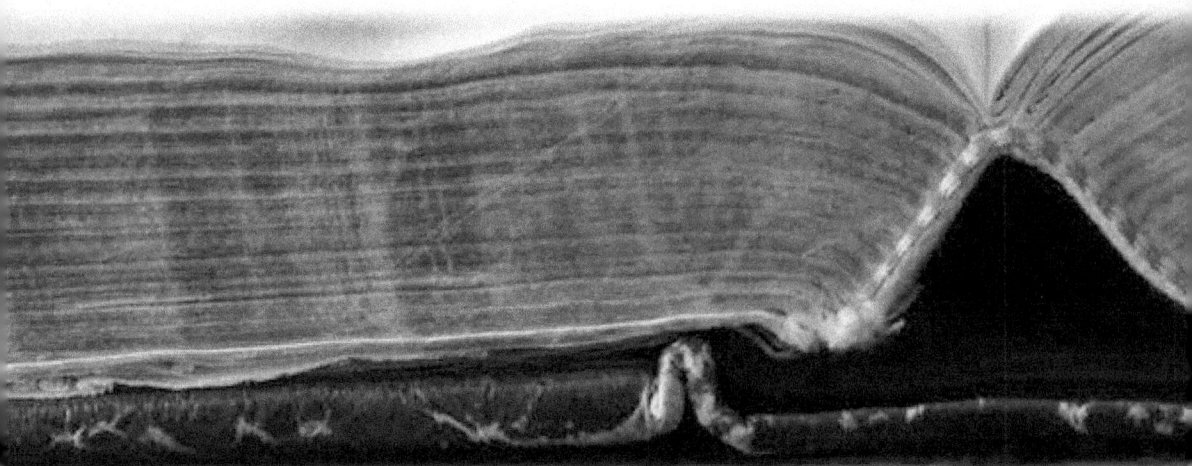

Part A.   **Board of Directors and Officers of the Board**

1.   **Role of the Board**

> ***Principle 1:***   *A successful Company is headed by an effective Board which is responsible for providing entrepreneurial and strategic leadership as well as promoting ethical culture and responsible corporate citizenship. As a link between stakeholders and the Company, the Board is to exercise oversight and control to ensure that management acts in the best interest of the shareholders and other stakeholders while sustaining the prosperity of the Company.*

Recommended Practices

The Board, being central in corporate governance and the highest governing body in the Company, should have a charter setting out its responsibilities, which may include the following:

1.1   exercising leadership, enterprise, integrity and judgment in its oversight and control of the Company so as to achieve the Company's continued survival and prosperity;

1.2   ensuring that the Board and its committees act in the best interest of the Company at all times;

1.3   ensuring compliance with the laws of the Federal Republic of Nigeria and other applicable regulations;

1.4   considering and approving the long-term and short-term strategies for the business of the Company and monitoring their implementation by management;

1.5   ensuring the establishment and implementation of a succession plan, appointment process, training mechanism and remuneration structure for both the Board and senior management of the Company;

1.6   being accountable to the Company as well as identifying and managing the relationship with shareholders and other stakeholders;

1.7   establishing and maintaining the Company's values and standards (including an ethical culture) as well as modelling these values and standards;

1.8   overseeing the internal audit function, approving the internal audit plan, and appointing and removing the head of the internal audit function on the recommendation of the committee responsible for audit;

1.9   establishing the Company's risk management framework and monitoring its effectiveness, setting the Company's risk appetite, receiving and reviewing risk reports;

1.10   providing oversight over Information Technology governance;

1.11 defining a formal schedule of matters specifically reserved for Board decision and matters delegated to Board committees and management;

1.12 overseeing the effectiveness and adequacy of the internal control system;

1.13 overseeing the Company's communication and information dissemination policy;

1.14 performing the appraisal of Board members and executive management;

1.15 ensuring the integrity of annual reports and accounts and all material information provided to regulators and other stakeholders; and

1.16 ensuring that management systems are in place to identify and manage environmental and social risks and their impact.

2. Board Structure and Composition

Principle 2: *The effective discharge of the responsibilities of the Board and its committees is assured by an appropriate balance of skills and diversity (including experience and gender) without compromising competence, independence and integrity.*

Recommended Practices

2.1 The Board should be of a sufficient size to effectively undertake and fulfil its business; to oversee, monitor, direct and control the Company's activities and be relative to the scale and complexity of its operations.

2.2 The Board should assume responsibility for its composition by setting the direction and approving the processes for it to attain the appropriate balance of knowledge, skills, experience, diversity and independence to objectively and effectively discharge its governance role and responsibilities.

2.3 The Board should consider the following factors in determining the requisite number of its members:

(a) appropriate mix of knowledge, skills and experience, including the business, commercial and industry experience needed to govern the Company;

(b) appropriate mix of Executive, Non-Executive and Independent Non-Executive members such that majority of the Board are Non-Executive Directors. It is desirable that most of the Non-Executive Directors are independent;

(c) need for a sufficient number of members that qualify to serve on the committees of the Board;

(d) need to secure quorum at meetings; and

(e) diversity targets relating to the composition of the Board.

2.4 The Board should promote diversity in its membership across a variety of attributes relevant for promoting better decision-making and effective governance. These attributes include field of knowledge, skills and experience as well as age, culture and gender. The Board should have a policy to govern this process and establish measurable objectives for achieving diversity in gender and other areas.

2.5 The Board should periodically invigorate its capabilities by ensuring the appointment of new members with relevant skills and fresh perspectives, while retaining valuable knowledge, skills, experience and diversity; and maintaining continuity.

2.6 No individual or small group of individuals should dominate the Board's decision-making.

2.7 The positions of the Chairman of the Board and the Managing Director/Chief Executive Officer (MD/CEO) of the Company should be separate such that no person can combine the two positions.

2.8 Directors may hold concurrent directorships. However, concurrent service on too many Boards may interfere with an individual's ability to discharge his responsibilities. To assist the Board in determining the appropriateness of concurrent directorships:

2.8.1 Prospective Directors should disclose memberships on other Boards, and current Directors should notify the Board of prospective appointments on other Boards. This information should be kept current by serving Board members.

2.8.2 The Board should consider the disclosed directorships, taking into account the number of other directorships and the responsibilities held, and determine whether the individual can discharge his responsibilities and contribute effectively to the performance of the Board before recommending such a person for appointment or continued service.

2.8.3 Directors should not be members of Boards of competing companies to avoid conflict of interest, breach of confidentiality, diversion of corporate opportunity and divulgence of corporate information.

2.9 The Chairman of the Board should not serve as chairman or member of any Board committee. The MD/CEO or an Executive Director should not serve as chairman of any Board committee.

2.10 A person (or group of persons) who is not a serving Director of the Company should not exercise any influence or dominance over the Board and/or Management. Such a person or group of persons would be deemed a shadow director as defined by extant laws.

3.   Chairman

Principle 3: *The Chairman is responsible for providing overall leadership of the Company and the Board, and eliciting the constructive participation of all Directors to facilitate effective direction of the Board.*

Recommended Practices

3.1   The Chairman's primary responsibility is to ensure the effective operation of the Board such that the Board works as a group towards achieving the Company's strategic objectives. He should also provide guidance to the MD/CEO and be available to him for regular communication.

3.2   The Chairman of the Board should be a NED and not be involved in the day-to-day operations of the Company, which should be the primary responsibility of the MD/CEO and the management team.

3.3   The MD/CEO or an Executive Director (ED) should not go on to be the Chairman of the same Company. If in very exceptional circumstances the Board decides that a former MD/CEO or an ED should become Chairman, a cool-off period of three years should be adopted.

3.4   The Chairman's functions should include the following:

   3.4.1   presiding over meetings of the Board of Directors and general meetings of shareholders;

   3.4.2   agreeing an annual Board plan with the Board;

   3.4.3   ensuring that the agenda for Board meetings is set;

   3.4.4   ensuring that the Board and its committees are composed of individuals with relevant skills, competencies and desired experience;

   3.4.5   ensuring that Board meetings are properly conducted;

   3.4.6   ensuring that the Board is effective and functions in a cohesive manner;

   3.4.7   ensuring that induction programmes are conducted for new Directors and a continuing education programme is in place for all Directors;

   3.4.8   ensuring effective communication and relations with the Company's shareholders and other stakeholders; and

   3.4.9   taking a lead role in the assessment, improvement and development of the Board.

3.5   The Chairman is responsible for ensuring that management provides the Directors with accurate, timely and adequate information.

3.6   The Chairman may interact with NEDs periodically.

4

4. **Managing Director/Chief Executive Officer**

Principle 4: *The Managing Director/Chief Executive Officer is the head of management delegated by the Board to run the affairs of the Company to achieve its strategic objectives for sustainable corporate performance.*

Recommended Practices

4.1 The Board may delegate any of its powers to the MD/CEO as it deems appropriate for the smooth operation of the Company.

4.2 The MD/CEO should have a broad understanding of the Company's business. He should demonstrate entrepreneurial skills, credibility and integrity and have the confidence of the Board and management.

4.3 The MD/CEO should establish a culture of integrity, conformance and performance which should be assimilated by personnel at all levels of the Company.

4.4 The functions and responsibilities of the MD/CEO should include:

    4.4.1 day-to-day management of the Company;

    4.4.2 proper implementation and achievement of the Company's strategic imperatives to ensure the sustainable development and growth of the Company;

    4.4.3 ensuring prudent management of the Company's finances and other resources;

    4.4.4 providing the Board with complete, accurate and timely information and documentation to enable it to make sound decisions;

    4.4.5 promoting and protecting the interests of the Company; and

    4.4.6 being the Company's leading representative in its dealings with its stakeholders.

4.5 The authority of the MD/CEO and the relationship between him and the Board should be clearly set out in a contract of employment.

4.6 The MD/CEO should declare any conflict of interest on appointment and annually thereafter. In the event that he becomes aware of any potential conflict of interest at any other point, he should disclose this to the Board at the first possible opportunity. Actions following disclosure should be subject to the Company's Conflict of Interest Policy.

4.7 The MD/CEO should not be a member of the committees responsible for remuneration, audit, or nomination and governance.

4.8   The MD/CEO may be appointed an NED in any other Company, provided such appointment is not detrimental to his responsibilities and is in accordance with Board-approved policy.

5.   Executive Directors

Principle 5:   *Executive Directors support the Managing Director/Chief Executive Officer in the operations and management of the Company.*

Recommended Practices

5.1   EDs should have a broad understanding of the Company's business in addition to possessing such other qualifications as may be needed for their specific assignments or responsibilities.

5.2   EDs should support the MD/CEO in the proper implementation and achievement of the Company's strategic imperatives, as well as prudent management of the Company's finances and other resources.

5.3   EDs should declare any conflict of interest on appointment and annually thereafter. In the event that they become aware of any potential conflict of interest at any other point, they should disclose this to the Board at the first possible opportunity. Actions following disclosure should be subject to the Company's Conflict of Interest Policy.

5.4   An ED may be appointed NED in any other company, provided such appointment is not detrimental to his responsibilities as an ED and is in accordance with Board-approved policy.

5.5   An ED should not be a member of the committees responsible for remuneration, audit, or nomination and governance.

5.6   The responsibilities and authority of EDs should be clearly set out in a contract of employment.

6.   Non-Executive Directors

Principle 6:   *Non-Executive Directors bring to bear their knowledge, expertise and independent judgment on issues of strategy and performance on the Board.*

Recommended Practices

6.1   NEDs should be chosen on the basis of their wide experience, knowledge and personal qualities and are expected to bring these qualities to bear on the Company's business and affairs.

6.2   NEDs should constructively contribute to the development of the Company's strategy.

6.3 NEDs should not be involved in the day-to-day operations of the Company, which should be the primary responsibility of the MD/CEO and the management team.

6.4 NEDs should have unfettered access to the EDs, Company Secretary and the Internal Auditor, while access to other senior management should be through the MD/CEO.

6.5 To facilitate the effective discharge of their duties, NEDs should be provided, in a timely manner, with reasonable support as well as quality and comprehensive information relating to the management of the Company and on all Board matters.

7. Independent Non-Executive Directors

Principle 7: *Independent Non-Executive Directors bring a high degree of objectivity to the Board for sustaining stakeholder trust and confidence.*

Recommended Practices

7.1 An Independent Non-Executive Director (INED) should represent a strong independent voice on the Board, be independent in character and judgment and accordingly be free from such relationships or circumstances with the Company, its management, or substantial shareholders as may, or appear to, impair his ability to make independent judgment.

7.2 An INED is a NED who:

7.2.1 does not possess a shareholding in the Company the value of which is material to the holder such as will impair his independence or in excess of 0.01% of the paid up capital of the Company;

7.2.2 is not a representative of a shareholder that has the ability to control or significantly influence Management;

7.2.3 is not, or has not been an employee of the Company or group within the last five years;

7.2.4 is not a close family member of any of the Company's advisers, Directors, senior employees, consultants, auditors, creditors, suppliers, customers or substantial shareholders;

7.2.5 does not have, and has not had within the last five years, a material business relationship with the Company either directly, or as a partner, shareholder, Director or senior employee of a body that has, or has had, such a relationship with the Company;

7.2.6 has not served at directorate level or above at the Company's regulator within the last three years;

7.2.7   does not render any professional, consultancy or other advisory services to the Company or the group, other than in the capacity of a Director;

7.2.8   does not receive, and has not received additional remuneration from the Company apart from a Director's fee and allowances; does not participate in the Company's share option or a performance-related pay scheme, and is not a member of the Company's pension scheme; and

7.2.9   has not served on the Board for more than nine years from the date of his first election.

7.3   The above-mentioned criteria for establishing the independent status of an INED are not exhaustive, but should be considered as examples of some of those relationships or circumstances which may impair, or appear to impair an INED's independent judgment.

7.4   The Board should annually ascertain and confirm the continued independence of each INED of the Company.

7.5   Reclassification of an existing NED into an INED on the same Board is not desirable.

8.   Company Secretary

Principle 8:   *The Company Secretary plays an important role in supporting the effectiveness of the Board by assisting the Board and management to develop good corporate governance practices and culture within the Company.*

Recommended Practices

8.1   Without prejudice to the provisions of extant laws, the Company Secretary should be a person with relevant qualifications and competence necessary to effectively discharge the duties of his office. The Board should ensure that the person appointed has the gravitas and objectivity to provide independent guidance and support at the highest level of decision-making in the Company.

8.2   Where the Company Secretary is an employee of the Company, he should be a member of senior management and should be appointed through a rigorous selection process similar to that of new Directors.

8.3   The Company Secretary should be properly empowered by the Board to discharge his duties and responsibilities.

8.4   The Company Secretary should have both functional and administrative responsibilities. The functional responsibility is to the Board through the Chairman, while administratively, he reports to the MD/CEO.

8.5   The Board should approve the performance evaluation of the Company Secretary.

8.6   In addition to his statutory functions, the Company Secretary should carry out the following duties and responsibilities:

    8.6.1   Provide the Board and Directors individually, with detailed guidance as to how their responsibilities should be properly discharged in the best interest of the Company;

    8.6.2   Coordinate the induction and training of new Directors.

    8.6.3   Assist the Chairman and MD/CEO in coordinating activities regarding the annual Board plan and with the administration of other strategic issues at the Board level;

    8.6.4   Notify Board members of upcoming meetings of the Board and its committees as well as other matters that warrant their attention;

    8.6.5   Compile Board papers and ensure that the Board's discussions and decisions are clearly and properly recorded and communicated to relevant persons in a timely manner;

    8.6.6   Provide a central source of guidance and advice to the Board and the Company on matters of ethics, conflict of interest and good corporate governance.

8.7   Under the direction of the Chairman, the Company Secretary's responsibilities include ensuring good information flow within the Board and its committees and between senior management and NEDs.

8.8   Subject to the provisions of extant laws, the appointment and removal of the Company Secretary should be a matter for the Board.

9.   Access to Independent Advice

Principle 9:   *Directors are sometimes required to make decisions of a technical and complex nature that may require independent external expertise.*

Recommended Practices

9.1   The Board should ensure that Directors, especially NEDs, have access to independent professional advice where they consider it necessary to discharge their responsibilities as Directors.

9.2   The Board should ensure that such independent professional advice is obtained as set out in the Company's governance policies and at the Company's expense.

10.   Meetings of the Board

Principle 10: Meetings are the principal vehicle for conducting the business of the Board and successfully fulfilling the strategic objectives of the Company.

Recommended Practices

10.1   In order to effectively perform its oversight function and monitor management's performance, the Board should meet at least once every quarter.

10.2   Every Director should endeavour to attend all Board meetings. The attendance record of Directors should be among the criteria for the re-election of a Director.

10.3   Minutes of meetings of the Board and its committees, as a record of what transpired at those meetings, should be prepared and sent to Directors on a timely basis. Such minutes should be formally reviewed and approved by the members of the Board or relevant Board committee at its next meeting.

11.   Board Committees

Principle 11: To ensure efficiency and effectiveness, the Board delegates some of its functions, duties and responsibilities to well-structured committees, without abdicating its responsibilities.

Recommended Practices

11.1 Board Committees

11.1.1   The Board should determine the number and composition of its committees as well as ensure that each is comprised of Directors with relevant skills and competencies.

11.1.2   Only Directors may be members of Board committees, while members of senior management may be required to attend committee meetings.

11.1.3   The terms of reference and composition of such committees should be set out in the Board-approved committee charter, which should be reviewed periodically.

11.1.4   The membership of Board committees should be reviewed and refreshed periodically.

11.1.5   Each committee should be composed of at least three members. Individual Board committee charters will indicate where INEDs are required.

11.1.6 To facilitate adequate oversight, the Board should establish committees responsible for nomination and governance, remuneration, audit and risk management.

11.1.7 The Board may combine any of the responsibilities mentioned in Section 11.1.6 on Board committees, taking into consideration the size, needs and other requirements of the Company.

11.1.8 The chairmen of Board committees should be appointed by the Board.

11.1.9 The Board should ensure that, in appointing members of the Board committees, there is a balanced distribution of power in respect of membership across committees so that no individual has the ability to dominate decision making and undue reliance is not placed on any individual.

11.1.10 The Company Secretary, or any other officer in the office of the Company Secretary, should be the secretary of all Board committees.

11.1.11 The agenda for the meetings of Board committees should be developed in consultation with the respective committee chairmen.

11.1.12 The timing of committee meetings should be well coordinated for the effective discharge of their duties.

11.1.13 At board meetings, the chairman of each Board committee should present a written report of the key recommendations made at all the meetings held by the committee since the last Board meeting.

11.1.14 Members of Board committees should devote sufficient time to the committees' work.

11.1.15 Board Committees may engage a consultant at the expense of the Company for the purpose of obtaining independent external expertise in carrying out their responsibilities. This should be done in line with the Company's policies.

11.1.16 Board Committees should be accountable to the Board for their own activities and performance.

11.2 Committee responsible for Nomination and Governance

11.2.1   The Board should consider assigning the responsibilities for nomination of members and oversight of governance matters to a stand-alone committee, or to any other committee capable of combining it with their existing functions, as is appropriate.

11.2.2   Members of the committee responsible for nomination and governance should be NEDs, and a majority of them should be INEDs where possible.

11.2.3   The chairman of the committee should be a NED.

11.2.4   The committee should meet at least twice a year or such number of times as may be appropriate to discharge its duties.

11.2.5   Among other things, the committee should have the duty to:

11.2.5.1   Review the structure, size, composition and commitment of the Board at least annually and make recommendations on any proposed changes to the Board;

11.2.5.2   Establish a formal and transparent process for Board appointments, including establishing the criteria for appointment to the Board and Board committees, reviewing prospective candidates' qualifications and any potential conflict of interest; assessing the contribution of current Directors against their re-nomination suitability, and making appropriate recommendations to the Board;

11.2.5.3   Identify individuals suitably qualified to become Board members and make recommendations to the Board for nomination and appointment as Directors;

11.2.5.4   Periodically determine the skills, knowledge and experience required on the Board and its committees;

11.2.5.5   Ensure that the Company has a formal programme for the induction and training of Directors;

11.2.5.6   Undertake the annual assessment of the independent status of each INED;

11.2.5.7   Ensure that the Company has a succession policy and plan in place for the Chairman of the Board, the MD/CEO and all other EDs, NEDs and senior management positions to ensure leadership continuity. Succession planning should be

12

reviewed periodically, with provision made for succession in emergency situations as well as long-term vacancies;

11.2.5.8 Deal with all matters pertaining to executive management selection and performance, including an annual evaluation of the performance of the MD/CEO and executive management.

11.2.5.9 Develop a process for, and ensure that the Board undertakes, an annual performance evaluation of itself, its committees, the Chairman and individual Directors, as well as the Company's corporate governance practices.

11.2.5.10 Ensure the development and periodic review of Board charters, Board committee charters and other governance policies, such as the code of ethics, conflict of interest and whistleblowing policies among others.

11.3 Committee responsible for Remuneration

11.3.1 The Board should consider assigning the responsibilities for the determination of remuneration policy and its application to executive management, performance evaluation, the adoption of incentive plans, and various governance responsibilities related to remuneration to a stand-alone committee, or to any other committee capable of combining it with their existing functions, as is appropriate.

11.3.2 Members of the committee responsible for remuneration should be NEDs, and a majority of them should be INEDs where possible.

11.3.3 It is desirable that the chairman of the committee be an INED.

11.3.4 The committee should meet at least once a year or such number of times as may be appropriate to discharge its duties.

11.3.5 The duties of the committee responsible for remuneration should include, among others:

11.3.5.1 Development of a formal, clear and transparent framework for the Company's remuneration policies and procedures;

11.3.5.2 Recommendation to the Board on the Company's remuneration policy and structure for all Directors and senior management employees.

13

11.4 Committee responsible for Audit

11.4.1   Without prejudice to the provision of extant laws on the Statutory Audit Committee, it is desirable for every Company to have a Board committee responsible for audit.

11.4.2   All members of the committee should be financially literate and should be able to read and understand financial statements. At least one member of the committee should be a financial expert, have current knowledge in accounting and financial management and be able to interpret financial statements.

11.4.3   For private companies, members of the committee responsible for audit should be NEDs, and a majority of them should be INEDs where possible.

11.4.4   In the case of the statutory audit committee, a chairman should be elected from amongst its members, and should have financial literacy.

11.4.5   The committee should meet at least once every quarter.

11.4.6   Subject to the provisions of extant laws, every public company should establish a statutory audit committee which shall perform the following functions:

11.4.6.1   Ascertain whether the accounting and reporting policies of the Company are in accordance with legal requirements and agreed ethical practices.

11.4.6.2   Review the scope and planning of audit requirements.

11.4.6.3   Review the findings in management letter in conjunction with the external auditor and management responses thereon.

11.4.6.4   Keep under review the effectiveness of the Company's system of accounting and internal control.

11.4.6.5   Make recommendations to the Board regarding the appointment, removal and remuneration of the external auditors of the Company.

11.4.6.6   Authorise the internal auditor to carry out investigations into any activities of the Company which may be of interest or concern to the committee.

11.4.7   The Board audit committee should have the following additional responsibilities:

11.4.7.1   Exercise oversight over management's processes to ascertain the integrity of the Company's financial statements, compliance with all applicable legal and other regulatory requirements; and assess the qualifications and independence of the external auditors, and the performance of the Company's internal audit function as well as that of the external auditors;

11.4.7.2 Ensure the establishment of and exercise oversight on the internal audit function which provides assurance on the effectiveness of the internal controls. On a quarterly basis, obtain and review a report by the internal auditor describing the strength and quality of internal controls including identification of any issues or recommendations for improvement raised by the most recent internal audit review of the Company;

11.4.7.3 Ensure the development of a comprehensive internal control framework for the Company, obtain appropriate (internal and/or external) assurance and report annually in the Company's audited financial report, on the design and operating effectiveness of the Company's internal controls over the financial reporting systems;

11.4.7.4 Oversee the process for the identification of fraud risks across the Company and ensure that adequate prevention, detection and reporting mechanisms are in place;

11.4.7.5 Discuss the interim or annual audited financial statements as well as significant financial reporting findings and recommendations with management and external auditors prior to recommending same to the Board for their consideration and appropriate action;

11.4.7.6 Maintain oversight of financial and non-financial reporting.

11.4.7.7 Review and ensure that adequate whistle-blowing policies and procedures are in place and that the issues reported through the whistle-blowing mechanism are summarised and presented to the board;

11.4.7.8 Review, with the external auditors, any audit scope limitations or significant matters encountered and management's responses to same;

15

        11.4.7.9 Develop a policy on the nature, extent and terms under which the external auditors may perform non-audit services;

        11.4.7.10 Review the independence of the external auditors in line with the policy referred to in Section 11.4.7.9 above prior to their appointment to perform non-audit services to ensure that where approved non-audit services are provided by the external auditors, there is no real or perceived conflict of interest, or other legal or ethical impediment;

        11.4.7.11 Preserve auditor independence, by setting clear hiring policies for employees or former employees of external auditors;

        11.4.7.12 Ensure the development of a Related Party Transactions policy and monitor its implementation by management. The Committee should consider any related party transaction that may arise within the Company.

11.4.8   At least once in a year, the committee should hold a discussion with the head of the internal audit function and the external auditors without the presence of management, to facilitate an exchange of views and concerns that may not be appropriate for open discussion.

11.5 Committee responsible for Risk Management

11.5.1   The Board should consider assigning the responsibilities for oversight of matters relating to risk management to a stand-alone committee, or to any other committee capable of combining it with their existing functions, as is appropriate.

11.5.2   Members of the committee responsible for risk management should include EDs and NEDs, a majority of whom should be NEDs.

11.5.3   Where the committees responsible for audit and risk management are separate, the Board should consider for one or more members to have joint membership of both committees for more effective functioning as this will enhance the discussions at meetings of both committees – the risk implication of audit matters will be discussed more extensively, and a knowledge of findings from the Company's internal audit activities will bring a unique perspective to the discussion of risk issues.

11.5.4   The chairman of the committee should be a NED.

11.5.5 The committee should meet at least twice every financial year or such number of times as may be appropriate to discharge its duties.

11.5.6 The committee should:

11.5.6.1 Review and recommend for approval of the Board, the risk management policies and framework, as well as assist the Board in its oversight of risk management strategy;

11.5.6.2 Review the adequacy and effectiveness of risk management and controls in the Company;

11.5.6.3 Exercise oversight over the process for the identification and assessment of risks across the Company and the adequacy of prevention, detection and reporting mechanisms;

11.5.6.4 Review the level of the Company's compliance with applicable laws and regulatory requirements which may impact the Company's risk profile;

11.5.6.5 Periodically review changes in the economic and business environment, including emerging trends and other factors relevant to the Company's risk profile and those trends which may threaten the Company's business model, key strategies, future performance, solvency and liquidity and make recommendations to the Board as appropriate;

11.5.6.6 Review and recommend for approval of the Board, at least annually, the Company's Information Technology (IT) data governance framework to ensure that IT data risks are adequately mitigated and relevant assets are managed effectively. The framework may include:

(a) Development of IT strategy and policy;

(b) Proactive monitoring and management of cyber threats and attacks as well as adverse social media incidents;

(c) Management of risks relating to third-party and outsourced IT service providers;

(d) Assessment of value delivered to the Company through investments in IT; and

(e) Periodic independent assurance on the effectiveness of the Company's IT arrangements.

11.5.7 The person charged with the responsibility for risk management should be a member of senior management of

17

the Company, a professional with relevant qualifications and experience and should be in attendance at meetings of the committee. The direct reporting line of this person should be to the MD/CEO and there should be an indirect reporting line to the committee responsible for risk management.

12.   Appointment to the Board

Principle 12:   A written, clearly defined, rigorous, formal and transparent procedure serves as a guide for the selection of Directors to ensure the appointment of high quality individuals to the Board.

Recommended Practices

12.1   The Board should approve the criteria for appointing Directors, as recommended by the committee responsible for nomination and governance. Such criteria should take into careful consideration the strengths and weaknesses of the existing Board, integrity, required competence and skills, knowledge and experience, capacity to undertake the responsibility as well as diversity, including gender diversity. In the case of specialised businesses, possession of requisite technical skill should be taken into account.

12.2   The committee responsible for nomination and governance should ensure that proposed Directors are fit and proper persons before recommending them to the Board for consideration for directorship positions.

12.3   Shareholders should be provided with biographical information of proposed Directors to guide their decision. Such information should include:

(a)   name, age, qualifications, country of primary residence and the ownership interest represented, if any;

(b)   whether the appointment is for ED, NED or INED, and any proposed specific area of responsibility or Board committee roles if any;

(c)   work experience and occupation;

(d)   current directorships and appointments;

(e)   direct and/or indirect shareholding in the Company and/or its subsidiaries; and

(f)   any other relevant information.

12.4   Every Director should receive a letter of appointment or contract of employment, specifying the terms and conditions of his appointment or employment.

12.5   The letter of appointment or contract of employment should cover the following issues:

18

(a)   duration of the appointment or tenure;
(b)   details of the remuneration;
(c)   summary of the rights, fiduciary duties and other responsibilities of the Director;
(d)   requirement to disclose any material interests in the Company and other entities carrying on business or providing services to the Company;
(e)   specific requirements, such as Board or Board committee meeting attendance;
(f)   formal induction programme or training for the Director to attend;
(g)   Board Charter, Code of Business Conduct and Ethics (attached as separate documents) and the Director's responsibility to observe same;
(h)   Board performance evaluation process used by the Company; and
(i)   any other relevant information.

12.6   The Company should state the processes used in relation to all Board appointments in its annual report.

12.7   Subject to the provisions of extant laws and the recommendation of the committee responsible for nomination and governance based on the results of the individual Directors' performance appraisal, Board members may offer themselves for re-election.

12.8   NEDs should serve for a reasonable period on the Board. However, it is necessary to reinforce the Board by continually injecting new energy, fresh ideas and perspectives. The Board should ensure the periodic appointment of new Directors to replace existing NEDs.

12.9   The tenure for the MD/CEO and the EDs should be determined by the Board. In determining the tenure of an ED, the Board should take into account his performance, the existing succession planning mechanism, continuity of the Board and the need for continuous refreshing of the Board.

12.10   The tenure for INEDs should not exceed three terms of three years each.

12.11   To resign, Directors should submit a written notice of resignation addressed to the Chairman.

12.12   Where a Director has concerns about the running of the Company which cannot be resolved and he elects to resign from the Board, such concerns should be detailed in a written statement to the Chairman for circulation to the Board.

13.   Induction and Continuing Education

Principle 13: *A formal induction programme on joining the Board as well as regular training assists Directors to effectively discharge their duties to the Company.*

Recommended Practices

13.1 The Board should establish a formal induction programme for new Directors of the Company to familiarise them with the Company's, strategic plan, operations, business environment, senior management, and the Directors' fiduciary responsibilities. The induction of new Directors should take place as soon as feasible after their appointment.

13.2 All Directors should participate in periodic, relevant, continuing education programmes to update their knowledge and skills and keep them informed of new developments in the Company's business and operating environment.

13.3 The outcome of the performance evaluation of the individual Directors should be taken into account in developing the Board training programme.

13.4 The training programmes should be at the Company's expense but should not be such that put undue strain on the Company's finances.

14.   Board Evaluation

Principle 14: *Annual Board evaluation assesses how each Director, the committees of the Board and the Board are committed to their roles, work together and continue to contribute effectively to the achievement of the Company's objectives.*

Recommended Practices

14.1 The Board should establish a system to undertake a formal and rigorous annual evaluation of its own performance, that of its committees, the Chairman and individual Directors. This process should be externally facilitated by an independent external consultant at least once in three years.

14.2 The evaluation system should include the criteria and key performance indicators and targets for the Board, its committees, the Chairman and each individual Board member.

14.3 The evaluation of the Board should consider the mix of skills, experience, objectivity, competence of members of the Board, its diversity (including gender), knowledge of the Company and its strategic direction, attendance at meetings, how the Board works together and other factors relevant to its effectiveness.

14.4 The result of the Board performance evaluation should be communicated to and discussed by the Board as a whole, while those of individual Directors should be communicated to and discussed with them individually by the Chairman.

14.5 Where the performance of a Director is considered to be unsatisfactory, the Board should provide appropriate training to address the identified gaps.

14.6 The results of a Director's performance evaluation should be considered in the Director re-election process.

15. Corporate Governance Evaluation

Principle 15: Institutionalising a system for evaluating the Company's corporate governance practices ensures that its governance standards, practices and processes are adequate and effective.

Recommended Practices

15.1 The Board should ensure that an annual corporate governance evaluation, including the extent of application of this Code, is carried out. The evaluation should be facilitated by an independent external consultant at least once in three years.

15.2 The summary of the report of this evaluation should be included in the Company's annual report and on the investors' portal of the Company.

16. Remuneration Governance

Principle 16: The Board ensures that the Company remunerates fairly, responsibly and transparently so as to promote the achievement of strategic objectives and positive outcomes in the short, medium and long term.

Recommended Practices

16.1 The Board should assume responsibility for the governance of remuneration by setting the direction for how remuneration should be addressed on a Company-wide basis.

16.2 The Board should approve policies that articulate and give effect to its direction on fair, responsible and transparent remuneration.

16.3 The remuneration policy should be designed to attract, motivate, reward and retain high performing human capital.

16.4 The Board should periodically confirm that the implementation and execution of the remuneration policy achieves its objectives.

16.5 Remuneration for NEDs should be fixed by the Board and approved by shareholders in the General Meeting.

16.6 The remuneration of the MD/CEO and EDs should be structured to link rewards to corporate and individual performances and include a significant component that is related to long-term corporate performance, such as stock options and bonuses. Mechanisms may be considered to align payment of certain components of the remuneration of the MD/CEO and EDs with the achievement of longer-term goals.

16.7 The MD/CEO and EDs should not be involved in the determination of their remuneration.

16.8 The Company's Remuneration Policy as well as remuneration of all Directors should be disclosed in the Company's annual report.

16.9 Companies should implement a clawback policy to recover excess or undeserved reward, such as bonuses, incentives, share of profits, stock options, or any performance-based reward, from Directors and senior employees.

16.10 Clawback can be triggered if the account or financial performance on which the reward was based is later found to be materially false, misstated, misleading, erroneous, etc. or in instances of misdemeanour, fraud, material violation of Company policy or material regulatory infractions.

16.11 The MD/CEO and EDs should not receive sitting allowances for attending meetings of the Board or its committees and Director's fees from the Company, its holding company or subsidiaries. Their remuneration should however encompass recompense for time spent on the Board, its committees, and related work.

16.12 NEDs should not receive performance-based compensation as it may lead to bias in their decision-making and compromise their objectivity.

16.13 NEDs may be paid sitting allowances, Directors' fees and reimbursable travel and hotel expenses. These payments, in addition to any other allowances and benefits made to NEDs, should be disclosed in the Company's annual report.

16.14 Subject to the provisions of extant laws, the Company may pay compensation for loss of office or retirement to Directors. In the case of the MD/CEO, EDs and senior management, the compensation payable for any loss of office or termination of appointment should be consistent with their contractual terms, fair and not excessive.

Part B.   **Assurance**

   17.   **Risk Management**

   Principle 17: *A sound framework for managing risk and ensuring an effective internal control system is essential for achieving the strategic objectives of the Company.*

Recommended Practices
The Board should:
17.1   ensure the establishment of a risk management framework that:
      17.1.1   defines the Company's risk policy, risk appetite and risk limits; and
      17.1.2   identifies, assesses, monitors and manages key business risks to safeguard shareholders' investments and the Company's assets;
17.2   formally approve the risk management framework and ensure that it is communicated in simple and clear language to all employees;
17.3   ensure that the risk management framework is integrated into the day-to-day operations of the business and provide guidelines and standards for management of key risks;
17.4   articulate, implement and review the Company's internal control systems to strengthen the risk management framework;
17.5   conduct at least annually, or more often in companies with complex operations, a thorough risk assessment covering all aspects of the Company's business and ensure that mitigating strategies have been put in place to manage identified risks;
17.6   obtain and review relevant reports periodically to ensure the ongoing effectiveness of the Company's risk management framework;
17.7   ensure that the Company's risk management framework is disclosed in the annual report; and
17.8   ensure that the risk management function is headed by a member of senior management who is a professional with relevant qualifications, competence, objectivity and experience.

18.   Internal Audit Function

Principle 18:   *An effective internal audit function provides assurance to the Board on the effectiveness of the governance, risk management and internal control systems.*

Recommended Practices

18.1   The purpose, authority and responsibility of the internal audit function should be clearly and formally defined in an internal audit charter approved by the Board.

18.2   Where the Board decides not to establish such a function, internally or outsourced, sufficient reasons should be disclosed in the Company's annual report with an explanation as to how the Board has obtained adequate assurance on the effectiveness of the internal processes and systems such as risk management and internal control.

18.3   The internal audit function should be headed by a member of senior management who is a professional with relevant qualifications, competence, objectivity and experience; and is registered with a recognised professional body.

18.4   The Board should ensure that the internal audit function is sufficiently skilled and resourced to address the complexity and volume of risk faced by the organisation.

18.5   The head of the internal audit function should:

18.5.1   Report directly to the committee responsible for audit while having a line of communication with the MD/CEO.

18.5.2   Have unrestricted access to the chairman of the committee responsible for audit as well as the Chairman of the Board.

18.5.3   Report at least once every quarter to the committee responsible for audit, on the adequacy and effectiveness of management, governance, risk and control environment; deficiencies observed and management mitigation plans.

18.5.4   Provide assurance to the Board by conducting periodic evaluations to determine the effectiveness and efficiency of the Company's internal control systems and make recommendations for enhancement or improvement.

18.5.5   Develop an annual risk-based internal audit plan which should be approved by the committee responsible for audit.

18.5.6   Liaise with other internal and external providers of assurance in order to ensure proper coverage and to minimise duplication of efforts.

18.6   There should be an external assessment of the effectiveness of the internal audit function at least once every three years by a qualified independent reviewer to be appointed by the Board.

18.7 The evaluation of the head of the internal audit function should be performed by the committee responsible for audit, and he may only be removed by the Board on the recommendation of the committee responsible for audit.

19. Whistle-blowing

Principle 19: An effective whistle-blowing framework for reporting any illegal or unethical behaviour minimises the Company's exposure and prevents recurrence.

Recommended Practices

19.1 The Board should establish a whistle-blowing framework to encourage stakeholders to bring unethical conduct and violations of laws and regulations to the attention of an internal and/or external authority so that action can be taken to verify the allegation and apply appropriate sanctions or take remedial action to correct any harm done. This framework should be known to employees and external stakeholders.

19.2 The Board should ensure the existence of a whistle-blowing mechanism that is reliable, accessible and guarantees the anonymity of the whistle-blower, and that all disclosures resulting from whistle-blowing are treated in a confidential manner. The identity of the whistle-blower should be kept confidential.

19.3 The Board should accord priority to the effectiveness of the whistle-blowing mechanism and continually affirm publicly, its support for and commitment to the Company's whistle-blower protection mechanism.

19.4 The team responsible for managing disclosures obtained through the whistle-blowing mechanism should:

  19.4.1 Review reported cases and bring them to the notice of the committee responsible for audit

  19.4.2 Provide the committee responsible for audit with a summary of reported cases, cases investigated, the process of investigation and the results of the investigations.

19.5 A whistle-blower can disclose any information related to a violation or suspected violation of any laws, internal policies, etc. connected with the business of the Company, its employees or stakeholders.

19.6 The Board should ensure that no whistle-blower is subject to any detriment on the grounds that he has made a disclosure. Where a whistle-blower has been subjected to any detriment, he may present a complaint to the Board and/or regulators. A whistle-blower who has suffered any detriment by reason of disclosure may be entitled to compensation and/or reinstatement as appropriate.

20.   External Auditors

Principle 20: *An external auditor is appointed to provide an independent opinion on the true and fair view of the financial statements of the Company to give assurance to stakeholders on the reliability of the financial statements.*

Recommended Practices

20.1   Subject to the provisions of any extant laws, the recommendation for the appointment, re-appointment or removal of an external auditor should be made to the Board by the committee responsible for audit.

20.2   External audit firms may be retained for no longer than ten years continuously. External audit firms disengaged after ten years continuous service may not be considered for reappointment until seven years after their disengagement. Where an external auditor's aggregate or cumulative tenure has already exceeded ten years at the date of commencement of this Code, such auditor should cease to hold office as an auditor of the Company at the Annual General Meeting to be held immediately after this Code comes into effect.

20.3   An external auditor may provide to the Company only such other services as are approved by the Board on the recommendation of the committee responsible for audit and such as does not create a self-review threat in line with the provisions of international auditing standards.

20.4   In order to preserve independence, there should be a rotation of the audit engagement partner every five years.

20.5   In order to preserve independence, there should be an appropriate cooling off period spanning at least three years between the retirement of a partner from an audit firm and his appointment to the Board of an audit client. Similarly, there should be a cooling off period before a Company can engage any member of the audit team as a staff member in the financial reporting function.

20.6   In order to ensure quality audit outcomes, the engagement partner and audit team should possess the knowledge, relevant skills and experience. Additionally, they should demonstrate a good understanding of the Company's business, be independent of the Company and approach their work with a high level of objectivity and professionalism – including applying internationally accepted audit standards in their work.

20.7 Where the Board is satisfied that the external auditor has abused its office, acted in a fraudulent manner, colluded in any fraud or engaged in any unethical practice, it may recommend the removal of such external auditor in accordance with the provisions of extant laws. Where a Regulator is satisfied that the external auditor of a Company has abused its office as auditor, it may request the Company to remove such external auditor in line with the provisions of extant laws.

20.8 Where external auditors discover or acquire information during an audit that leads them to believe that the Company or anyone associated with it has committed an indictable offence under any law, they should report this to the Regulator, whether or not such matter is or will be included in the Management Letter issued to the committee responsible for audit and/or the Board.

Part C.   Relationship with Shareholders

21.   General Meetings

Principle 21: *General Meetings are important platforms for the Board to engage shareholders to facilitate greater understanding of the Company's business, governance and performance. They provide shareholders with an opportunity to exercise their ownership rights and express their views to the Board on any areas of interest.*

Recommended Practices

21.1   General Meetings should be conducted in an open manner allowing for free discussions on all issues on the agenda. Sufficient time should be allocated to shareholders, particularly minorities, to participate fully and contribute effectively at such meetings.

21.2   The chairmen of all Board committees and of the Statutory Audit Committee should be present at General Meetings of the Company to respond to shareholders' inquiries.

21.3   The venue of a General Meeting should be accessible to shareholders, to ensure that shareholders are not disenfranchised on account of the choice of venue.

21.4   Notices of General Meetings shall be at least 21 days from the date on which the meeting will be held. Copies of the annual reports, audited financial statements and all other information pertaining to any resolution to be voted upon – including voting or proxy instructions and relevant papers – that will enable members prepare adequately for the meeting should be despatched along with the notice.

21.5   The Board should ensure that unrelated issues for consideration are not lumped together at General Meetings. All matters to be considered should be clearly and separately set out. Separate resolutions should be proposed and voted on for each substantive issue.

21.6   The Board should ensure that decisions reached at General Meetings are properly and fully implemented as governance directives.

22. **Shareholder Engagement**

Principle 22: *The establishment of a system of regular dialogue with shareholders balances their needs, interests and expectations with the objectives of the Company.*

Recommended Practices

22.1 The Board should develop a policy that ensures appropriate engagement with shareholders. The policy should be hosted on the website of the Company.

22.2 The Chairman of the Board, or other designated persons as specified in the policy referred to in Section 22.1, may interact with shareholders in order to help develop a balanced understanding of shareholder issues and ensure that their views are communicated to the Board.

22.3 The Board should encourage institutional investors to:

22.3.1 Positively influence the standard of corporate governance and promote value creation in the companies in which they invest.

22.3.2 Monitor conformance with the provisions of this Code and raise concerns as appropriate.

22.4 The Board should ensure that dealings of the Company with shareholder associations are always transparent and in the best interest of the Company.

23. **Protection of Shareholder Rights**

Principle 23: *Equitable treatment of shareholders and the protection of their statutory and general rights, particularly the interest of minority shareholders, promote good governance.*

Recommended Practices

23.1 The Board should ensure that:

23.1.1 shareholders at annual general meetings preserve their effective powers to appoint and remove Directors of the Company;

23.1.2 all shareholders are treated fairly and equitably. No shareholder, however large his shareholding or whether institutional or otherwise, should be given preferential treatment or superior access to information or other materials;

23.1.3 minority shareholders are adequately protected from abusive actions by controlling shareholders;

23.1.4 the Company promptly renders to shareholders documentary evidence of ownership interest in the Company and related instruments. Where these are rendered electronically, the Board should ensure that they are rendered to shareholders promptly and in a secure manner; and

23.1.5 all shareholders understand the ownership structure of the Company, and support them in this by making available, current information on the ultimate beneficial owners of the major shareholdings or any shareholders owning, controlling or influencing five percent (5%) or more of the Company's shares.

23.2 At all times, Directors should act in good faith and with integrity in the best interests of all shareholders, and provide adequate information to shareholders to facilitate their investment decisions.

Part D.   Business Conduct and Ethics

24.   Business Conduct and Ethics

> ***Principle 24:*** *The establishment of professional business and ethical standards underscores the values for the protection and enhancement of the reputation of the Company while promoting good conduct and investor confidence.*

Recommended Practices

24.1   The Board should clearly model a top-down commitment to professional business and ethical standards by formulating and periodically reviewing the Code of Business Conduct and Ethics.

24.2   The Board should be responsible for monitoring adherence to the Code of Business Conduct and Ethics to ensure that breaches are effectively sanctioned. This may be delegated to the committee responsible for nomination and governance.

24.3   The Code of Business Conduct and Ethics should include the following:

24.3.1   Directors and senior management of the Company should act honestly, in good faith and in the best interests of the Company in accordance with legal requirements and agreed ethical standards;

24.3.2   Directors owe a fiduciary duty to the Company, together with a duty of care, skill, diligence and loyalty in fulfilling the functions of their offices and exercising the powers attached to those offices;

24.3.3   Directors should undertake diligent analysis of all proposals placed before the Board and act with the level of skill expected from Directors;

24.3.4   Directors should not make improper or prejudicial use of privileged information and should not disclose non-public information except where disclosure is authorised or legally mandated;

24.3.5   Directors should not take advantage of their position for personal gain or to compete with the Company;

24.3.6   Directors should not engage in conduct likely to discredit the Company, and should encourage fair dealing by all employees with the Company's customers, suppliers and competitors;

24.3.7   Directors should encourage the reporting of unlawful or unethical behaviours and actively promote ethical behaviours and the protection of those who report violations in good faith; and

24.3.8   Directors, management and other employees shall have an obligation to comply with the principles of the Code of Business Conduct and Ethics at all times.

24.4   The Code of Business Conduct and Ethics should:

(a)   commit the Company, its Board, management and other employees, contractors, suppliers (under contractual terms) and other company-controlled entities to the highest standards of professional and ethical behaviour, business conduct and sustainable business practices;

(b)   be designed with due consideration of the interests of the Company, its management and employees;

(c)   receive its implementation commitment from the MD/CEO and executive management;

(d)   be sufficiently detailed as to give clear guidance to users; and

(e)   be formally communicated to all persons to whom it applies.

24.5   Companies are encouraged to explore formal mechanisms for engagement and communication with stakeholders, including the use of alternative dispute resolution mechanisms and associated processes.

25.   Ethical Culture

Principle 25: *The establishment of policies and mechanisms for monitoring insider trading, related party transactions, conflict of interest and other corrupt activities, mitigates the adverse effects of these abuses on the Company and promotes good ethical conduct and investor confidence.*

Recommended Practices

25.1   The Board should ensure:

25.1.1   The establishment of policies on insider trading, related party transactions and conflict of interest.

25.1.2   That insiders are precluded from buying and selling any security in breach of their fiduciary duty and other relationship of trust and confidence while in possession of material, privileged, non-public and price-sensitive information about the Company.

25.1.3   That insiders are precluded from engaging in unlawful or improper transfers of assets and profits out of companies for their personal benefits or for the benefit of those who control the companies.

       25.1.4   The disclosure of all transactions between related parties, whether natural persons or bodies corporate, including whether such transactions have been executed at arm's length and on normal market terms. This disclosure should be made prior to the conclusion of the transaction, if they exceed a disclosure threshold as determined by the Board.

25.2 The policy on conflict of interest should be communicated, supported and monitored to provide reasonable assurance that all potential conflict of interest situations will be disclosed. The policy should be guided by the following:

       25.2.1   Directors should promptly disclose any real or potential conflict of interest that they may have by virtue of their membership of the Board.

       25.2.2   A Director may not be present during the time any matter in which he has an interest is being decided and should not seek to participate or influence any discussions or negotiations relating to that matter.

       25.2.3   If a Director is not certain whether he is in a conflict of interest situation, the Director concerned should discuss the matter with the Chairman of the Board, the Company Secretary or the chairman of the committee responsible for nomination and governance for advice and guidance.

       25.2.4   If any question arises before the Board as to the existence of a real or perceived conflict, the Board should by a simple majority determine if a conflict exists. The Director or Directors potentially in the conflict of interest situation should not be present during any discussion and voting on the issue.

       25.2.5   Directors who are aware of a real, potential or perceived conflict of interest on the part of a fellow Director, have a responsibility to raise the issue promptly for clarification, either with the Director concerned, the Chairman of the Board or the chairman of the committee responsible for nomination and governance.

       25.2.6   Disclosure by a Director of a real, potential or perceived conflict of interest or a decision by the Board as to whether or not a conflict of interest exists should be recorded in the minutes of the meeting.

       25.2.7   All directors should declare any conflict of interest on appointment and annually thereafter. In the event that they become aware of any potential conflict of interest at any other point, they should disclose this to the Board at the first possible opportunity. Actions following disclosure should be subject to the Company's conflict of interest policy.

25.2.8   No person who has served at directorate level or above, leaving the services of a relevant regulatory institution, for any reason, should be appointed as a Director or top management staff of an institution that has been directly supervised or regulated by the said regulatory institution until after three years of the disengagement of such executive or senior management staff from that regulatory institution.

Part E.   Sustainability

26.   Sustainability

> ***Principle 26:*** *Paying adequate attention to sustainability issues including environment, social, occupational and community health and safety ensures successful long term business performance and projects the Company as a responsible corporate citizen contributing to economic development.*

Recommended Practices

26.1   The Board should establish policies and practices regarding its social, ethical, safety, working conditions, health and environmental responsibilities as well as policies addressing corruption.

26.2   The policies should include the following:

   26.2.1   the Company's business principles, practices and efforts towards achieving sustainability;

   26.2.2   the management of safety issues including workplace accidents, fatalities, occupational and safety incidents;

   26.2.3   plans and strategy for addressing and managing the impact of serious diseases on the Company's employees and their families;

   26.2.4   the most environmentally beneficial options particularly for companies operating in disadvantaged regions or in regions with delicate ecology, in order to minimise environmental impact of the Company's operations;

   26.2.5   the nature and extent of employment equity and diversity (gender and other issues);

   26.2.6   training initiatives, employee development and the associated financial investment;

   26.2.7   opportunities created for physically challenged persons or disadvantaged individuals;

   26.2.8   the environmental, social and governance principles and practices of the Company; and

   26.2.9   corruption and related issues.

26.3   The Board should monitor the implementation of sustainability policies and report on the extent of compliance with the policies.

Part F.   Transparency

27.   Stakeholder Communication

Principle 27: *Communicating and interacting with stakeholders keeps them conversant with the activities of the Company and assists them in making informed decisions.*

Recommended Practices
27.1   The Board should adopt and implement a stakeholder management and communication policy.
27.2   The Board should ensure that the reports and other communication issued to stakeholders are in clear and easily understood language and are posted on the Company's web portal. This information may include description of structures of the Board and management among others, frameworks, policies and other material information about the Company.
27.3   Communication with stakeholders and the general public should be governed by the principle of timely, accurate and continuous disclosure of material information on the activities of the Company so as to give a balanced and fair view of the Company, including its non-financial matters.
27.4   The Board should establish an investors' portal on the Company's website, where the communication policy as well as the Company's annual reports for a minimum of five immediately preceding years and other relevant information about the Company should be published and made accessible to the public in downloadable format.

28.   Disclosures

Principle 28: *Full and comprehensive disclosure of all matters material to investors and stakeholders, and of matters set out in this Code, ensures proper monitoring of its implementation which engenders good corporate governance practice.*

Recommended Practices
28.1   The Board should ensure that the Company's annual report includes a corporate governance report that provides clear information on the Company's governance structures, policies and practices as well as environmental and social risks and opportunities.
28.2   The Company's corporate governance report should include the following:
    (a)   composition of the Board of Directors, stating the names and classification of the Chairman, the MD/CEO, EDs and NEDs

as well as INEDs. This information should also be on the Company's website and other publications of the Company;

(b) the plan for achieving gender diversity set by the Board in accordance with its diversity policy, the progress towards achieving them and the proportion of women employees in the whole organisation, including women in executive management positions and women on the Board;

(c) Board appointment process including a summary statement on induction and training of Board members;

(d) evaluation process for the Board, its Committees and individual Directors as well as the assessment of the corporate governance practices in the Company;

(e) Directors standing for re-election;

(f) composition of Board committees including names of chairmen and members of each committee;

(g) description of the roles and responsibilities of the Board committees and how the committees have discharged those responsibilities;

(h) the number of meetings held by the Board and its committees during the year and the attendance of individual Directors at those meetings;

(i) cumulative years of service of each Director, the external auditor and the external consultant who performs the Board Evaluation or Corporate Governance Evaluation at the end of the reporting period;

(j) statement on the availability or otherwise of the Code of Business Conduct and Ethics for Directors, management and other employees;

(k) highlights of human resource policies and internal management structure, including relations with employees, employee share-ownership schemes and other workplace development initiatives;

(l) highlights of sustainability policies and programmes covering social issues such as corruption, community service, including environmental protection, serious diseases and matters of general environmental, social and governance (ESG) initiatives;

(m) highlights of the policy and cases of clawback being pursued by the Company; and

(n) a list of all the fines and penalties (including date, amount, and subject matter) imposed on the Company by regulators at the end of the reporting period.

28.3   The report should specify the nature of any related party relationships and transactions as follows:

    28.3.1   their purpose and financial magnitude necessary to understand whether the transactions have been at arm's length and that the Company has not suffered any loss or disadvantage from such transactions.

    28.3.2   any Director's interest in contracts either directly or indirectly with the Company or its subsidiaries and holding companies.

    28.3.3   the name of the Director, his classification, the nature and details of the transaction and the Director's interest therein: provided that the disclosures required do not include the Director's service contract.

    28.3.4   any contracts with controlling shareholder(s), their group networks and associates.

    28.3.5   The names of the parties and the nature of the transaction, and the value (monetary or other value) involved in the transaction.

28.4   The Board should use its best judgment to disclose any material matter even though not specifically required by this Code to be disclosed if in the opinion of the Board such matter is capable of affecting the present or anticipated financial condition of the Company or its status as a going concern. The onus of proof of such possible negative effect is on the Board.

28.5   The annual report should contain a statement by the Board on the Company's level of application of this Code arising from the results of its corporate governance evaluation.

28.6   Where the Board has engaged independent experts in evaluating and reporting on the extent of application of this Code, they should name the consultant and include a summary of the report (provided by the consultant) in the Company's annual report.

28.7   A Director who has serious concerns about the activities of a Company should ensure that the following are promptly raised to the Board for resolution:

    (a)   any unreported cases of conflict of interest, insider trading, related party transactions, fraud or any illegal or suspected illegal activities;

    (b)   the impairment of the external auditor's independence and objectivity, or failure to approach his work with an acceptable degree of professional scepticism;

    (c)   any violation of this Code, extant laws and regulations, and disregard for accounting standards, auditing standards or financial reporting requirements;

      (d)   the impairment of the independence of the Board or any of its committees; or

      (e)   condoning of unethical behaviour and conduct in the Company.

28.8 The annual report should contain a statement by the Board on the Company's ESG activities. This should be reviewed by an appropriate Board committee and may be subject to independent review.

28.9 The Company should establish policies and procedures for the identification, communication and response to concerns from stakeholders.

Part G.   Definitions

29.   Definitions

29.1   In this Code, unless the context otherwise requires:

29.1.1   "chief financial officer" means a person appointed as the chief financial officer of a Company by whatever name designated;

29.1.2   "close family member" means those persons who may be expected to influence, or be influenced by, that person in his dealing with a Company;

29.1.3   "Company" means a Company incorporated under the Companies and Allied Matters Act, Cap. C20, Laws of the Federation of Nigeria 2004;

29.1.4   "concessioned" or "privatised" companies means companies hitherto owned or operated by a government (Federal or State) and ceded or sold to private investors;

29.1.5   "control" refers to a situation where a person is exposed, or has rights, to variable returns from his involvement with a Company and has the ability to affect those returns through his powers over the Company;

29.1.6   "corporate citizenship" means the social responsibility of businesses and the extent to which they meet legal, ethical, economic and environmental responsibilities;

29.1.7   "detriment" includes dismissal, termination, demotion, retirement, redundancy, undue influence, duress, withholding of benefits and/or entitlements, blacklisting, withdrawal of patronage and any other act that has a negative impact on the whistle-blower;

29.1.8   "Director" means a person duly appointed by the Company to direct and manage the affairs of the Company;

29.1.9   "ethics" means moral principles that govern a person's behaviour or the conduct of an activity;

29.1.10   "executive management" means the Chief Executive Officer and other persons having authority and responsibility for planning, directing and controlling the day-to-day activities of the Company, whether or not they are members of the Board of Directors of the Company;

29.1.11   "extant laws" means any law or statute in force in the Federal Republic of Nigeria;

29.1.12   "financial expert" means a person who understands and interprets generally accepted accounting principles and financial statements;

29.1.13 "financial literacy" means the possession of the basic set of skills and knowledge that allows an individual to understand financial statements to make effective and informed decisions;

29.1.14 "general meeting" includes the Annual General Meeting, Statutory Meeting and the Extraordinary General Meeting;

29.1.15 "insider" means the following:

    (a) any person who is connected with the Company in one or more of the following capacities:

        (i)   a Director of the Company or a related Company;

        (ii) an officer of the Company or a related Company;

        (iii) an employee of the Company or a related Company;

        (iv) any shareholder of the Company who owns five percent (5%) or more of any class of securities or any person who is or can be deemed to have any relationship with the Company or member;

        (v) members of the statutory audit committee of a Company; and

        (vi) any person involved in a professional or business relationship who has access to inside information by virtue of his relationship to (i) to (v) above.

    (b) any of the persons listed in paragraph (a), who by virtue of having been connected with any such person or connected with the Company in any other way, possesses unpublished price-sensitive information in relation to the securities of the Company, and any reference to unpublished price-sensitive information in relation to any securities of a Company is a reference to information which:

        (i)   relates to specific matters relating or of concern (directly or indirectly) to that Company, that is, is not of a general nature relating or of concern to that Company; and

        (ii) is not generally known to those persons who are accustomed to or would be likely to deal in those securities but which would, if it were generally known to them be likely materially to affect the price of those securities;

29.1.16 "joint control" refers to a situation where more than one person, working together, exercise control over a Company;

29.1.17 "listed Company" means a Company which has any of its securities listed on any recognised stock exchange;

29.1.18 "Managing Director/Chief Executive Officer" means the head of Management delegated by the Board to run the Company;

29.1.19 "regulator" or "regulatory authority" means the Financial Reporting Council of Nigeria and other sectoral regulators as may be appropriate;

29.1.20 "regulated private companies" means private companies that file returns to any regulatory authority other than the Federal Inland Revenue Service and the Corporate Affairs Commission;

29.1.21 "related party/company" means a person or Company that is related to the Company that is preparing its financial statements.

    a. A person or a close member of that person's family is related to a reporting Company if that person:

       i. has control or joint control of the reporting Company;

       ii. has significant influence over the reporting Company; or

       iii. is a member of the key management personnel of the reporting Company or of a parent of the reporting Company

    b. An entity is related to a reporting Company if any of the conditions in IAS 24 applies.

29.1.22 "significant influence" refers to the power to participate in the financial and operating policy decisions of a Company, but not control them;

29.1.23 "significant shareholder" means a person whose shareholding, directly or indirectly, consists of at least five percent (5%) of the Company's paid up capital or voting rights;

29.1.24 "stakeholder" includes shareholders, employees, analysts, creditors, customers, regulators, vendors, host community, non-governmental organisations and government;

29.1.25 "Statutory Audit Committee" refers to the committee responsible for audit, which public companies are required to constitute by extant laws;

29.1.26 "whistle-blower" means any person(s) including the employee, management, Directors, customers, service providers, creditors and other stakeholder(s) of a Company who report any form of unethical behaviour or violations of laws and regulations to the appropriate internal authority or regulators.

29.2   In this Code:
      29.2.1   words importing the masculine gender include females; and
      29.2.2   words in the singular include the plural and words in the plural include the singular.

Outcomes-Based Governance

Glossary of Terms

Term	Definition
Accountability	This term depicts the responsibility/duty of explaining one's actions or decisions. Within the context of corporate governance, it usually means that the Board of Directors must have a duty of accountability towards stakeholders. It is important to note that although discharge of duties can be delegated to others, the duty of accountability cannot be delegated.
Africapitalism	The term was coined by Mr Tony O. Elumelu, CON. It is an economic philosophy based on the belief that Africa's private sector must play a leading role in the continent's development as such the concept calls on businesses to make decisions that will increase economic and social wealth ad promote development in the communities within which they operate. The principles of Africapitalism include; entrepreneurship, long-term investments, strategic sectors, development dividend, value-added growth, regional connectivity, multi-generational development and shared purpose.
Agenda	A list or programme of items to be discussed at a meeting.
Articles of Association	This is one of the governing documents of an organisation. It outlines the rules governing the conduct of the company's affairs such as powers, appointment process, etc.
Assurance	Assurance in the context of corporate governance is the process by which stakeholders are able to rely on the successful conduct of business by an organisation as well as sound internal processes, efficient decisions making and accurate information. This is primarily achieved through an effective internal audit process and assurance model. The duty for assurance is placed on the governing body.
Auditor	This is a person appointed by an organisation (usually by the shareholders in a general meeting) to report on whether

Term	Definition
	the accounts of the company present a true and fair view of the company's affairs. Auditors are appointed by, and responsible to, the members of the company and must report to them on the true position of the accounts prepared by the directors.
Audit Committee	The committee responsible for overseeing the company's external audit process, performance of the internal audit function, discussing and recommendation risk management policies and for monitoring the internal control process.
Bankruptcy	This is when a corporation is insolvent in the sense that its liabilities exceed its assets.
Best Practice	This represents the policies and guidelines that are considered to be the standard to which organisation's should strive to achieve.
Board	This is a group of appointed persons who are collectively responsible for running the affairs of an organisation.
Board Diversity	This is the extent to which the members of the board represent varied segments of society in terms of gender, race, professional background, experiences and even character traits.
Board Performance Evaluation	This is a periodic assessment of the performance of the board (individual and collective). It may be self-assessment (by the board members themselves) or by a third party. It may also be qualitative or quantitative.
Board Structure	This represents the make-up of the board in terms of size, demography, profession, independence, etc.
Chair, chairman, chairperson	This is the person responsible for presiding over the board of directors' proceedings/meetings. The Chair ensures that procedures are followed, decorum is maintained and provides general leadership.
Committee	This is a group of individuals (usually directors) to whom a duty/function has been delegated, for example, audit committee, nominations committee, remuneration committee, etc.
Company	A company is a legal entity formed to engage and operate a business. There are various types of company including, private companies, public companies, companies limited shares, unlimited companies, companies limited by guarantee.

Term	Definition
Company limited by guarantee	This is a company having the liability of its members limited by the Memorandum of Association to such amount as the members may respectively undertake to contribute to
	the assets of the company in the event that the company is wound up.
Company limited by shares	This is a company having the liability of the shareholders of the company limited by the Memorandum of Association to the capital originally invested, i.e. the liability of members is limited to such amount, if any, unpaid on the shares respectively held by them. It may be private or public. They account for a majority of the company.
Company secretary	A company secretary is responsible for the efficient administration of a company by ensuring compliance with statutory and regulatory requirements as well as the enforcement of board decisions. It is a vital role and has become multifaceted in recent times.
Compliance	This is the process by which an entity ensure that its activities align with required and voluntary requirements (codes, applicable laws, regulations, best practices) from regulators as well as with best practices.
Comply/apply or Explain	This is a system of corporate governance under which companies are not legally required to adopt recommended governance standards but are only to issue a statement explaining whether they are in compliance with the standards or reasons for non-compliance.
Comply/apply and	This was introduced by the King IV Report. It stipulates that an
Explain	explanation should be provided in the form of a narrative account, with reference to practices that demonstrate the application of the principle. The application should demonstrate which recommended or other practices have been implemented and how these achieve and give effect to the principle. It suggests that the application of all the principles is assumed and companies should explain the practices that have been implemented to give effect to each principle.
Control Systems	Control Systems (usually internal) is a mechanism of corporate governance in the form of guidelines and procedures that enables a company to prevent operating

Term	Definition
	losses resulting from a range of factors such as negligence, theft, error, technological malfunction, etc. Controls systems play an important role in corporate governance systems and enable a company prepare accurate financial statements.
Corporate Actors	This consists of the key players in corporate governance who have the utmost power in corporate governance. They usually include shareholders and directors but could also include regulators, employees and host communities.
Corporate citizenship	Corporate citizenship is the concept that recognises that organisations are members of the communities within which they operate and of the global community, as such organisations must commit to ethical behaviour by balancing stakeholders' needs. If further proposes that companies must not only contribute their business activities but must also make investments in the local community as the same is essential for their long-term success.
Corporate Social Responsibility (CSR)	This is how companies manage their business activities to produce and overall positive impact on society. It covers a range of factors such as sustainability, social impact, ethics, etc. It ensures that companies integrate social and environmental concerns in their business operations, establish community partnerships and have goals that are philanthropic and charitable in nature.
Corporate Strategy	This is the identified, developed and implemented goal or direction of a company. It affects the manner and process in which business activities are carried out.
Director	This is an officer of an organisation who forms part of the governing body of the organisation. Directors may be executive, independent or non-executive
Dividends	This is a payment made to members out of a company's distributable profits, in proportion to their shareholding.
Due Diligence	This means vetting issues that affect the business thoughtfully and carefully. Directors and officers of a company have a duty of due diligence in their activities.
Duty of Care and skill	This is a fiduciary responsibility that requires directors to in carrying out their corporate duties act in the same manner as a reasonably prudent person would and to

Term	Definition
	ensure that the interests of the company are catered for. It is important to note that a higher degree of expertise and standard of competence is generally expected from directors in managing the affairs of the company.
Emerging Markets	The concept of emerging markets or economies was introduced by the International Finance Corporation in the 1980s. It represents rapidly growing and volatile economies. Emerging economies have low to middle per capita income; they mimic the economy of developed nations but do not fully meet the requirements to be classified as one.
Ethics/Business Ethics	Ethics is a set of principles of right conduct or a system of moral principles, while business ethics are the principles guiding an organisation's conduct of its activities, internal relations and interactions with external stakeholders.
Executive Director	Executive directors are directors in charge of the day to day running of the affairs of the company. They tend to be full-time employees.
Fiduciary Duty	This duty arises as a result of the relationship of trust between directors and members. It requires directors to act in a manner that is legally becoming of their office and which places the interests of the company ahead of theirs.
Governing Body	The Board of Directors is the governing body of every entity.
Governing Document	This is any document that outlines the aims, purposes, rules and procedure of an organisation. They include articles of association, constitution, etc.
Independence	This means to be free from conflict of interest that may impair objectivity.
Independent Directors	(Sometimes known as an outside director). This is a director who has no material relationship with the company. They generally are not entitled to remuneration or payment other than sitting fees.
Integrated Governance	This is a system of control by which sustainability frameworks are implemented in an organisation's activities in other to ensure value creations for the company and stakeholders in the long term.

Term	Definition
Internal Audit	This is the process of evaluating and receiving independent assurance that an organisation's risk management and internal control systems are accurate and effective.
Investors	An investor is a person who offers capital usually with the expectation of receiving financial returns.
Keiretsu network	(system, series, grouping of enterprises) This is a Japanese term that denotes a system of interrelation between companies by cross-shareholdings to form a robust corporate structure. Under the Keiretsu network, boards tend to be large, predominantly executive and often ritualistic.
Liability	This is the implication of failure to comply with obligations of a legal or regulatory nature.
Management	This is the process of administering and controlling the affairs of an enterprise.
Meeting	This is simply an assembly of persons for a particular purpose.
Member	Within the context of corporations, a member is shareholder in a company limited by shares and a guarantor in a company limited by guarantee.
Memorandum of Association	This is a governing documents of an organisation that is prepared during the formation process of a company to define its relationship with shareholders. It is usually filed at the relevant regulating body such as the Corporate Affairs Commission (CAC) in Nigeria and the Companies and Intellectual Property Commission (CIPC) in South Africa during the incorporation process.
Minutes of Meeting	This is a record of the occurrences during a meeting.
Non-Executive Director	This is a director who is not involved in the day to day running of the affairs of an organisation, rather they provide an oversight function as well as sit on committees saddled with sensitive issues such as remuneration of executive directors. Non-executive directors are also sometimes considered as independent directors or external directors.
Operating Risk	This is the risk of loss resulting from failed internal control systems, people, external factors, reputational damage, etc.
Risk	Risk entails the likelihood of loss from unexpected or uncontrollable outcomes entailed in conducting business.

Term	Definition
Risk Management	This is the process by which a company identifies and manages its risk exposure as well as reduce adverse outcomes of risk.
Risk Tolerance/Appetite	This is the extent to which a company is able to pursue its strategic objectives. It is the level and type of risk that an organisation is willing to encounter in its business activities. Organisations have different risk appetites depending on their corporate strength, objectives, culture and sector.
Proxy	This is a person authorised by a member to attend and votes in its place at a company's general meeting. Generally, members/shareholders have the statutory rights to appoint a proxy.
Quorum	This is the minimum number of persons required to be present at a meeting for same to be constitutionally valid. This usually provided for by the governing law or documents.
Reputational Risk Control	This is the extent to which an organisation protects its intangible assets of corporate reputation.
Resolution	This is a formal decision taken by an organisation through its governing organs (the members of the board).
Shadow Director	This is a person who has an influence on directors and under whose directions directors are accustomed to act. They usually tend to be active/majority shareholders.
Shares/Stock	This represents units of ownership interest in an organisation.
Share capital	This is the sum that has been invested by shareholders i.e. the funds a company raises in exchange for issuing an ownership interest in the company.
Shareholder/ Stockholder	This is a person who holds shares or stock in a company.
Stakeholder	This any person who has a stake or an interest in a company. They can be internal such as members, employees, etc. and external such as customers/consumers, regulators, host communities, etc. They have the ability to influence the company and are also influenced by the company.
Statutory	A legal requirement place on an entity.

Term	Definition
Succession Plan	This is a strategy for directing the long-term success of companies by ensuring the smooth passing on of leadership positions and replacing those in authority when the need arises. An effective succession plan can mitigate the harsh effects that losing boards members may present. Developing and maintaining a succession plan is usually the responsibility of the nominations committee. In recent times, the company secretary also has a huge rule to play in succession planning by advising the board on its structure, composition and on its succession plan.
Security	This entails the protection of the assets of an entity from threats and danger.
Transparency	This simply means openness, honesty and accuracy in providing information to stakeholders.
Ultra Vires	This is an act beyond one's power or authority.
Whistleblowing	This is the act of informing the appropriate authorities/management of a perceived wrongdoing or misconduct of another. Usually in the context of corporate governance, a whistleblower is typically an employee who draws the attention of management to wrongdoings of another employee.